SUPER BIRD

OTHER BOOKS BY DONALD P. EVANS

NEVELE PRIDE: Speed 'n' Spirit
BIG BUM: The Story of Bret Hanover
HOOKED on HARNESS RACING

SUPER BIRD

The Story of Albatross

Donald P. Evans

SOUTH BRUNSWICK AND NEW YORK: A. S. BARNES AND COMPANY
LONDON: THOMAS YOSELOFF LTD

© 1975 by A. S. Barnes and Co., Inc.

A. S. Barnes and Co., Inc.
Cranbury, New Jersey 08512

Thomas Yoseloff Ltd
108 New Bond Street
London W1Y 0QX, England

Library of Congress Cataloging in Publication Data

Evans, Donald P
    Super bird; the story of Albatross.

    1. Albatross (Race horse)   I. Title.
SF343.A5E9   798'.46   73-10520
ISBN 0-498-01351-0

PRINTED IN THE UNITED STATES OF AMERICA

CONTENTS

Acknowledgments 7

Chapter 1 13
Chapter 2 17
Chapter 3 24
Chapter 4 29
Chapter 5 36
Chapter 6 41
Chapter 7 48
Chapter 8 56
Chapter 9 63
Chapter 10 73
Chapter 11 81
Chapter 12 91
Chapter 13 104
Chapter 14 122
Chapter 15 131
Chapter 16 140
Chapter 17 152
Chapter 18 158
Chapter 19 167
Chapter 20 173
Chapter 21 181
Chapter 22 191
Chapter 23 208
Chapter 24 220

Appendix 235

Index 239

ACKNOWLEDGMENTS

This could have been a more complete book—a better book—had three key figures in the Albatross story been willing to take part in the telling of that story. Bert V. James, Alan J. Leavitt and Dr. J. Glen Brown were all invited to answer questions and express their views in this biography. For reasons of their own, they decided to remain on the sidelines.

Mr. James very nearly participated as the book was being constructed, but was apparently stricken with a case of second thoughts at the last minute because, as he indicated in a letter to me, he felt that his comments would be used in a controversial way and not as a matter of opinion and fact. Mr. James also expressed concern that I might pull my punches in reporting facts about Stanley Dancer, so as not to jeopardize my relationship with that gentleman, and he expressed his reluctance to contribute in any way to the continuation of any ill feelings or feud between himself and Mr. Dancer or the current owners of Albatross.

Mr. James, at least, was good enough to turn me down early in the game, back at a time when I was assembling information for the biography. Not so with Mr. Leavitt. Mr. Leavitt waited 167 days—until the manuscript was completed—before giving me an indication that he was sitting out the book. And when he did write, he took the opportunity to accuse me of a strong personal bias in Stanley Dancer's favor, and to question the objectivity of the forthcoming book, even though he barely knows me and could not possibly have known what I had written in the volume. Mr. Leavitt also expressed his concern that his continuing success as a syndicator of Standardbreds would be seriously and adversely affected if either his integrity or character was to be impugned, and he concluded by saying that his lawyer would want to communicate with my publisher.

In any event, Mr. Leavitt *did write,* which is more than can be said for Dr. Brown. I am still waiting for his response to my request for answers and comments.

By now, the reader may have the impression that this is a controversial book. I don't agree. It certainly wasn't meant to be. Initially, I started out to write a rather complete biography of a great harness horse as I had done in the case of Bret Hanover and Nevele Pride

(*Big Bum: The Story of Bret Hanover* and *Nevele Pride: Speed 'n' Spirit*). I knew there were hard feelings involved in the Albatross story; everyone in harness racing, or anybody who bought a newspaper in April of 1972 knew that. I did not mean to make the feud the crux of the story—the great pacer and his incredible accomplishments were the things—and I don't believe I have. By the same token, I did not mean to avoid the controversy, and I haven't.

I have no quarrel with Messrs. James, Leavitt and Brown, nor with their right to refrain from participating in the preparation of this book. There were many others who *did make* major contributions, however, and I must thank them. Publicly. In print.

Stanley Dancer, one of the busiest, most industrious men I have ever met, was patient, cooperative and cordial throughout several long interviews and many phone calls, and you can't ask for more than that. I have tried mightily to keep my admiration for this great horseman at a minimum, and I have more than likely failed. While Stanley has his detractors, as all successful men do, I freely admit I am not one of them. I have never gotten over the fact that Dancer was a farm boy with a sixth grade education who parlayed pride, native ability and determination into world fame and wealth. The people who knock America would do well to study his life story. It could only happen here.

Meeting Louis and Hilda Silverstein was one of the fringe benefits that came my way in writing the biography. Louis Silverstein, like Stanley Dancer, was another giant product of the American system, although Silverstein had the added burden of a serious physical handicap in his climb up the ladder. Mrs. Silverstein is a lady, a real lady from the old school—rich in compassion, generosity and loyalty. You will read of her loyalty—her husband's as well—in this volume. It grieves me—and everyone who knew him—that Mr. Silverstein's life had to end before the publication of this book.

John F. Simpson, Sr., and his good right hand, Murray Brown, helped in many ways, too. Simpson, who rose from comparative obscurity in the mid-1940s to eventually head the world's largest horse breeding farm, is a frank, let-the-chips-fall-where-they-may kind of man who parted with time and wisdom in large amounts as the information for this book was being assembled. Brown sits atop the harness racing sport like a wise, young owl, surveying it on all sides.

A very special thanks must go to Harry Harvey, the sensitive horseman who transformed a scrawny, unwanted colt into a world champion, only to lose him when the greatness began to blossom in earnest. It literally took months to coax Harvey into talking for the record, the memory of losing the colt being so painful. But when he did open up, he was magnificent, relating his experiences with both color and clarity. It wouldn't have been much of a book without him.

John (Tic) Wilcutts, Mark Lydon and Charles Kenney, three of the five individuals who bred Albatross, were most helpful as well, although it must have cost them something to talk so frankly of the big fish who got away. Gentlemen, may another Albatross turn up in the future of each of you.

Joe Wideman and Roger Pritchard, the faithful caretaker and night watchman of Albatross respectively, were warmly cooperative, as were horsemen Herve Filion, Jack Bailey, Bruce Nickells, Vernon Dancer, Harold Dancer, Sr., and Ronnie Dancer.

No book such as this gets written without the help of the United States Trotting Association and its excellent staff, so my thanks go out to the giant unit itself as well as to Stan Bergstein, Larry Evans, Ed Keys, George Smallsreed and Tom White. There isn't a publicity arm of any sports body in the nation to match the USTA's, and the men I have named are the reasons for its greatness.

I received a personal assist from Paul Hofstetter, Jr., of the *Chicago Tribune*, and I borrowed bits and pieces of information from a multitude of daily newspapers. The pages of *Horseman & Fair World*, *Harness Horse* and *Hoof Beats* magazines were plundered for facts, and I found colorful, accurate reporting in each.

The publicists of many tracks where Albatross raced were badgered for anecdotes, information and photos, and most responded in fine fashion. For service above and beyond the call of duty, I must lavish extra praise upon the late Kurt Stehmann, Charlie Stokes, Bruce Stearns, Fran Smith, Dave Wasserman, Bob Wellman, Bill Galvin, Bob Beslove, Biff Lowry, Denis McGlyn, Warren Eves, Ed Walsh, Dave Herman, Earl Flora and Albert Trottier.

Three fine harness racing veterinarians—the Drs. Edwin Churchhill, John Steele and Bert Miller—shared some of their vast knowledge with me, earning themselves little more than my gratitude.

A special gold star must go to two other great people who invested much time and energy in this volume—Miss Margaret Hart, who has been minding my grammar and spelling since I was a cub reporter on the Rome, N.Y., *Daily Sentinel*, and Bill Taylor, the Vernon Downs track photographer who was my man Friday throughout my travels in researching the biography.

Last but most assuredly not least, I must say thank you to Jane Evans, for typing, typing, typing and to Marta Evans for keeping the noise down to an acceptable level while the typewriter and I fought the good battle.

SUPER BIRD

1

Louis Silverstein was steaming.

"Unbelievable," he growled as the elevator sped toward the lobby. "Cut and dried. All wrapped up and tied with a ribbon. Never had a chance. Why in hell did they bother to invite us in the first place?"

Silverstein, a semiretired industrialist and full-time philanthropist from Philadelphia, was sharing the elevator with his attorney, S. Jay Cooke, also of Philadelphia. It was Monday, March 27, 1972, and the two were fresh out of a meeting in a posh apartment in the Hampshire House hotel, Central Park South, New York City. During the course of the brief and stormy parley, majority interests in the Albatross Stable had voted to remove Stanley Franklin Dancer as trainer-driver of world champion pacing horse Albatross.

Louis Silverstein, staring trancelike at the door of the plunging conveyance, was firmly entrenched some 180 degrees the other side of the majority decision.

"How can they do this terrible thing, Jay?" he demanded rhetorically of the lawyer. "Have they lost their sanity? Have they forgotten so soon what this man did with that horse last year? Twenty-five wins, two seconds and a third in 28 starts? More than $550,000 in earnings, an all-time high for a harness horse in a single season? A win record of 1:54.4, the fastest race mile ever recorded in the sport? Landslide election as harness horse of the year? Can all that be swept away so quickly?"

"Louis, with them it seems to be a case of 'What's he done lately?'" the lawyer offered gently.

"But it isn't right, Jay. It isn't fair, and I can't let them get away with it. Why, they'll destroy this great man, Stanley Dancer. They'll ruin him. He's a proud man, and he loves that horse. They'll do great harm to his reputation . . ."

Silverstein's frustration had grown to suffocating proportion as the oust-Dancer movement had rapidly taken shape. Dancer had brought Albatross up from his Pompano Park, Florida, winter training headquarters for an early start to the pacer's 1972 season. The champion, hailed as the Big Bird by sports writers across the land, had then stunned the writers and his adoring public by losing his first three races to a rejuvenated problem pacer called Isle Of Wight.

While there may have been logical explanations for the defeats—there were in Dancer's mind, surely—Albatross stable members Bert V. James, Alan J. Leavitt, Leon Machiz and Ira Helman, along with proxy Dr. J. Glen Brown, were not buying them. In their view, each Albatross loss sliced tens, even hundreds of thousands of dollars from his eventual value as a Standardbred sire. They wanted Mr. Dancer's scalp before the horse suffered additional humiliations. The dissidents, representing 70 percent of the pacer's ownership, had effectively performed the scalp surgery at the Hampshire House gathering.

It was an action, they were aware, that would rattle the windows, if not rock the foundations of the harness world.

Silverstein, with anger mounting as he and Cooke left the hotel and hailed a taxi for the ride to Pennsylvania Station and the return to Philadelphia, was spokesman for the remaining 30 percent of the pacer—10 percent each held by his wife Hilda, Mrs. Hazel D. Shriner of Taneytown, Maryland, and John W. Rollins of Wilmington, Delaware.

Mrs. Silverstein, Mrs. Shriner and Rollins were all devoted champions of Stanley Dancer, able and eager to back the New Egypt, New Jersey, horseman with faith, finances, or both. None was more vociferous in his devotion than 77-year-old Louis Silverstein, who looked upon Dancer as a son and was prepared to fight for him with parental ferocity.

He was still fuming as the cab, in fits and starts, proceeded down Seventh Avenue. "Did you hear that one guy at the meeting, Jay?" he boomed at the attorney. "He says to me, 'Silverstein, the thing I hold against Stanley Dancer is the fact that he doesn't have humility. He refuses to sit down and tell us how he's going to drive the race.' My God, he thinks Stanley's in the garment business; that he should report to them about a carload of goods he's about to buy. The guy doesn't realize that racing a horse is like no other business. The driver doesn't know what's going to happen until the gate leaves. And there's no way of telling what the other horses and drivers are going to do.

"And how about the other guy, the one who kept saying Stanley was ruining the horse? 'All I know,' he says to me, 'is that three weeks ago we had a horse worth five million dollars. Now Dancer loses three straight with him and the horse is worth maybe two and a half million, tops.' Then he tells me. 'You know, Silverstein, we planned to put this horse to stud down at Lana Lobell Farms, and in three years you wouldn't have heard anything more about Hanover Shoe Farms.'

"You get that, Jay? These guys think they can put Hanover out of business. In three years, yet. That's the kind of people we're dealing with!"

"They do seem to be in control of the situation, though," Cooke pointed out. "They've got the numbers."

"I know, I know," Silverstein replied irritably. "But I can't roll over and play dead. I can't give up. I've got to do *something*. I can't permit them to take the horse away from that man. Not after the magnificent season he had with him last year. Not after all the terrible physical pain he went through to drive him in every single race. I've got to fight them!"

"I know how you feel . . ." Cooke began.

But Silverstein wasn't listening. Nor was he seeing the bustle outside the vehicle—businessmen, tardy from lunch, scurrying along the sidewalk, shoppers idly peering into store windows, angry traffic stacked up at the intersection. His mind was busy. Slashing at the problem. Sifting through past experiences. Pondering possibilities. Stalking alternatives.

"An injunction, Jay!" he roared, startling the cab driver.

"An injunction?"

"Yes. Is it possible?"

"To keep the horse in the Dancer stable?"

"Yes."

"Based on the ground that it was clearly understood from the inception of the syndicate that Stanley Dancer would train and drive the horse as long as he races?"

"Exactly."

This had been one of the major points advanced by Silverstein and Cooke during the rocky session in the apartment. When the Albatross syndicate was formed, they claimed, it was flatly stipulated that Stanley Dancer would handle Albatross through the balance of the horse's racing career. Why else would long-time Dancer patrons, people who hardly needed the profit such an arrangement might bring, join a bunch of strangers in such a business venture?

"It could work if we got right on it, got our papers in before they make some kind of legal move," the attorney granted cautiously. "But, Louis, even if we succeeded, it might only be a temporary solution. Let's face it, they still have the numbers."

"Yet it would provide me with some breathing room, give me some time to come up with a plan."

"Such as?"

The wheels were turning now, the gears meshing, the juices flowing. The scent of battle had chased the gloom, installed a glint in the eye. Lou Silverstein, a victor over a physical disability that would have invalided the average man, was partial to quick decisions. They had helped him amass a fortune in the textile industry, and they had served him well in his later career—raising and contributing funds for giant improvement projects at the University of Pennsylvania Hospital.

"Maybe buy those guys out," he announced.

"Who would buy them out?" Cooke asked with growing suspicion.

"Maybe me."

"Alone?"

"If it's necessary. Jay, my mind's made up; I'm determined to save that horse for Stanley Dancer. If I have to, I'm prepared to buy those guys out myself. I could have Stanley race him while I hunt around for investors to form a new syndicate."

The taxi had pulled up to the entrance of the mammoth underground train station, but Cooke signaled the driver to be patient. "Louis," the lawyer said slowly, "You may be talking in the neighborhood of two million dollars to acquire the other 70 percent of Albatross. And suppose there is something wrong with the horse, as those men suggest?"

"Stanley Dancer says he's perfect, and that's enough for me."

"Well, then, suppose he gets hurt and has to retire. Or suppose he reaches normal retirement and you still haven't found a substantial investor, someone interested in standing him at stud. You don't own a breeding farm, you know, and, frankly, you're a little old to start one now."

"Jay, my boy, you sound like a lawyer," Dancer's head cheerleader responded almost gaily. "If worst came to worst, I'd just have to tell Hilda to clear the furniture out of the living room and we'd have to keep him there."

Cooke could only stare at his client.

"Come on," Silverstein urged. "Let's get back to Philadelphia and get those injunction papers started."

2

Three years earlier, it would have been inconceivable that some of the most important people in harness racing would be squabbling over Albatross, tossing around figures like two, three and even five million dollars.

Lord knows that his breeders, five star-crossed individuals who rather remind one of the folks who bought passage on the maiden voyage of the Titanic, would not be haunted today had they possessed even the slightest inkling. Four members of the quintet gave up Albatross, his dam and a full sister in a package deal that netted each a cool profit of $72. The fifth member did not fare nearly so well.

It may well have been the most one-sided transaction since the Manhattan Indians swapped the deed to their island to Peter Minuit for $24 worth of tasteless gewgaws.

John E. (Tic) Wilcutts, a rapier-shaped horseman from the Pennsylvania-Maryland-Delaware racing circuit, was the prime catalyst in the conception of Super Bird. Wilcutts owned the mare who produced the champion. He also planned, plotted, schemed and manipulated the breeding which yielded the colt. Then he let the youngster—and his valuable kin—slip through his leathery hands. By that time, four of his acquaintances were also aboard the sinking ship. Today, they share Wilcutts's residency in the land of what might have been.

Neither nescience nor naiveté had anything to do with the loss, it should be pointed out. The five breeders represented more than a solid century of experience in the racing game. It was plain and simple, unadorned, old-fashioned rotten luck all the way.

But then good fortune and Tic Wilcutts have never been what you'd call close cronies.

The slender reinsman, so diminutive in his youth that the owner of Man O'War tried to persuade him to leave school for a career as a Thoroughbred jockey, was one of the restless, action-seeking young men who graduated from World War II military service and drifted into harness racing. He only dabbled in the sport in the beginning, tinkering with other people's discarded racing stock, and did not win his first race until 1951. From that point on, his progress was steady. When he managed to stay healthy.

The "book" on Wilcutts reads like this: "One of the top drivers in the country. Resourceful, adaptable, excellent post man, and has the ability to drive any horse." Then it continues, "Only a series of accidents, cutting into his racing opportunities on several occasions, has prevented him from being among the sport's all-time race winners."

The book is accurate. He has won as many as 165 races in a year, and 10 times that number over his career. He has a dozen track driving championships to his credit, including crowns picked up at the old Baltimore Raceway, Laurel Raceway, Rockingham Park, Scioto Downs, Liberty Bell Park and Brandywine Raceway. Trotters and pacers he has handled over the years have won more than four million dollars. He has long been one of the most adroit, most in-demand catch-drivers in an industry which suffers from no shortage of talented reinsmen.

Racing spills have been his Achilles heel. Busy drivers blessed with daring have always been susceptible to accidents. "I don't give a damn how good or how careful you are," Castleton Farms trainer-driver Glen Garnsey once commented, "you go to post enough times and you're bound to get crunched." Wilcutts has been a living, limping illustration of Garnsey's remark. A pair of serious accidents sidelined him for all but a tiny portion of the 1962 season. Smaller calamities put him on the shelf in the mid-1960s. A murky, ominous cloud has seemed to hover over his head through most of his years at the races, forcing him to become a prolific reader of get-well cards.

The cloud was also firmly in place when he attended the annual Standardbred Sales Company auction in Harrisburg, Pennsylvania, in the autumn of 1965. A yearling called Toledo Hanover, bought in part by basketball star Wilt Chamberlain, was one of the stars of the show, although Wilcutts's tastes were more modest. He was there to pluck a colt or two out of the sales ring for his patrons. He was also there to add an inexpensive youngster to his own small collection of Standardbreds—preferably a pacing filly who might race well for him, then go on to a second career as a broodmare.

Voodoo Hanover seemed tailor-made for him. Almost too good to be true. She was a daughter of Dancer Hanover, one of the hottest young sires in the land, and she seemed to have all the physical equipment necessary for success and prosperity at the races. Wilcutts, puffing an ever-present mini-cigar, could not believe his luck when auctioneer George Swinebroad knocked the filly down to him on his bid of $3,500.

The filly's name alone should have put him on his guard.

Voodoo Hanover, encamped at Wilcutts's winter training headquarters at Pinehurst, North Carolina, was a conundrum, an enigma from the start. But let Tic tell it:

"The filly was pacing bred; so I naturally put the hopples on her as soon as she was broken. She didn't want to pace, however; she wanted to trot. Since there was some trotting blood in her family,

John (Tic) Wilcutts plotted and planned the breeding of Albatross. (USTA photo)

I figured, okay, I'll try her on the trot. I trained her down to 2:25 and she was real good gaited. Didn't interfere or anything. But fooling with her gait had taken a lot of time. It was getting late then, and since I hadn't kept her in many stakes or anything, I thought, well, I'll turn her out this year.

"When she turned three, I picked her up again. I was determined to train her on the pace this time, but she still had it in her head that she was a trotter. Off came the hopples and I trained her the way she wanted to be trained—on the trot. I got her down to 2:25 again, although she just seemed to hang there. Wouldn't or couldn't go any faster. She'd trot a quarter in maybe 32 seconds, but that was it. She had no brush, no lick, so I said to myself, you're wasting your time. I dug out the hopples for the third time.

"She was a long time hitting a pace—I mean she was really tough, fighting me all the way—but eventually she gave in. We got along pretty well toward the end of the Pinehurst training; so I took her with me to Liberty Bell in March. She'd been in 2:15 pretty handy, and I got to thinking maybe I've got a real nice pacer here. Just about the time I was getting my hopes up in early April, she fractured a bone in her knee. All the time and effort went down the drain."

The first phase of Wilcutts's plans—to race the filly—was shattered along with the youngster's knee. Disappointed but undaunted at this stage, he began to think of Phase II. Voodoo Hanover, the frustrated race filly, would have to bail him out in the role of a broodmare.

Tic knew precisely which stallion from the hundreds available he wanted for his filly. The sire's name was Meadow Skipper. Four years earlier Tic had seen Meadow Skipper and Overtrick lock horns in one of the greatest, grittiest duels witnessed at the Lexington Red Mile. Overtrick had won the battle by a slender nose, but Wilcutts had been so impressed with both horses that he vowed he would one day send broodmares to each. He'd sent a mare to Overtrick, and now it was Meadow Skipper's turn. That was his decision, and he never strayed from it.

Skipper, a son of Dale Frost-Countess Vivian, had recently wound up a brilliant, four-season campaign at the races. He had been bred and sold by Christy S. Hayes of Columbus, Ohio, and Hall-of-Famer Delvin Miller had brought him out, racing him—with a big assist from Paul Crilley—as a two-year-old for owner Hugh Grant. Then the Clearview Stables of Winthrop, Maine, bought him, with venerable horseman Earle Avery handling him through the remainder of his career. When his shoes were pulled at the end of the 1965 season, Skipper's lifetime record showed countless stakes victories, a win mark of 1:55.1 and earnings of $428,057. Amazingly, the fleet pacer, battling such awesome contemporaries as Overtrick and Country Don, had accomplished all this despite intermittent sieges of unsoundness.

Wealthy sportsman Norman S. Woolworth was the owner of Clearview Stables. Woolworth, along with David R. Johnston, also owned Stoner Creek Stud, Inc., a major breeding farm in Paris, Kentucky, and it followed that the young stallion would reside and practice his new and important trade at Stoner Creek.

His impeccable pedigree, sparkling race record, reputation for gameness and handsome conformation made Skipper a natural for stud service. His service book was filled almost as soon as it was opened in 1966, his first season at stud. The same was true for 1967, when Wilcutts was looking to breed his Voodoo Hanover to the promising young sire. But Tic was hopeful that he had an entrée—an "in."

"I'd had a mare, Peg's Lady, down at Stoner Creek for two or three years, trying in vain to get her in foal," he explained. "I figured maybe Charlie Kenney, the farm manager, would kind of feel sorry for me and give me a break with Voodoo Hanover, somehow let her in to Meadow Skipper."

Kenney, a veteran of both Thoroughbred and Standardbred breeding, listened with a sympathetic ear. He was not very encouraging, however. Skipper's book was closed, like the advertisements said, and Tic would be wise to look elsewhere if he wanted his mare bred in 1967.

Halted at the front door, the trainer went around to the rear. He took the matter up with Dr. John Peters, then the track veterinarian at Liberty Bell Park and a man not without some influence among breeding farm managers, including one in Paris, Kentucky. Tic extolled the virtues of his mare—mainly her bloodlines, since she hadn't really revealed any others—and bemoaned the fact that he wasn't able to secure a booking to Meadow Skipper.

"Tell you what," Dr. Peters offered. "You let me buy a piece of the mare and I think I can persuade Charlie Kenney to let her in."

"You're in," the trainer agreed readily.

Peters, who promptly turned his share over to his wife Elizabeth, made a fervent, plaintive telephone appeal to Kenney. To no avail. Skipper was booked solid. The chances of working Voodoo Hanover into the stallion's schedule were on a par with those of a Clydesdale trying to win the Hambletonian.

Chagrined, Peters reported back to Wilcutts, who now had a partner, but still no booking.

Soon he had two partners. Mark M. Lydon, the young assistant racing secretary at Liberty Bell, resided at the Holiday Park Apartments in Northeast Philadelphia. So did Tic Wilcutts. The Lydon, Wilcutts and Peters families, all good friends, were in the habit of gathering socially from time to time. Sipping highballs together on a Sunday evening shortly after Dr. Peters's abortive effort to bring Charlie Kenney around, the talk eventually centered upon Wilcutts's trials and tribulations with Voodoo Hanover. Lydon, a former school teacher and football coach who was elevated to Liberty Bell racing secretary in 1972, declared that he wanted into the mare's blossoming syndication.

"Get your money up," charitable Wilcutts replied.

The syndicate now had three members. What it still lacked was an engagement to the popular young stallion at Stoner Creek, and it was time to play the trump card. The trio of fledgling partners was in complete agreement that the way to a man's heart was not necessarily through his stomach. It could also be accomplished through a man's son. It was convenient, to say the least, that Stoner Creek

Mark M. Lydon

manager Charlie Kenney's son, John S. Kenney, was a young veterinarian who was practicing right there at Liberty Bell. And who employed Dr. John Kenney? Why, Dr. John Peters, of course.

Invite Dr. Kenney into the syndicate, the reasoning went, and Charlie Kenney could hardly refuse their request. Better yet, invite both Kenneys to join the group!

"So John Kenney called his dad and got the job done," Wilcutts said, recalling the coup. "But first he checked the mare's breeding and looked her over from stem to stern. He told his father that she was well bred and looked good, good enough to go to Skipper. I doubt that even John could have slipped her past his father if she hadn't had a touch of class in both pedigree and looks. While Skipper's book was full just as Charlie had been telling us, somewhere along the line a mare had to drop out and we got in."

Voodoo Hanover had her date with Meadow Skipper, and the breeders of Albatross were intact: John E. (Tic) Wilcutts, veteran horseman badly in need of a rabbit's foot; Elizabeth B. Peters, attractive wife of the track veterinarian; Mark M. Lydon, rising young track official; Dr. John S. Kenney, assistant to Dr. Peters and son of the man with the keys to Meadow Skipper, and Charles A. Kenney, highly respected breeding farm manager who would unwittingly play a larger role in harness racing history than he ever thought or sought.

Wilcutts had the mare appraised, and a $1,500 value was placed on her. Mrs. Peters, Lydon and the two Kenneys all wrote $300 checks to Tic, and the venture was under way. Later they would all have to chip in to pay Meadow Skipper's stud fees, stakes nomination fees for the foals and the mare's board at Stoner Creek.

"I don't know what we expected when it all started," Lydon reported after the Albatross story was history. "How in hell could anyone foresee a thing like that!"

3

Voodoo Hanover was mated with Meadow Skipper on four occasions in May of 1967, with the product of that union—a bay colt—foaling on May 8, 1968.

His birth created little commotion, either at the bustling, 730-acre Stoner Creek farm in Kentucky or up at Liberty Bell Park, where four of his breeders were busily pursuing their occupations in the waning days of the William Penn Racing Association's spring meeting.

The colt was checked by Charlie Kenney, the fifth member of the breeding team, who found him to be healthy and complete in every respect—a head, neck, shoulders, withers, hind quarters, four legs, and a tail about the size of a gray squirrel's. He stood good and straight, certainly a plus, but it occurred to Kenney that he might well turn out to be a small, rather undistinguished looking horse when he reached maturity. All of this the farm manager passed on to his partners in Philadelphia.

While Kenney's report seemed to be lacking in enthusiasm, it was welcome news that Voodoo Hanover had thrown a stud colt. Colts generally bring more money than fillies at auction, and the breeders fully intended to sell the colt as a yearling—more than likely as part of the Stoner Creek consignment (with the farm as agent)—at the annual Tattersalls fall sale at Lexington. "In fact, we were hoping to sell a colt out of the mare every year," Mark Lydon reported.

As the days went by and none of the other partners volunteered to name the suckling, Kenney took it upon himself to do the honors. Many years earlier, while employed by the Coldstream Stud Thoroughbred farm, Charlie had bred a farm-owned mare named Lull to a stallion called Mate. The "Mate" reminded him of a sailing vessel and its crew, while the "Lull" made him think of a lull in the wind—in sailing parlance, a "calm." Spliced together, the two terms seemed to suggest Samuel Taylor Coleridge's *Rime of the Ancient Mariner*, the gloomy saga of a sailing man becalmed without food, drink or hope, who puts the lid on his fate by slaying the sacred albatross. Charlie called the Thoroughbred colt Albatross.

The young horse was a fine sprinter. According to Kenney, he was the fastest half-miler training at Hialeah Park, Florida, that year, and raced successfully in the shorter dashes. He couldn't handle the longer distances, however, and his usefulness as a race horse was limited, his career short.

When a colt by Meadow Skipper-Voodoo Hanover came along, he began to wax nautical again and pulled the Albatross name out of his memory for the Standardbred foal. He conferred it upon the colt after receiving the blessings of the United States Trotting Association, which approves all names. Had the Thoroughbred Albatross been a famous horse, the USTA would have turned down his request.

For years the horse's name would intrigue people, causing sports writers and fans alike to wander through Coleridge's long poem in an effort to find some deeper meaning, some closer connection between the horse and poem. The best anyone could do, including Kenney, was to tie the "Skipper" from Meadow Skipper to the doomed sailor in the work, and the "Voodoo" from Voodoo Hanover to the ominous albatross of the poem.

While the albatross of the rime portended harm for the mariner, the Albatross of Standardbred racing presented a mixed bag to the folks closest to him over the years—thumping ill fortune for some; wild and wonderful success for others.

Charlie Kenney, running the big and busy farm, made it his business to keep a watchful eye on Albatross, looking on as the tangle of legs, bones and head began to take shape, began to resemble a horse.

Tic Wilcutts and Dr. John Peters saw the colt only once in the 14 months he roamed the pastures of the Kentucky farm. Wilcutts and Peters were in Lexington in late September, 1968, for the races and auction sessions at the Red Mile, and drove the short distance to Stoner Creek for a look at the youngster they had bred. They wandered through the fields until they spotted Voodoo Hanover and knew the colt by her side had to be Albatross.

"I wouldn't say he was the best looking weanling in the field, but he was by far the cleanest one—there wasn't a pimple on him," Wilcutts recalled. "He wasn't a handsome colt or anything like that. And he was definitely on the small side."

It was the last time either would see the young horse until he was racing as a two-year-old, starting to write a thick chapter in the harness racing history books.

Kenney continued to see a great deal of him. He saw him weaned (that painful experience when the frightened colt is separated from his mother), and he saw him mope and squeal and fuss and fight and eventually adjust to his new surroundings with the other "orphaned" youngsters at the farm. Kenney was on hand when Albatross and all the other weanlings arbitrarily celebrated their first birthday on January 1, 1969, and he was there when Voodoo Hanover dropped her second foal by Meadow Skipper, a filly who would eventually be called Doc's Fritzi.

Charlie Kenney saw Albatross at all stages of his young life and he was not impressed. The colt did not possess that special spark that often kindles a fire in the mind and chest of a veteran breeding man like Kenney. All the parts were there in proper proportion, but welded together, the unit seemed bland to the farm manager. Bland and small.

And Charlie, who had directed three of her matings with Meadow Skipper (the last of which was unsuccessful), did not think much of Voodoo Hanover either. Voodoo and Albatross—peas from the same genetic pod.

"The colt was perfectly sound, but, to be perfectly frank, I just didn't 'like' him nor his dam, and so advised the members of the partnership," he confessed with candor years later when lesser men would have been rushing to cover their tracks in a similar situation.

"It is important to remember that Meadow Skipper's first crop had barely started racing, and certainly nothing spectacular had happened to draw my attention to Meadow Skipper's future brilliance as a sire," he also pointed out.

"In any case, I set about recommending that if I could get a buyer for Voodoo Hanover (then barren from her 1969 breeding), her suckling filly and her yearling colt, the package should be sold."

In all, 24 months had elapsed since a desperate and determined Tic Wilcutts had syndicated his mare and gained her a booking to Meadow Skipper. In the interim, the partners had shared the cost of two $1,500 breedings to Skipper and some $3,000 worth of board bills on the mare and her yearling son. What they had to show for their money was an unproven broodmare, her smallish son and a suckling daughter.

Now Charlie Kenney, one of the wisest, most experienced breeders in the industry, was urging that they sell the whole package . . . that they bail out, scram while the scramming was good. His recommendation was contained in a letter to Wilcutts.

Dr. John Kenney, knowing his father's reputation and trusting his judgment, was agreeable. So was Mark Lydon, who felt he was only along for the ride and would yield to the senior Kenney's greater wisdom.

Tic Wilcutts and John Peters, who was acting for his wife, were stunned by the unexpected proposal.

"I couldn't understand why the Kenneys would want to get out after we'd paid the stud fees for two years, after we'd gone that far," Wilcutts said. "I simply couldn't understand it at all.

"Doc Peters and I appeared to be the only ones against selling, and we talked of buying the other partners out. But it seemed as though we had to come up with the money in a hurry, and it was a bad time of year for both of us. We had to pay income taxes, social security and workmen's compensation on our help and it kind of left us cramped for cash."

Peters also suggested that the two of them attempt to coax the balance of the breeders into keeping the colt, with Wilcutts to train him. Tic declined, however, citing the fact that there were too many owners involved. Tic, like most harness trainers, had always tried to steer clear of arrangements like that.

Charlie Kenney's recommendation that the syndicate liquidate its equine holdings was initially advanced in early June of 1969. The actual sale of the three-horse package was not culminated until late July. In the meantime, Wilcutts and Peters, the two reluctant sellers, were guilty of "letting the matter slide," in Wilcutts's words.

"That's where we made the mistake, of course," he said later. "I could sense that we were doing wrong."

While Kenney did not go so far as to advertise the parcel of horses he had for sale, he did mention it to enough people for word to spread. Up in Avella, Pennsylvania, not far from Pittsburgh, there was a man who was anxious to break into the breeding business. He had his antenna out for broodmares to populate a horse farm he had leased at Avella. He was also in the market for young horses he might send to the sales as a consignment from his farm—a sort of trial run for the day when he would be raising his own youngsters and sending them to the auctions. He was immediately receptive when his trainer brought the Voodoo Hanover package to his attention.

The deal was consummated by telephone. The man bought Voodoo Hanover, Albatross and the suckling filly for $11,000. The entire transaction was handled by gentlemanly Charlie Kenney, who neither praised nor knocked the horses, and the buyer's trainer. The rest of the syndicate's partners were either willing or, at least, *passive* spectators, accepting the sales price.

Albatross and all the incredible wealth, records and glory he would generate were lost to them.

Mark Lydon, at the time, was satisfied with the sum that Kenney had managed. "True, we hadn't gotten rich on the deal, but then we hadn't lost anything either—except for poor Tic Wilcutts. Owning one-fifth of the mare and foals, I wound up with a profit of $72 when we sold. We also picked up some breeder's fees later on when Albatross won the Founder's Plate at Roosevelt."

Equipped with a buoyant personality, the young racing secretary has taken his brush with fame and fortune in stride. "I've been the target of a lot of ribbing over the years, but it hasn't really bothered me," he insists today. "I'm not bitter. Everybody makes a mistake; that's what racing is all about. Somebody gets lucky; somebody gets unlucky. That's the name of the game, I guess."

On several occasions, Lydon, working in the racing departments of Liberty Bell and Brandywine Raceway, had the dubious pleasure of putting races together that featured Albatross. "I always rooted for him," he says. "In harness racing, you sell a horse, you want to see him do good."

Likewise, Tic Wilcutts professes no malice over losing a world champion in such an almost casual manner. The cross of self-recrimination he bears is reserved for the broodmare he permitted to slip away. "Look at it this way," he explains, "if we had held on to the mare, we could have earned $25,000 or more on every foal she had. As for Albatross, well, we were going to sell him anyway. That was always the plan. The great career that he had would have been the thing that would have made the mare's foals so valuable in the future."

Unquestionably, Tic Wilcutts is the unsung hero of the Albatross story. He is the man who picked Voodoo Hanover out of the stampede of yearling fillies sold in 1965. He is the man who was willing to invest time, effort and faith in the filly, straining to get her to the races. He is the man who stubbornly insisted that she be bred to Meadow Skipper. And he is the man who perceived that it was an error to part with the mare.

And if there is to be a hero in the early portion of the Albatross saga, there must also be a goat. That role belongs to Charlie Kenney. He will have it no other way. "I should have gotten the bonehead prize of the year for selling that colt, his dam and his sister," he says flatly. "I'll take that responsibility. Those other people were innocent bystanders. I should be made to look foolish."

Frank, honest words from a frank, honest man. Typical of an individual who remains 10 feet tall in Standardbred breeding today. For every faulty judgment that Kenney has made during his long and distinguished tenure in racing, there are a hundred successful trotters and pacers boosting his reputation over the nation's race tracks. His partners knew then—and they know now—that Charlie Kenney is a man of great skill and integrity.

There is one thing they did not know at the time Albatross slipped from their grasp. Because it was not important at that point, and because it would have meant nothing to them, Kenney did not bother to tell them the name of the man who bought the Albatross package.

It was James. Bert V. James.

4

Bert Vansickle James—a bulky, reserved, rather dour man with a mustache, who burst upon the harness racing scene like an instant summer storm that whips together over the Great Lakes, then roars away to batter the neighboring land masses with hardly a whisper of warning . . .

. . . The sort of individual who not only seems to emerge full blown from thin air, but casts a giant shadow from the first moment his outline becomes visible.

His entry into racing was so unusual, his progress so spectacular, his conduct so atypical and his departure as a major force so rapid, that he barely left the sport's biographers with a chance to catch their breath, let alone prepare his biography.

As recently as 1965, nobody very much had heard of Bert James outside of the good folks who bought new and used cars in the Windsor, Ontario, area of Canada, right across the river from Detroit. James owned a General Motors agency—Cadillacs and Chevrolets—in Windsor and did very well with it, comfortably providing for a pretty wife and six attractive children.

The chrome chariots of Detroit were his prime interest until an optimistic horseman from nearby Windsor Raceway wandered into his showroom one day and revealed a hungry appetite for a Cadillac. While the horseman yearned for the big, glossy vehicle, he was painfully short of cash. He offered to swap James his old car and three high-mileage harness horses for the Caddy. On a whim, James agreed. As quick as you can say Adios, he was in the racing game. Come hell or high and very turbulent waters.

James quickly sold one of the steeds for $500. A second was claimed from him for $1,000. The third was Senator Eric, a nine-year-old pacer who had averaged some $2,500 a year in earnings during his long stint at the races. Suddenly, with what came to be known as the James's magic working for him, aging Eric found new vigor and new speed. He was a bearcat instead of a pussycat. Over the next 18 months the invigorated oldster picked up $13,000 for his satisfied owner, and sent the Canadian car dealer into high gear in the Standardbred business.

Other race horses followed as James quickly expanded his horizons. He paid $40,000 for the two-minute pacer Hope Time and watched from the clubhouses and paddocks of many tracks as the young horse earned himself out in a single season. The pacer, who had left James's stable by that time, had more than $212,000 on his card in 1972.

Breeding was next for the ambitious James. He had become interested in the famous Armstrong Brothers' racing and breeding organization at Brampton, Ontario, and decided to pattern his own operation after theirs. He was aiming high. The Brothers Armstrong, masters of a 300-acre, 300-horse farm near Toronto, had bred or campaigned, or bred *and* campaigned, some of the most glittering names in harness racing annals—champions like Armbro Flight (1:59; $493,602), Governor Armbro (2:00.2; $365,539), Dottie's Pick (1:56.4; $263,978) and Countess Adios (1:59.1; $303,773), the last of which they owned in partnership with Hugh Grant.

In 1967, he made his move. He sold the Windsor auto dealership —it was a big one, grossing eight million dollars at its peak—and leased a rambling, 475-acre farm from Mr. Harness Racing himself, Delvin Miller. Called Bancroft until the James clan rechristened it the James Boys Farm, the big spread had been the Miller family homestead for nearly two centuries.

Soon there were members of the James family fanning out across its acres. The family roster, listed in a *Harness Horse* magazine advertisement in 1970, three years after the invasion occurred, included: "Bert James, President . . . Donna James, Administration . . . David James, Farm Manager . . . Albert James, Administration . . . Peter James, Student-Farm . . . Jeffrey James, Veterinary College."

Missing from the list were son Bert James Jr. and daughters Mary and Judy, who presumably visited the farm if they were not actually headquartered there.

The James gang had landed in Avella, Pennsylvania, in force.

Borrowing pages from the Armstrong Brothers' book, James planned to stand no stallions at the farm, preferring to buy into stallion syndicates or send the mares to other stud horses available. And like the Armstrongs with the "Armbro" tag they conferred upon their yearlings, the James Boys came up with the "Jambo" prefix for their youngsters. Foals born the first year were given second names starting with the letter "A", so the farm's initial crop would contain a Jambo Adonis, Jambo Adam and Jambo Allan. Foals born the second year were due to be called Jambo Belle, Jambo Byrd and so forth.

Bert James Sr. and his eldest son, David, were on the prowl for likely candidates for their broodmare band. It was no soft assignment since most of the major breeding farms in the land, enterprises like Hanover Shoe Farms, Castleton, Walnut Hall and Almahurst, are constantly scouting for promising mares, too—with healthy checkbooks at the ready. So are the nation's smaller breeders. Finding a filly or mare with a pretty pedigree and decent racing record is generally either a lucky stroke, expensive proposition, or both.

The Jameses were still struggling to assemble their fledgling band in 1969 when Charlie Kenney was striving to find a new home for

Voodoo Hanover. While Kenney did not "like" her, Voodoo did boast a pretty pedigree, if not a decent racing record. And she did come complete with a pair of foals.

An alert, ambitious and sensitive Pennsylvania horseman named Harry M. Harvey was Bert James's lodestone in the acquisition of Voodoo Hanover & Co. It was Harvey who heard of Kenney's mission to peddle the three-horse parcel, and it was Harvey who persuaded James to buy it.

Harvey's background in racing is an interesting one. He was born

Family portrait: Albatross and Harry Harvey.

and raised on a New England farm. As a teenager, he set his sights on a harness racing career and went about preparing himself for it as though he had selected brain surgery or nuclear physics. The late Thomas S. Berry was a top Grand Circuit trainer of the day; so Harvey decided that he would study under him. He bombarded Berry with letters asking for a groom's job. The famous trainer, a sort of harness racing "Harvard" in Harvey's eyes, ignored the young man for many months. Finally he relented, more to stop the flow of letters than to oblige a determined young disciple.

Harvey traveled the length of the country with Berry, grooming and later training his great Grand Circuit champions and scrutinizing the master's work in the stable and on the race track. When he felt he had earned his bachelor's degree, Harvey moved on, seeking his master's as assistant trainer to fast-rising young horseman Delvin Miller. Miller gave him horses to drive, good ones, and it was Harry Harvey in the bike when Helicopter won the Hambletonian Stake in 1953. At 29, Harry was the youngest man to ever win the Hambo until 27-year-old John Simpson Jr. came along with Timothy T. in 1970.

Harvey trailed Jim Arthur in the Miller Stable hierarchy, however, and realized that Miller and Arthur would be getting the top stock to drive for years to come. With his training and driving opportunities limited, he voted yes when Miller asked him to become superintendent of Miller's Meadow Lands Farm at Meadow Lands, Pennsylvania in 1954. He remained there for a dozen years, running the farm and supervising the breeding activities of Adios, the world's premier equine sire, until the magnificent stallion died in 1965. When Del Miller reduced his breeding operation after Adios's death, Harvey moved to his own Arden Hills Farm nearby and expanded his personal Standardbred breeding endeavors, standing such solid but unheralded sires as Majestic Hanover, Express Rodney and Vicar Hanover.

Operating a modern breeding farm in the face of growing competition did not provide him with the income he needed, however. He began to step up his training and driving efforts, labors of love which had been virtually dormant during his many seasons as manager of Miller's Meadow Lands.

"In this day farms are expensive and there is just not that much money in $500 stud fees," he told *Hoof Beats* magazine interviewer Tom White. "So it was a matter of economics that I returned to training."

By 1969 he was constructing a rather large contingent of colts and raceway horses, and his deep maroon driving colors and novel helmet—he wears a silk cover over the hard hat in the manner of European drivers and Thoroughbred jockeys—were becoming more and more familiar around North America's racing ovals.

One of his patrons was Bert James. James, in settling into his

Delvin Miller, Mr. Harness Racing himself, played several roles in the Albatross story. (James Ponter drawing)

new James Boys Farm, had asked Del Miller to recommend a reputable trainer for his racing stock. It would be nice, he said, if the trainer worked out of the Pittsburgh area. Miller hastened to suggest Harvey, who was practically a neighbor, and James accepted his advice. With some of the former Cadillac dealer's horses in his stable —two or three at a time—a grateful Harvey took it upon himself to help James in his quest for broodmares.

Harry was acting as a sort of procurer—in the best sense of the word—for patron James when he steered him onto Voodoo Hanover and her two children. To say that Harvey located the three-horse package for James, however, is to reduce the situation to its most rudimentary form. Actually, the play was Kenney-to-Lydon-to-Rooney-to-Harvey-to-James, a quadruple reverse which calls for some explaining.

Charlie Kenney, after gaining his partners' approval to sell the mare and foals, had urged each of the syndicate members to roll up his or her sleeves and help in the effort to locate a buyer.

Mark Lydon was doing exactly that when he tried to tout Timothy J. Rooney onto the three-horse parcel. Rooney, a tall, youngish member of the famous sports-minded Rooney family which operates the William Penn meeting at Liberty Bell as well as the Pittsburgh Steeler football team, was a frequent visitor to Liberty Bell. His brother John was president of the meeting (Tim would bcome president of Yonkers Raceway when the family bought control in 1972), and Tim was friendly with assistant racing secretary Lydon.

Tim Rooney wasn't interested in the proposition, but had a friend who might be—Harry Harvey. Harvey had trained an occasional horse for him over the years, was an ardent fan of the Steelers and enjoyed personal ties with the Rooney family.

Harvey, who was shifting his emphasis from breeding to training and driving, wasn't interested, but had a friend who might be—Bert James.

Thus, James ended up with the ball.

Harry knew that his neighbor and client was not only searching for well-bred mares, but was also hoping to put together a small band of yearlings to take to the 1969 sales. James hoped to gain some valuable selling experience before his first major farm consignment headed for the sales rings in 1970.

In addition to his desire to assist James, Harvey had a paternal interest in the deal outlined by Tim Rooney. He was a knowledgeable fan of Meadow Skipper, the sire of the two foals that were involved in the three-horse parlay.

"I was always fond of Meadow Skipper because he was raised at Del Miller's farm while I was there," he pointed out. "His dam, Countess Vivian, was supposed to have been bred to Adios that year, but the old horse was ailing at the time, so she ended up going to Dale Frost instead. I followed Skipper throughout his racing career, knew how game he was to be racing so well with splint problems, and was positive he would make a pretty damn good sire."

The more he thought about the deal, the more enthusiastic he became in his discussion with James.

"Sounds all right to me," James agreed without undue hesitation. "If you think it's worthwhile, go ahead and buy them for me."

Harvey then called Kenney at Stoner Creek Stud. "I'd known Charlie Kenney for a long time, dating back to the days when I was with Tom Berry," Harry recalled.

"I knew he was as honest as anybody in the business, and that he's realistic and frank about his own product. He wasn't too high on the mare, Voodoo Hanover, but he did tell me she'd recently dropped a nice looking filly foal. 'And the mare's got a yearling colt, too,' he added. 'I don't really know what to tell you about him. He doesn't look too sharp, on the small side and all, though he doesn't look all that bad either. He's a growthy kind of colt, and his legs are all right . . .'"

Harvey asked the price of the three and Kenney quoted him a figure of $11,000. He also inquired about a finder's fee—where a percentage of the sale price goes to the man who locates a buyer—and was told it was impossible since the breeders had nearly the whole $11,000 tied up in the original cost of the mare, stud fees, nomination fees and board. Horsemen with less integrity than Harry Harvey have been known to tinker with the price tag and manufacture their own finder's fee.

"Even so, my man will take them," the trainer instructed the farm manager. "I'll see that he sends you a check, and that he arranges for a van to pick the colt up."

It was agreed at the time of the sale that Voodoo Hanover would remain at Stoner Creek the rest of July as the farm tried for the third time to get her in foal to Meadow Skipper (the mating which didn't take). Her weanling daughter, of course, had to stay with her, leaving only the yearling colt for immediate delivery.

"By the way, what do they call that colt?" Harvey asked.

"He's called Albatross," Kenney answered.

5

Harvey had mixed emotions when he first laid eyes on Albatross a few days after he arrived at the James Boys Farm. Bert James looked on stoically as Harry circled the yearling, studied him from every angle, and offered a verdict:

"He's not what you'd call real cute, Bert, but then he's got some good points. He's an angular kind of colt, not too big, but long barreled. He's got good legs, just about the way you want them, and he's got a long neck and a pretty good-sized head. He'll grow into that head, which means he'll be a bigger horse one day."

The trainer, nervously running a hand through his thick brown hair as he reported, was passing on an opinion that would be echoed by nearly every veteran horseman who saw Albatross during the first year and a half of his life. There was little outstanding about the colt when you considered him as a collective entity, yet it was difficult to fault him in any one area. Time would be the agent that would mold all the parts into one of the slickest, most efficient racing machines produced since the arrival of Imported Messenger, the sport's foundation stallion, on American shores in 1788.

Harvey, if anything, was being a bit generous in his remarks, he confided later. It was he, after all, who had urged James to part with $11,000 for Albatross and his two relatives. Privately he was hoping the mare and her filly foal would flash a little more style, grace and size when they showed up at the James Boys Farm.

James seemed unperturbed over the trainer's hedgy appraisal. For good reason. Whatever the colt looked like—Bret Hanover or Old Shep—he was planning to sell him within three months. His plan was to send him to the October auction in Lexington, where his breeders had originally plotted to peddle him. But he was too late to get him catalogued and had to shoot for the Standardbred Horse Sales at Harrisburg in November instead.

He and his eager sons were also simonizing two other yearling colts for the Harrisburg vendue, a Thorpe Hanover son called Saint Clair Bit (to be renamed Pretty Boy) and a Right Time offspring named Saint Clair Bill (due for a name change to Flag Time). Harry Harvey, practically indispensable to the neophyte breeder at the time, uncovered that pair as well.

Another of Harvey's patrons, Dick Obenchain of Pittsburgh, had bred the colts and was looking to sell them privately. "Dick was asking $10,000 for the two when I told Bert about them," Harry said. "He and his son David went over with a checkbook, and brought them back. That's how quick Bert was."

So the James Boys Farm had a token consignment of three yearlings when the family—and ever-helpful Harry Harvey, who had his own colts to sell—headed for the Pennsylvania capital on Monday, November 3, 1969. Bert James left home with a jaunty spirit—he had visions of selling Albatross alone for $11,000—but returned rather subdued after his brush with the major league buyers and sellers. In Harvey's words, the Harrisburg auction "was a disaster for James."

As always, it was the largest, most important Standardbred sale of the year. A total of 838 horses, 532 of them yearlings, changed hands during the four-day affair. Also changing hands was $5,335,200 in cash. All the top horsemen were there, the Stanley Dancers, Herve Filions, Billy Haughtons, George Sholtys, Joe O'Briens, Frank Ervins, Del Millers and Del Camerons. The big buyers—K. D. Owen, J. Elgin Armstrong, Leonard J. Buck, Fred L. VanLennep, Norman S. Woolworth, Louis Resnick and Thomas A. Dexter among them—were also on hand. The market was brisk, the bids high: $125,000 on Froelich Hanover (later renamed Dexter Hanover), $57,000 on Bob Hanover, $50,000 on Breton Hanover.

It was one hellish place, and one hellish time, for a comparative greenhorn with three unheralded yearlings to get his feet wet. James went to the sale with three yearlings and came home with two of them.

He did manage to sell Pretty Boy (Saint Clair Bit) to Dudley C. Dahle of Farmington, Connecticut, for $1,900. And he had Flag Time (Saint Clair Bill) sold for something in the neighborhood of $5,500 until the prospective purchaser checked the colt out in his stall at the rear of the huge sales arena and decided there was something wrong with his eyes. The new owner had a veterinarian verify his suspicions, and the sale was off. The buyer and the vet were both wrong, but that was little consolation to James at that moment.

While James was hoping for $11,000 on Albatross—he thought perhaps he could recoup the sum he had paid for the colt, his dam and sister on the sale of Albatross alone—he was realistic enough to expect less. He and Harvey, while the happy bedlam of the auction swirled about them, had set "bottom" figures on the colts he was selling. In the case of Albatross, the floor was $7,000. If the bidding did not reach that sum, James would not sell. He would "bid in" the colt and take him back to the farm, either to sell privately at a later date or to train for the races. He would have to pay a sales commission on the figure reached, but the action would protect him from bargain hunters who might grab the youngster for a song.

To carry it off, he needed a sympathetic accomplice to "run the colt up" if necessary. He needed someone to offer at least an illusion of interest in the horse if little existed, and he needed someone to provide some opposition if only one other party chose to bid on him. James again turned to Harvey for help.

Harry, himself, could not be the confederate. His face was too familiar to the hundreds in the hall, and his affiliation with James was hardly a secret. He scoured the crowd for a friendly countenance, spotted Tim Rooney, and prevailed upon the personable, agreeable young track executive to handle the chore. It was the same Tim Rooney who had declined to purchase Albatross three months earlier, turning the proposal over to Harvey.

Albatross, preened to the best of the Jameses' abilities, was hip number 130 in the sales ring. He was marched around and around the ring while the auctioneers loudly hailed his rather limited credentials and the bidding opened. The interest in him was hardly what would be termed intense. Even with Rooney performing admirably from one side of the ring, James still could not get his $7,000 for the colt. The last legitimate bid on him was $6,800, with Rooney dutifully upping it to $7,000 to save the horse for James.

(Several years later Charlie Kenney, Tic Wilcutts and Mark Lydon, three members of the quintet which bred Albatross, would all take a measure of comfort from the fact that James was unable to sell the colt at that price. "It helped to prove that we weren't such giant jackasses," Wilcutts commented. "James was willing to let him go at $7,000 and couldn't find a buyer.")

The angels were on James's side, although he was unconsciously doing his level best to shake them. No sooner had he signed the slip, which, in effect, saved the future world champion for himself, than he was accepting a suggestion from Harvey that the two of them circulate through the arena in search of a buyer for Albatross. "I still think we can sell him," the trainer said. Straining fate a little further, James acquiesced.

Billy Haughton was one of the horsemen who failed to succumb to Harry's sales pitch. Harvey had pegged the ultrasuccessful Haughton as a possible candidate because Billy has no built-in prejudice against inexpensive colts. Haughton trains 100-plus yearlings each year, and many of them are horses he has snatched out of auctions for as little as $5,000, $4,000, $3,000 and even $2,000. With some 3,700 victories and more than $19 million in purses won through 1973, Billy has proven that class and big price tags are not always synonymous.

Harvey found Haughton in breeder Max C. Hempt's hospitality trailer, sampling some of Hempt's refreshments after the sales session, and tried to arouse his interest in Albatross. Haughton, easygoing and one of the most popular figures in the sport, listened attentively and studied the colt's breeding in the catalogue. Finally he handed the book back to Harvey, grinned and shook his head neg-

Great horseman Billy Haughton drove Seton Hanover against Albatross. (James Ponter drawing)

atively. "Too much white paper for me," he commented, referring to the unproven producing records of both the colt's dam and sire.

While Sweet William was aware that Meadow Skipper's first crop had yielded some creditable freshman pacers, he was waiting for more evidence that Skipper would make a great sire. And Albatross's dam, Voodoo Hanover, was sporting neither a racing nor producing record of any kind.

Had Haughton been the least bit interested in Albatross's pedigree, it probably would have gone no further than that. The colt's lineage, at that point, was about all he had going for him. The

90 or so days at the James Boys Farm had done little to improve his looks, not that the James family had not bombarded him with oats and curry combs. Flag Time, the yearling falsely accused of having faulty vision, "was a big, strapping youngster, looking like he was full of promise," according to Harvey. Albatross, as late as the Harrisburg sale, "was on the scrawny order, not carrying a bit of extra weight, sort of nondescript looking."

The trainer did not want to see James get stuck with two colts, be forced into taking them home and having them trained. One should be sacrificed, Harry felt, and that one should be Albatross. It was for that reason that Harvey nudged James into a sales campaign after the colt had left the sales ring, where he had failed to bring $7,000.

Once converted to the trainer's way of thinking, James was out selling hard, like in the days of pushing Eldorados back in Windsor. He did some detective work and came up with the names of the men who had bid $6,800 on Albatross in the ring, the last genuine offer before Tim Rooney had jumped in to preserve the colt for James. They were members of the Stafford harness racing clan in Cherry Hill, New Jersey—a family of solid Standardbred breeders, trainers and drivers.

"What do you know about them?" James asked Harvey.

"They're good, substantial people," Harry said.

"I think I'll go see them."

The next day Bert located them in the smoky, clamorous hall and tried to sell them Albatross on the spot. The Staffords were tempted, but were not prepared to act that quickly. They wanted to secure a partner to help share the cost. A figure of $6,500 was mentioned.

That was the best that either James or Harvey could manage—a shaky "maybe."

James headed back to Avella with two of the three yearlings he had shipped to the sale—the muscular, striking looking Flag Time and the small, mousy Albatross. He had learned much at the auction, taken it on the chin a couple of times, but was still adamant about cracking the Standardbred breeding industry. And he still had a shot at selling the smaller colt.

A few days later he was contacted by one of the Staffords, who told him they wanted the youngster and would send a van for him. The van never arrived. With Albatross in a kind of limbo, James called a member of the Jersey racing family. "I'm sorry," he was informed, "our partner bought another horse, so we'll have to forget the deal."

A grim Bert James then called Harry Harvey. "That Albatross colt . . ." he started.

"What about him?" Harvey asked.

"I want him trained."

40

6

It was early December, 1969, before Albatross was vanned the short distance from the James Boys Farm to the Arden Fairground, where his training was to start. He was already three weeks behind the rest of the yearlings in Harry Harvey's stable, and the trainer could only shrug ruefully as the little horse backed down the ramp of Bert James's trailer.

"He might make a pacer," owner James remarked as a groom snapped a lead shank to the colt's halter.

"He might," the trainer replied solemnly.

For Harvey, it was a case of taking some bad with the good. He had other yearlings for James, including the handsome Flag Time, and James was not the kind of man you could get choosy with. You either accepted all his colts, runts included, or you got nothing.

"Do the best you can with him," the owner added.

"I'll give it a real try," the trainer promised.

If Harry had reservations about Albatross at the outset—and he did—they were only reinforced during the colt's early days in his stable. The young horse offered but one small clue to his future greatness, and it was a hint that Harvey would just as well have done without at the time.

Albatross had *spirit*.

"Spirit? He had that, all right. Man, did he have spunk," Harvey recalled years later. "The first thing he did when I got him was kick hell out of his stall. I mean he wouldn't quit. He was at it day and night, slamming away at the walls until I thought he'd level the barn or kill himself.

"I don't mean to convey the idea that he was a mean colt, because he wasn't. Not at all. It was simply that he was a stud colt, and he felt real good. He was bored and restless, full of vinegar. And he about drove us nuts."

Harvey and his crew of veteran caretakers wrestled with the problem for weeks. They shifted the colt from stall to stall in an attempt to find a neighbor, another horse, with charisma enough to attract his attention, keep him occupied. In vain. Then they tried him in a corner of the barn where he could peer out the windows and watch all the activity outside. Forget it.

Nothing worked until his trainer stumbled on the idea of an O'Brien Paddock—a smallish, fenced in, portable enclosure. He bought one, installed it in the centerfield of the fairground track, and turned his high-voltage colt loose in it. Throughout the winter and early spring, the spunky yearling spent the better part of the daylight hours in the paddock, bucking, lunging, galloping and pacing his excess energy away. It wasn't the ultimate solution, but it was a valuable tool while he was being taught the rudiments of pacing.

Albatross broke easily—"No problems," said Harvey—and accepted the bit, harness and jog cart without a major skirmish. He balked at the hopples, however, resisting the plastic hoops with savage cleverness. All dressed up to go pacing, he would decide to shed the hopples, trying to kick himself over the jog cart shaft to do it. Harvey decided that he had better jog him most of the time to save a rate increase in his workmen's compensation plan because of injured grooms.

That was fine with Joe Luster, the first of a parade of caretakers assigned to Albatross during his 14 months under Harvey's wing.

On the move, the Meadow Skipper son was reasonably well gaited, although he showed a tendency to "wing" his left front leg—toss it somewhat to the side instead of straight ahead. He wore flat shoes in front (half-round, half-swedge behind), and Harry was tempted to tinker with his shoeing in an effort to rid him of the habit. He pondered the action for days, then voted against it. Similar experiments with other horses had not panned out for him, so he decided to stand pat and see what time and nature could do to solve it.

With all his minor faults, Albatross was showing progress, and Harvey began to "like" him. "By mid-January, he was showing me little flashes of speed that kind of surprised me," the colt's tutor reported. "We were going the right way of the track by then, and I'd let him ramble a little—not much, a hundred feet or so—and he could move out pretty good."

There was another small point that endeared him to Harvey. "I couldn't help but notice that his respiration was outstanding. His ability to convert oxygen into energy was as good— better, really—as any horse I'd ever seen. While it was no guarantee that he would be a great horse, I knew that he could not even be a good one without proper breath control."

After two full months of training, Albatross was accepting the hopples and correcting the winging habit, but his stall-kicking routine was still giving his trainer fits. Paddock exercise and all, the colt was still full of hell at night, whiling away the hours by bouncing his hoofs off the sides of the stall. At one point he slammed the wood so hard and so consistently that he made himself lame in a rear leg. In desperation, Harvey padded his stall, which reduced the chances of serious harm. "But I never really got him over the kicking thing," he confessed.

Then other small idiosyncrasies began to blossom. Bursting with nervous energy, Albatross seemed to be a veritable cornucopia of pesky inclinations. When Harry trained him with other horses, he became competitive, grabbing into the bit and straining to race them. He was also unalterably opposed to having another horse kick dirt in his face. Struck by a chunk or two of soil, he would pull himself off the rail and charge past the offender, unless Harvey happened to be feeling particularly virile at the moment.

At high speed—brushing, as it's called—he was guilty of making little skipping breaks. He would lose his rhythm, break stride for an instant, then land back on the pace. Harvey fretted over this stunt until he recalled that Dale Frost, Del Miller's world champion out of the past, had the same tendency in his youth. Harvey had helped to train Dale Frost, and had seen him outgrow the habit. So would Albatross, he reassured himself, since Albatross happened to be a grandson of Dale Frost.

And then there were the ducks and dives. "Before I began to train him in a blind bridle, or sometimes a Kant-See-Back, he'd give me a real thrill," his trainer reflected. "We'd be motoring along okay and suddenly he'd spot something in the infield, a piece of paper or something. Then he'd duck and dive, trying to avoid it. His reflexes were so unbelievably quick that you never got a warning. I thought for sure I was going over the fence with him a couple of times."

By mid-March, however, Harvey was prepared to put up with all the high jinks, all the colt-fashion stunts Albatross could ever hope to fashion. The impossible had happened. The small, scraggy, common looking colt who had gone unsold at Harrisburg was suddenly the brightest light in the Harvey stable. He had caught and passed his larger contemporaries, all of whom had enjoyed a head start in training on him. Sporting new inches and pounds—no longer the ugly duckling—he was fulfilling all the bits and pieces of promise he had shown his trainer during his 100 or so days of training. Harvey had seen it coming—the bursts of speed, his superior breathing apparatus, his love of competition—yet he could scarcely believe it.

"I was training about a dozen two-year-olds in addition to Albatross. Two of them, Joeys Byrd and Flag Time, seemed outstanding from the beginning, while two or three others looked like they were going to be class individuals. But all of a sudden this little horse, Albatross, could handle them all with ease. He kept getting better and better until along about the middle of March, it was obvious that he was far better than anything else I had."

Bert James, with time on his hands since son David was running the breeding operation, was a constant visitor to Harvey's training headquarters at the Arden Fairground. James was there maybe five mornings a week watching his colts in their training routines (and harassing grooms, according to Harvey). If he looked a little smug as he chewed on his big Windsor cigar, he had a perfect right. Two of his young horses had, in effect, been rejected at the Harrisburg auction only a few months earlier. Yet there they were, training like prospective champions and heading the Harvey stable charts. One of them, in fact, was the undisputed star of the barn.

James did not push Harry for a prognosis of Albatross's future. And Harvey did not volunteer one. "I'm from the old school," the trainer said. "I hate to blow a horse out of proportion; I'd rather have him make good on his own. It's easy to get high on one and it's easier to have one go the other way. So I never offered James any glowing reports. It kind of made sense, too, because I had no idea how good he was in relation to the high-priced colts training in Florida. I kept my mouth shut and my fingers crossed."

He also kept Albatross circling the half-mile fairground track, a little faster each and every week. About the first of April he began to train him in a set with a veteran trotter called Oaklands Yank. Joe Garrett, an older man and a Harvey friend, had the trotter at Arden, getting him ready for the 1970 racing campaign. For Garrett, it was a labor of love. He trained the horse all winter long, more for the pure joy of training than for the limited riches the trotter was likely to garner during the season. Oaklands Yank could only trot a mile in 2:08 or so and had no brush to speak of, yet Garrett was prepared to race him against any horse who wandered up alongside him on the training track.

Harvey decided that Oaklands Yank would make a perfect match for young Albatross. Harry had been training his colt in near-isolation, trying to cure him of grabbing on when another horse came near. But the start of the racing season was drawing nearer, and it was imperative that he learn to behave in the company of others. The trainer was bent upon making a usable race horse out of him, one who could be raced from off the pace and not simply on the front end. Hotheaded front runners rarely wind up in the winner's circle, Harry knew. The charmed area is generally reserved for a trotter or pacer who bides his time back in the pack, conserves his energy, then makes a big move in the late stages of the contest.

Harry would keep Albatross tucked in behind Oaklands Yank for seven-eighths of the mile before pulling him off the rail and letting him have his head. At first it was a tough and tight battle to see which horse would finish first. Soon, however, the younger horse was breezing past the veteran without Harvey having to crack him with the whip, shake the lines at him, or even cluck to him. There was no question in the minds of either Harvey or Garrett that Albatross was clearly something special.

Bert James, leaning on the fence and watching his colt swish past the older trotter, had come to the same conclusion and was champing at the bit to learn exactly how special he was. He was pressing Harry to start the colt in a race at the earliest possible moment—

Albatross, still on the small and slender side as a 2-year-old, limbers up for Harry Harvey. (USTA photo)

like on May 20, when a mini-purse colt contest was scheduled at The Meadows, a pari-mutuel track only a stone's throw away.

Harvey, a graduate of the more conservative Tom Berry school of horsemanship, would have preferred to wait a while longer . . . to give the colt more seasoning, more honing. But Bert James was a difficult man to buck. He was a businessman and believed he could make his mark in racing by applying the cold, logical techniques of the business world to the sport. You had a car in the showroom; sell it. You had a horse ready to race; race him. It was an attitude not shared by the majority of citizens in the harness racing world, most of whom had fared pretty well under the old, more leisurely, more courtly rules. It was also an attitude which would set him at odds with some of the most potent people in the industry before Albatross was ready for retirement.

Harry Harvey, at the time, was anxious to please. Hopping out of semiretirement as a trainer-driver, he had enjoyed a fine year in 1969—258 starts, 90 wins, $140,269 in purses won and a .508 Universal Driver Rating System average, which was tops in the nation for drivers with from 200 to 300 races. The training fees he had earned, coupled with his percentage of the purses he had won, had helped shore up his income. He could stand the prosperity. He had a large and costly farm to maintain and a wife and four children to provide for. The children, he hoped, would receive the college education he had missed.

The year 1970 shaped up as an even better one. Maybe even a vintage year. He had a few more colts than in 1969, and the Class of '70 seemed more precocious, more promising. More important, one of his pupils, Albatross, gave every sign of being the kind of horse that most trainers wait an entire career for—generally in vain. He was not about to lose him by being obstinate with the owner. If James wanted to test the colt, the colt would be tested.

The countdown to Albatross's debut went smoothly until the first week in May, when Harvey went out one afternoon to retrieve him from his portable paddock and found him injured. Scurrying back and forth in the wire mesh enclosure, he had apparently overreached himself and damaged a leg. The tendon sheath on the right front leg had filled somewhat, and Harry Harvey was one shaken, dejected horseman.

"It scared hell out of me. I was so sick I could have cried. Here was this great colt, training like a world-beater, only two weeks away from his first race, and he was hurt. And in a tendon, of all places."

Nobody had to tell Harvey that tendon injuries have probably disabled more horses, ended more racing careers, than any of the dozens of other evils that can befall a race horse.

He and James conferred quickly, tossed the names of several top veterinarians back and forth, and settled upon Dr. E. R. Buckley of Painesville, Ohio. They called Buckley, a specialist in horse lameness with decades of experience, and were advised to van the colt out to his clinic without delay.

The good doctor examined the horse, counseled that he did not believe the injury was serious, and began to treat him. The filling was soon gone, the leg back to normal. "I don't think it will bother him any," the Ohio vet advised. "You can go on with him."

Harvey offered a silent prayer of thanksgiving. Then he took the colt home, trained him briskly on two more occasions, and hauled him the short distance to The Meadows.

7

It was 7:30 p.m., 30 minutes before the regular racing program was scheduled to begin. The seven two-year-old pacers were already on the track, nervously parading over the tartan surface. The Meadows would have a crowd of 3,465 that night. Maybe half that number had arrived. The fans were settling into grandstand seats, enjoying their dinners in the clubhouse restaurant, or leaning across the apron fence while the colts limbered up.

Betting was prohibited. Interest in the race was desultory at best, except for the paddock area where trainers, owners, grooms and a smattering of track employees jostled for position to watch the contest. Fans care little for non-betting baby races. Horsemen love them.

A token purse of $300 was at stake. The first five finishers would share in it, with the cash being handed out on a sliding scale. The winner would pick up $150; the fifth horse $15. Obviously, racing experience was the real prize in the affair.

In the field were Fortune Hanover, Trotwood Willie, Cool It, Armbro Laddie, Justarrived, Game Cash and Albatross. There was some decent breeding represented in the group, sons of Lehigh Hanover, Thorpe Hanover, Overtrick and Gamecock, although the high-priced, highly touted colts out of Florida were still winding up their training elsewhere—at places like the Lexington Red Mile, Atlantic City Raceway and Vernon Downs. Or were already racing on the Grand Circuit.

Albatross, with a jittery Harry Harvey in the sulky behind him, had drawn the seven-post and would start on the far outside. Harvey was just as well satisfied. Freshman Standardbreds going to post for the first time have sometimes been guilty of shocking breaches of decorum. The outside post is generally the safest spot in the line-up if one or more entries decide to tango instead of pace.

Suddenly it was post time. The starting gate was moving. The seven baby pacers were forming behind it. Albatross's racing career was under way.

As the gate pulled away, leaving the seven scrambling for position, Harvey headed his pacer straight for the front of the pack. Albatross rolled along willingly. He was parked out as the youngsters reached the quarter-pole in 33.1 seconds, but was safely on top as the half-pole arrived in 1:06.1. The field was stretched out behind him in Indian file fashion.

Harry Harvey was thoroughly enjoying himself, bouncing along in the bike, the spring breeze whipping at his silks as he and Albatross coasted along the backside of the track. He glanced behind him, saw no rival mounting a threat, and let his pacer out a notch or two. Albatross responded with a big kick which saw him cover the final half-mile in 1:01.1. He had three and a half lengths on Game Cash at the wire, with Justarrived getting up to claim third money.

It was almost too simple. First crack out of the box and Albatross owned a 2:07.2 victory.

The fact that his pacer had won did not surprise trainer Harvey. His sizzling second half did. He'd only trained the colt in 2:12 before starting him, and here he was pacing the last four furlongs in 1:01.1. It surprised Harvey, delighted Bert James, drew some oohs and aahs from the paddock assembly, and created a small stir within the industry when the two weekly racing magazines—*The Harness Horse* and *The Horseman & Fair World*—carried results of the race in their next editions.

Tic Wilcutts and Mark Lydon, two of the five Albatross breeders, were dazed when they read about it. "The moment I saw what he'd paced that last half in, I knew damn well we'd made a big mistake," Lydon said grimly. "I'd heard some reports that the colt was training well at Arden, but I had no idea he was that good. Tic? All he could think of was the fact that we'd let that mare get away."

Over in New Egypt, New Jersey, Stanley Dancer leafed through the magazines, spotted Albatross's victory, and commented to his brother Harold that it looked like Harry Harvey had brought out a nice colt.

Down in Hanover, Pennsylvania, John Simpson Sr., president of the Hanover Shoe Farms, read of the race and tucked the results away in his mental file. Simpson, heading the world's largest horse breeding operation, makes it his business to keep abreast of performances such as Albatross's.

The roles of Wilcutts and Lydon in the Albatross story had ended. Those of Dancer and Simpson would begin later.

Bert James, risking a rare smile as Albatross glided under the wire a big winner in his first start, was all for packing up his colt and sending him on to the Grand Circuit, harness racing's vagabond major league. That's where the money was.

"I don't know, Bert," Harvey commented cautiously. "I'm not sure that's such a good idea. The colt hasn't had all that many work miles in May, and he's only got that one race under his harness. If we take him out to The Geers, we're liable to bump heads with Flying Bret, Jolly Roger, or maybe both of them."

"I think he can hold his own," James said.

"But, Bert, those horses have had several starts," Harvey persisted. "Why, that Flying Bret has already won in two minutes and a piece. I really don't think we're ready to meet that kind yet."

As usual, James prevailed. Albatross, with a lone win in a $300 baby race on his card, was en route to Hazel Park, Michigan, for a match against the young Goliaths.

Flying Bret, a son of the mighty Bret Hanover, was the nation's fastest freshman colt at that stage of the season. Trained and driven by Charlie Clark for owners Alan and Ira Kristel of Howlett Harbor, New York, Flying Bret had rocked the racing world by winning in 2:00.4 in his third career start at Lexington on May 15. No one could remember a two-year-old going that fast so early in the season.

Jolly Roger was another of the Florida-trained freshmen who had headed north from the Sunshine State with a booming reputation. He had been one of the training leaders at Pompano Park, and had already won in 2:05.2 at Atlantic City. He was also a full brother to Most Happy Fella, a three-year-old in 1970 who would pace in 1:55, win pacing's Triple Crown, and be voted sophomore Pacer of the Year before the year was out. Both colts, sons of Meadow Skipper-Laughing Girl, were in the talented hands of Stanley Dancer.

The Geers Stake for two-year-olds at Hazel Park drew 14 entries in 1970. The large field caused racing secretary William C. Connors to split the affair into a pair of divisions, each worth $13,550. Albatross received mixed blessings in the draw. He was lucky enough to avoid Flying Bret, who landed in the second division, but had to face Jolly Roger. Roger, Albatross and five contemporaries were slated to do battle in the early dash.

The butterflies flitting about in Harvey's stomach felt like eagles this time as he eased Albatross up behind the starting gate. He knew he had a class colt, possibly even a great one. But this was the Grand Circuit. He was taking on the best of the southern-trained youngsters, and Harry was pessimistic. So were the Hazel Park fans, 9,081 strong, who sent Jolly Roger away as the even money favorite and Albatross off as a better than 4 to 1 shot.

Both the trainer and the punters were off target.

Albatross was slow leaving the gate. He was sixth and parked out at the quarter. He was fourth and parked out at the half. He was still fourth and still parked out at the three quarters, and Harvey was wondering when his overworked little horse would call it quits. As the field rounded the last turn and headed for home, he had his answer: Albatross was not about to quit. He suddenly forged ahead of the pacesetting Jolly Roger and still had a neck on the favorite as they slammed past the finish. The time for the mile was 2:06.3.

It was a remarkable performance. Albatross had been on the limb the entire mile, never getting to the rail where the route to the wire is shortest. And he had defeated some of the top Roarin' Grand colts in the land, including the highly regarded Jolly Roger.

The pari-mutuel board in the infield indicated that he had paid $10.80, $3.80 and $2.80. He would never be that generous again.

Harvey was jubilant, although his joy was tempered later in the evening when a colt named High Ideal scored an equally shocking upset over previously unbeaten Flying Bret in the second division of the Geers. High Ideal, another son of Bret Hanover, paced a 2:04.1 mile over the Hazel Park five-eighths track to dethrone the reigning champion. To worrywart Harvey, High Ideal's triumph meant there was still another fierce contestant to be faced by his horse.

The Grand Circuit moved on to Sportsman's Park, Chicago, and so did Albatross. With his sparkling win at Hazel Park, it was taken for granted he would make all the stakes events on his calendar. Even the prudent Harry Harvey had to admit the colt deserved the chance to mix it with the big names and compete for the big purses. So long as he remained sound and healthy.

The June 4 race at Sportsman's Park was the American National for two-year-olds. Nineteen trainers entered their youngsters, forcing another two-division slice. A bounty of $9,500 was at stake in each dash.

Albatross, racing out of the seven-hole for the third time, faced nine rivals in the early division and simply overpowered them. He paced in 2:04.3—his third life mark in as many outings—and scored by three and a half lengths over Bret's Brat, yet another of the Bret Hanover offspring who seemed to be sprouting from everywhere.

Most of the tougher foes had ended up in the second half of the event, with Flying Bret and Jolly Roger proving their equal skills by finishing in a dead heat for win in 2:03.

When the harness racing journals came off the presses the following week, Albatross, Flying Bret and Jolly Roger all had their photos on the covers. 1970 was shaping up as one of the most competitive seasons ever in the contest for two-year-old pacing honors.

Following the Sportsman's Park match, Albatross had a 17-day gap in his stakes schedule. Not one of the people who had been close to him in the first year and a half or so of his existence—the five breeders, James or Harvey—had ever envisioned that he would be one of the Grand Circuit's brightest stars in June of 1970. As a result, he wasn't as heavily staked as some of the other youngsters on the tour.

His trainer and owner were both concerned that he would become rusty, lose his edge in the interim. Harvey got on the phone, hunting a race for him. He was looking for a conditioned (non-stakes) event for two-year-olds and found it at Northfield Park, near Cleveland.

He took on six rather pedestrian opponents and left them all 10 or more lengths up the race track. He earned only $500 for his

Two-year-old Albatross with a full head of steam up. Harry Harvey is in the sulky. (USTA photo)

troubles, although the contest was noteworthy in two respects. It was Albatross's first journey over an off-track, and he created a minus pool—actually a pair of them—for the first time. There wasn't enough cash wagered on the other horses to pay minimum prices on him. He left the track holding the bag for $134.75 and $26.68 respectively in the place and show pools. Forcing the track to minus was something of a distinction, putting him right up there with the likes of Bret Hanover and Nevele Pride.

Heading back on the stakes trail, his record reflected four starts, four wins, earnings of $12,175 and a mark of 2:04.3.

The happy bubble was about to burst, however.

An even dozen colts faced starter Henry Folger in the $8,133 Reading Futurity at Laurel Raceway, Maryland, on June 25. Harry Harvey, scoring his colt in front of the grandstand, was not in the best of moods. Albatross had not warmed up well. He was rank, bullheaded, and tossing his head around. And a sudden, hard rainstorm had helped to dampen both his spirits and his racing silks. Harvey was impatient for the race to get started.

Albatross was never a contender in the contest. He broke stride an instant before the gate pulled away, and Harvey could not get him to hit a pace until the big field had passed the quarter-pole.

"It was awful," the trainer remembered. "While the chart did not show it, he was making little skipping breaks the rest of the way to the three quarters. He'd pace maybe 50 feet, then break stride again. He skipped like that all the way to the turn for home."

The Meadow Skipper son was eighth at the quarter, a shaky sixth at the half, fifth at the three quarters and fifth at the head of the stretch. Then he found some footing that agreed with him and practically yanked Harvey out of the sulky with his brush down the stretch. Fairly flying the final furlong and a half, he cut his vast deficit to five lengths and finished third behind Jolly Roger and Race Byrd.

"In my mind, it was the greatest effort of his young career," Harvey said. "He galloped the first quarter and lost ground on three, four, or even five breaks, yet he managed to pace his individual mile in 2:03.3.

"The fans were all talking about Dancer's Jolly Roger, who had won in 2:02.3, but Albatross's mile had convinced me that he was the best of the crop. It was the first time that I had permitted myself to believe that."

The conviction that he was handling the nation's grandest freshman pacer did not put his trainer's mind at ease. Harvey was awake most of the night, probing for reasons for the colt's curious behavior. He reflected that Meadow Skipper had made several breaks during his racing span, and wondered if heredity had anything to do with it. He quickly discarded that theory. He also discounted the possibility that Albatross might be unsound. Over the next few days he experimented with the colt's rigging, but eventually returned to the old tack. None of the changes seemed to either improve or harm the horse's way of going, although Harry did decide to tie his tongue in future races.

"In the final analysis, I had to believe it was the race track," he said. "The colt had raced great at The Meadows, which also has a tartan track, but I think the water bothered him at Laurel. It was such a vicious storm during the evening that it left puddles on the tartan surface. I believe he made a skip every time he hit one of the puddles. Coming home, the water had run off and there was plenty of sand on the track. He liked the footing there and really got rolling."

Bert James accepted Albatross's first loss with surprising composure and grace. "You can't expect to win them all," he told the trainer. Harvey, bolstered by Albatross's erratic but awesome trip at Laurel, wasn't at all sure that he agreed with the owner.

"Even then I don't think Bert really knew what a fantastic colt he had," Harry said. "That would come later."

While young Super Bird fared no better than third in the Reading, he had finished in front of nine other classy two-year-olds. One of them was a colt by the name of Nansemond. It was a name that would crop up from time to time over the next two and a half years.

Albatross was back on the winning track nine nights later. He picked up another lifetime speed badge—2:03.3—in turning back 11 foes in the $13,020 Canadian Juvenile Stakes at Garden City Raceway, St. Catherines, Ontario. Jolly Roger was missing from the field, although the swift High Ideal, with Keith Waples driving, was among Bird's victims.

His victory was so breezy—he paced the last half in 59.1 to win by two lengths—that it was difficult to imagine the tables would be turned in less than a week—that it would be High Ideal in the winner's circle and Albatross returning to the paddock for an early bath.

The site was venerable Richelieu Raceway in Montreal, the cornerstone of modern harness racing in Canada. Albatross had arrived there after a long and hot van ride from Toronto. When Harvey flew into Montreal on the morning of the race, July 10, a groom was waiting to tell him the colt had been running a temperature of 104 two days earlier.

The caretaker had sensibly called a veterinarian, who could find nothing wrong with him beyond the fever. "I wouldn't call it virus," the vet had offered. "More than likely it's a reaction to the long trip from Toronto. Tell the trainer it should be all right to race him if the temperature goes down."

Harvey, hearing all this when he arrived, was tempted to scratch his horse. But the fever was gone and Albatross felt sharp and fit in his warm-up miles. He was in the first of two $16,610 divisions. Stablemate Flag Time, racing in the second dash, had also run a temperature earlier in the week.

High Ideal was again driven by Keith Waples. The Bret son had the rail and shot away from the gate like a Cape Kennedy launching. Harvey, steering Albatross out of the two-hole, could not beat his rival away, so he nursed his horse into a spot directly behind the pacesetter. The two favorites raced like that down to the half, where Harvey observed that Waples had backed his horse off and was obviously saving him.

With the half-pole slipping by in 1:04.2, Harvey jerked Albatross off the rail and hustled him up alongside High Ideal. They were head and head at the six-furlong mark, and Harvey was reasonably certain his horse would win it in the scramble home. He was wrong, however. High Ideal, with Bret Hanover's blood flowing through his veins, paced the final panel in 28.4. Albatross was a neck behind at the wire.

Harry Harvey, weary and somber, drifted into another session of soul-searching on the flight back to Pittsburgh. Had the fever earlier in the week taken the edge off his horse? Had he started him back too quickly after the fast mile at Toronto? Had he driven him badly, been out-maneuvered by Keith Waples? Or was he simply engaging in wishful thinking by brashly believing Albatross was the top freshman pacing colt in the land?

An affirmative answer seemed possible for any one of the first three questions, he decided. He had to vote no on the fourth, however. Albatross *was* the best. He merely needed the right race, the right night, the right field and the right track to prove it conclusively.

8

Vernon, New York, is a small, pleasant village along Route 5, some 16 miles west of Utica. Not much happens in Vernon in winter. The 1,100 residents trudge through the snow to pick up their mail at the Post Office, stop in for a coffee at the Rexall Drug Store, transact a little business at the National Bank, or sample a toddy at the Village Inn. Sure, the Burton Livestock Exchange is open through the winter months, but on the whole, the town battens down the hatches and waits for spring.

The tempo begins to pick up about April 15. The snow has disappeared—or, at least, is disappearing—and the traffic grows heavier on Peterboro Street, especially where it meets the mouth of Ruth Street. Mobile homes of all shapes and sizes are tugged around the corner, roll down Ruth and vanish over the hill near the Livestock Exchange. Horse trailers and vans, carrying anywhere from one to 12 horses, lumber along the same route, as does a stream of autos, station wagons and pickup trucks.

Soon it's difficult to find a table for lunch at Willie Law's or the Charlebois Brothers' restaurants. Postmaster Jim Dam is busy selling postal boxes. The Foodland Store is hiring help. Seats are at a premium at the bar of Les Carney's Nutshell Inn. Lee Lagoy has picked up the pace of his hair-clipping.

Spring has arrived in Vernon. Of almost equal consequence, Vernon Downs is opening.

You wouldn't call Vernon Downs a plush harness racing plant. It's not in the same league with Pompano Park, Florida, or Scioto Downs, Ohio, certainly. But it is charming, roomy and complete, and boasts some of the prettiest track grounds found anywhere. More important, it is constructed around an unusual three-quarter-mile racing oval which is lightning fast because of its dimensions and composition. The United States Trotting Association gives it an official speed rating of 2:01.4, meaning that only Lexington's Red Mile is supposed to be faster. Through 1974, Vernon had hosted almost 500 two-minute miles, including slashing tours of 1:54 by Bret Hanover and 1:55 by Adios Harry.

Many of the Grand Circuit's leading trainers, men like Ralph Baldwin, John Simpson Jr., Billy Haughton, Clint Hodgins, Frank

Ervin and George Sholty, send all or part of their colt contingents to Vernon in May and June. They train and sharpen their youngsters over the big, safe Vernon oval and use the track as a kind of Grand Central Station, shipping the colts to stakes engagements, then shipping them back. The procedure generally continues through Grand Circuit Week in late July or early August.

Roarin' Grand Week is the high point of the Vernon season as it is for all 20-plus member tracks. The cream of North America's two and three-year-old Standardbreds turn up from all points of the compass for the six or seven nights of rich racing action. The track's nearly 1,100 stalls are taxed to the limits as racing secretary Jerry Monahan uses every device short of a shoe horn to fit the visitors in. Motels in the Vernon area are likewise filled as the Roarin' Grand trainers, drivers, owners, caretakers and their retinues seek accommodations. The village, booming from the start of the track's season in April, is strained to the seams by the influx.

In 1970, the Grand Circuit arrived at Vernon Downs on Monday, July 27. Albatross was already there, jogging in the mornings and spending his afternoons peering out the stall door, watching the other Circuit fillies and colts arriving. He was prepping for his stakes event —the Andy Kerr Memorial Pace—and he did not have long to wait. The race, honoring the late and great Colgate University football coach, was the lead-off event on the Circuit agenda at Vernon.

Sixteen trainers had thought enough of their charges to enter them in the Kerr. A split was necessary, and Harry Harvey was so anxious to learn who his rivals would be that he phoned Walter Bonafice, the assistant racing secretary, two days in advance of the contest.

"You landed in the softer end of it, Babe," Bonafice told him. "You're the best."

Harvey had had too many dealings with Bonafice to let it go at that. "Who's in there with him?" he asked suspiciously. Pressed, the racing official listed the field, which included Flying Bret, Race Byrd, Winning Worthy, H. T. Luca and Paulos Hanover. "That's the softer division?" Harvey inquired skeptically.

"Would I lie to you?" Bonafice demanded. "Jolly Roger, Seton Hanover, Tarport Skipper—they're all in the second division. You toss a two-minute mile at them cats in your end of it and you'll jerk their bridles off. Harry, you got a piece of cake."

Harvey, thinking about it, had to agree that the draw had been kind to him. Nobody had to tell him how tough Jolly Roger was. And Seton Hanover, handled by Billy Haughton for the Farmstead Acres of Glen Head, New York, was unbeaten. In his division, only Flying Bret gave him any real concern. Albatross had never met Flying Bret—they had raced in different divisions in the past—but the Bret Hanover colt had been trailing off some after his spectacular early success.

But was Albatross prepared to pace in two minutes at that stage of the season, as Bonafice suggested he must? Harvey figured he'd have his answer come Monday night.

It turned out to be a rare night for racing. It was warm, pushing 76 degrees at race time, and the blue, gold and white Grand Circuit pennants decorating the clubhouse entrance stood lank and lifeless, meaning there was no appreciable wind to buck. Vernon's big miracle mile—the roomy oval with a quarter-mile chute leading into it—looked like a giant ribbon of beige silk under the lights.

Remembering his gritty mile at Richelieu, Harvey had decided that his colt did not want for gameness, so he chose to race Flying Bret for the lead. The Bret Hanover colt, in the hands of Charlie Clark, was in the habit of setting the pace.

The two co-favorites swept down Vernon's long chute as though the purse for the Kerr division were $94,000 instead of $9,400. As the pair sailed out of the chute and onto the main track, Harvey looked over at his rival, noticed that he was laboring, and decided he had him beaten. The electronic timer, reading 27 seconds flat to the quarter, gave him a momentary shock, but Albatross was pacing so effortlessly that he quit worrying.

"From that point on, while it seems impossible, I was simply buggy riding," he reported later. "My horse got to the half in 57.3 and the three-quarters in 1:27.4, and still he was gliding along without strain. Race Byrd started to come at us past the three quarters, and my first inclination was to dig into my colt. But Albatross let him move up to the wheels of the bike, then he just kind of swelled up and spurted ahead, even though he was going a hell of a clip at the time. I never did get after him, although I kind of half-heartedly shook the lines at him halfway down the stretch. He won by a solid length over Paulos Hanover, who made a big move at the end to get second money."

Harvey, stealing a quick glance at the timer as he flashed under the wire, was shocked. The figures 1:57.4 were up there.

It was a national season's record that would stand throughout the entire 1970 campaign.

"The thing that rocked me the most was the fact that he had turned in a clocking like that so easily. It was the one time when I felt he could have gone a substantially better mile had I worked on him a little. I felt he could have gone a full second faster, if not more," he pointed out.

A full second faster would have erased Bullet Hanover's name from the record book. Bullet Hanover was history's fastest two-year-old pacer. His 1:57 record, set in 1959, had come in August over the Indianapolis, Indiana, mile track. And it had been set in the middle of the afternoon when racing ovals are at their peak of speed.

John F. Simpson Sr., the man who had driven Bullet Hanover to the world mark, was on hand at Vernon that night to see Alba-

Harry Harvey, still on good terms with Bert James at the time, poses with James and his wife after fleet filly Saucy Wave scored easy win at Vernon Downs. Vernon racing secretary Jerry Monahan and family present trophy. (Vernon Downs photo)

tross in his incredible mile. Simpson was most impressed. "I liked his gait, his deportment on the track, the way he carried himself, the set of his head," he stated years later. "It was my first look at him and I liked everything I saw. Of course, his magnificent mile spoke for itself."

Simpson, heading the Hanover Shoe Farms dynasty by then, had a few more important facts for the mental dossier he was maintaining on Albatross.

As for Harry Harvey, well, he had the kind of evidence he needed to bolster his private contention that Albatross was the valedictorian of a clearly exceptional class of two-year-old pacing colts. His conviction remained hard and firm after watching the second half of the Kerr Pace, won by Seton Hanover in 1:59 flat.

Albatross would lose one more race during the season, but Harvey would contend that the defeat "should be charged to driver and owner."

In the interim, the Meadow Skipper offspring was fated to go another big mile, and the sports writing fraternity was bound to begin toying with his unusual name. Earl Watson, publicity director of

Pocono Downs, was one of the early writers to get into the act. Following Albatross's smashing triumph at Pocono, Watson wrote in the harness magazines:

"*It's becoming increasingly evident that Albatross is misnamed. Hawk, falcon, eagle—or perhaps The Jet—would be more appropriate.*

"*Bert V. James' two-year-old pacing sensation, who gained super pacer status with his 1:57.4 clocking at Vernon Downs on July 27, zipped off a 1:59.1 clocking to establish a new Pocono Downs record for his age and gait in capturing his division of the $33,736 Hanover-Hempt Stake on Saturday night.*

"*The stakes event, which lured 25 starters, was split into three divisions with Scot Time (2:03) and Seton Hanover (2:00.2) emerging victorious in the other sections.*

"*But, it was Albatross who left the fans buzzing in the third and final division. The Meadow Skipper colt was turned loose in the stretch by Harry Harvey and soared home by 3½ lengths after fractions of 28.4, 59.2 and 1:29.4. It was Albatross's seventh win in nine starts.*"

The Pocono affair was on August 8. Dame Fortune quit smiling on the little horse—or took a vacation, at the very least—on August 14. Just when Albatross, Harvey and James were scheduled to appear before the home folks.

The Albatross entourage was back at The Meadows, where it had all begun months before, when Lady Luck turned off the grin. Harvey's colt drew the nine-post in a 10-horse field for the $17,370 Arden Downs Stake. Then owner Bert James complicated the situation by constructing a game plan. And trainer-driver Harvey compounded it by following the plan.

"James had the habit of scrutinizing the field for every race," Harvey explained. "He would study the program lines and talk to people who were familiar with the other horses in the event. Then he'd come and discuss what he'd learned with me. It was simply a discussion, nothing more. He never actually told me how to drive the horse.

"At The Meadows, however, he was more concerned than usual about Albatross's post position. Drawing the nine-hole, the colt had to start in the second tier, and Bert was afraid he'd get locked in and be caught back in traffic. This time he was rather insistent that I barrel him out of there, head straight for the top."

Harvey argued against the strategy. The horse due to start in front of him in the first tier could leave the gate well, he reasoned. Albatross could follow him away and gain a comfortable spot on the rail. He could make his move after the early traffic thinned out.

Then a pair of scratches developed in the field—one of them a horse in the front tier, the other the 10-horse alongside Albatross in the second wave. While the rules stated that Albatross could not move

Young horseman Eddie Dunnigan scored early victory over Albatross. (James Ponter drawing)

up to the first row, he could leave the gate behind any horse that Harvey chose. The danger of getting trapped in a pocket was considerably lessened.

The trainer took the precaution of discussing the situation—and the rules—with starter Dick Williams. "Don't worry," Williams said reassuringly, "we'll see that you get away all right." The starter, at Harvey's urging, relayed the same message to owner James.

"But Bert remained unconvinced," Harry remarked. "He seemed

to have a premonition the colt would get pinned to the rail with horses all around him and we wouldn't be able to shake free in time to win the thing. I was torn between doing what I felt was right and pleasing the owner."

Grudgingly, he chose to please the owner.

When the field departed, Harvey and Albatross trailed the seven-horse away. They swept around the horse on the far outside and made a beeline for the front. Albatross had the lead at the quarter-pole, but he had to earn it with a 29-second brush over the five-eighths-mile track. Rushing to the front and then making the big sweep from the far outside to the rail had cost him some sting. Harry was hoping to back him off and give him a breather when Charlie Clark suddenly appeared with Flying Bret.

No rest was possible as Albatross held his opponent at bay, whipping past the next two poles in 1:00.3 and 1:30.3. Flying Bret's bid was finished by this point—he backed through the field and finished eighth—but Harvey still could not permit his colt to relax. Seton Hanover, reined by young Eddie Dunnigan, had been trailing him like a vulture, and Harry sensed that Seton would be out and coming within the next few seconds.

Midway through the final turn, Albatross had two lengths on his new foe, yet Harvey knew he was in trouble. For the first time in his young career, Bird was getting leg weary. The gap was closing. Dunnigan, sitting in for boss Bill Haughton, was working furiously on his horse. Harvey was also rapping Albatross. At the wire it was Seton Hanover. By a slender nose in 2:00.2, the last quarter, turn and all, in 29.4.

Harvey was despondent. "We blew it," he said. "It was, after all, only an eight-horse field. Yet, to please the owner, I had barreled him out of there like there were 15 horses in the race. It was a particularly bitter defeat for me because I knew he was better than those other colts."

From that time forward, Harvey kept his own counsel, plotted his own strategy. And Albatross would not taste defeat again that season.

9

The Fox Stake, raced at the Indiana State Fair in Indianapolis, is one of those hallowed harness racing happenings which gush with prestige, overflow with riches and offer a year's lease on a trophy about the size of Mount Everest.

The Fox, in business since Sep Palin guided Red Pluto to a comfortable victory over Lafayette in 1927, has entertained nothing but the fanciest freshman pacers year after year, and its winners have included The Widower, Adios, Knight Dream, Good Time, Torpid, Bullet Hanover, Bret Hanover, Romeo Hanover, Best of All and Laverne Hanover.

The gentlemen who have driven the Fox winners are the same gentlemen whose racing silks, soft and hard hats, whips, stopwatches and statuettes are on display at the Hall of Fame of the Trotter in Goshen, New York—Mr. Palin, Tom Berry, Henry Thomas, Vic Fleming, Del Miller, Frank Ervin, Curly Smart, Joe O'Brien, Billy Haughton, John Simpson Sr. and Ralph Baldwin, to scratch the surface.

It was a race, contested in heats in the traditional manner, which Harry Harvey wanted desperately to win in 1970.

As an aide-de-camp to Tom Berry and then to Del Miller, Harvey had sweated his way through several sweltering afternoons at the Indianapolis Fairground, looking on enviously as his bosses paraded colts to post in the Fox. Circumstances, mainly his long, self-imposed exile at Miller's breeding farm, had denied him a ride in the classic stake, much as he longed for one.

In 1970, he deduced, he would not only get his ride, but very possibly add his name—and the name of his horse—to one of the little golden plaques running up and down the face of the gargantuan Fox trophy.

It was a warm and pleasant vision that entertained him straight through the morning of August 15, when he checked Albatross's stall at Arden Downs and discovered his stakes-winner suffering from a royal case of colt virus. The youngster was running a mild temperature, acting lethargic and commencing to drip at the nose.

Harvey groaned. A single glance told him he was in trouble. It was obvious the malady was more serious than the brief run of fever Albatross had conquered at Richelieu Raceway in Canada. A colt virus is unpredictable at best, dangerous at worst.

The next three weeks were nearly traumatic for the trainer as the tides of Albatross's health rose and fell. The fever would vanish one day, reappear the next. His nose was dripping mucus every day. Curiously, he quickly shook the sluggishness and let his handler know that he felt good. Even frisky.

"We shipped him over to my farm and turned him out," Harvey recollected. "It was the first time he'd been turned loose since he started racing, and he raised vicious hell running and ramming around in the paddock. I had to pull him out of there, but he was no better in the stall, causing all kinds of commotion because he obviously felt pretty good."

To save wear and tear on both the horse and his barn, Harvey waited until his temperature was back to normal, then trained him lightly. He had a slight reaction to the session, but nothing too serious. Optimistically, Harvey and James decided Albatross could make an August 27 stakes date at Brandywine. They shipped him over to the Delaware track, but when he stepped down off the trailer he was sporting a temperature of 1:03.2. Harry scratched him and sent him back to the farm.

"He had a low-grade infection and couldn't seem to shake it," Harvey said. "So we had a horse that wasn't really sick, but not really well, either. And all the time I'm thinking about the Fox Stake. I knew I couldn't start him in the Fox if he didn't have some training miles in him, including at least one fast one.

"Finally he got to a point where I could train him three slow miles, around 2:20. He came through it pretty good, so I brought him back four days later and sent him a 2:03.4 mile over the half-mile track. It was the fastest I ever trained him in all the time I had him. He finished well and I brought him back in 2:12.

"Bert was as anxious as I was to start him in the Fox, so we shipped him out to Indianapolis. We'd never given him a needle before, but this time we went the vitamin route pretty good —vitamins B-12 and C. We were also using an oxygen mask on him, giving him medicated oxygen about 30 minutes a day to clear up the infection in his head and throat. In fact, we used the mask on him the rest of the season.

"He seemed healthy for the Fox, though I had some reservations concerning his chances. They were all there, all the great colts we'd been racing, and I didn't think my colt had the miles in him to keep him tight enough to beat them."

Harry Harvey was about to become the first man to recognize a novel fact about Albatross: That he could remain as sharp as a Miami Beach dude on an absolute minimum of training. That a layoff of two, three, or even four weeks from competition only served to make him that much tougher when he did return to action. It was a trait which would reveal itself time and time again as his racing career continued.

Race Byrd, Seton Hanover, Paulos Hanover, Tarport Skipper, Dexter Hanover—they were all there when Harvey's colt paraded for the $71,030 Fox on Sunday afternoon, September 6. The fairground track, struck by a series of heavy showers which forced a two-day postponement of the contest, was officially listed as "good" at race time.

Off-track and all, Albatross captured the Fox with straight heat victories in 1:59 and 1:58.3. Harvey made big, sweeping moves with him early in both heats, finishing with four and a half lengths over Local Time and Tarport Skipper in the first, and a single length over Race Byrd and Count Bret in the second.

Only Bullet Hanover had put a pair of faster miles back to back in the Fox—1:57 and 1:59—and the first was a world record that was still alive and well 13 years later. And Bullet's historic journey was over a fast track.

Harvey, interviewed by Indiana Governor Edgar D. Whitcomb in the winner's circle, was appropriately humble in his comments. He lauded his horse, pointing out that Albatross had been ailing with a virus, yet was super tough despite the fact that he was going a pair of heats for the first time. Sympathizing with the gentleman who was holding the Fox trophy during the ceremonies, he kept his remarks on the brief side.

Albatross, with four two-minute victories to his credit, was still fighting the sniffles nine nights later when he paced a 2:02.3 mile in the mud to win a $12,500 division of the Matron Stake at Wolverine Raceway, near Detroit. It was his first test in honest-to-goodness mire, and he passed it with flying colors. A mud-spattered Harry Harvey, joined by Bert James and members of the James family, collected the Matron's silver ornament from wry USTA publicist Larry Evans.

The Albatross team was then out of racing action for two weeks. Super Bird had temporarily run out of stakes engagements, though another near-calamity soon turned up to rescue Harvey, James and the colt from boredom.

Harvey shipped the pacer back to the Arden Fairground for relaxed training to keep him up for his next assignment, the Star Pointer Pace at big Yonkers Raceway on September 28. Since a little fever had shown up in the colt's front ankles after his recent races, the trainer decided to work on them during the break in his schedule.

Out of the horsemen's ancient arsenal of fever-fighting weapons, he chose the poultice.

A veterinarian friend (Harvey declined to identify him, apparently to insure a continuation of the friendship) prepared a pair of wax-based poultices for the colt. Harry patted and squeezed them into place after a training session five days before the Yonkers race. Then he shipped the horse to the New York track, instructing groom Randy Blackhurst to remove the bandages when the colt arrived. The idea was that the poultices would work to remove the fever while Bird was en route to the metropolitan track.

Harvey remained back at Arden, but Bert James drove up to Yonkers. James was at the track shortly after Albatross checked in. He watched as caretaker Blackhurst worked on the horse's legs. Five minutes later he was on the phone to Harvey. "We're in bad trouble!" he reported breathlessly.

"What do you mean?" Harvey demanded.

"Those poultices. We took them off and all the hair on the horse's ankles came with them. His legs are swelling like crazy. They're big as stovepipes!"

"My God!" the trainer exclaimed. "Hang on, I'm on my way."

Harvey hurried to Yonkers, rushed to Albatross's stall, peered at the legs, and was sick. They were every bit as bad as James had reported. Worse, if anything. Great gobs of hair were missing from the ankles and fetlocks. The swelling had reached up to the tendons. The legs were thick, hot and puffy.

Fighting panic, Harry called the veterinarian who had prepared the plasters. He was told the poultices contained nothing which could have caused such a reaction. Since *something* had caused it, however, the vet prescribed bathing the legs in ice water and rubbing them with cod liver oil. "Keep jogging him," the vet added.

Harvey and his stable crew "worked on him to beat hell, night and day," and the swelling gradually went down, the fever slowly subsided. A day before the race, when the colt had to be scratched if he was to be routinely withdrawn, Harvey had Yonkers track veterinarian Dr. Robert L. Kennedy look him over. Dr. Kennedy said the remaining swelling was not serious and not painful to the horse. Albatross was fit to race if Harvey chose.

"So we raced him," Harvey said later. "But I have to admit, I felt guilty. His legs looked terrible. Anybody looking at him had to think we were nuts racing a great horse like Albatross on legs that looked like that."

The puffy ankles and tendons bothered Albatross not one iota. The colt was leaving from the nine-post in the second tier, a fact that again disturbed owner James, who was wandering about the paddock like a CIA agent, gathering information for a grand design to win the race. Harvey, burned once by James's obsession with unfortunate post positions and traffic problems, dutifully listened to the owner, but ignored his suggestions. Instead, he went to Harold (Sonny) Dancer Jr., who was handling the horse due to leave the gate in front of him. Dancer assured him that his horse, who had made a break in his last start, was now in good form and would move out with haste, permitting Harvey and Albatross to follow him away without danger. Harvey was grateful for Dancer's frank tip. "He wanted to beat me, but he knew what a great horse I had and didn't want to see him lose on a fluke—like getting fouled up at the gate," Harry said in tribute.

Albatross wove his way through traffic, was parked out at the half in 59.4, and made his move heading for the three quarters. He blazed to the front on the backside of the half-mile track and roared off to win by eight lengths in 2:00.1. His driver said he "came off the last turn with almost uncontrollable speed, winning eased up."

The colt with the fat and bald legs had set a stakes record for the $27,747 Star Pointer. It was also a national season's mark for half-mile tracks.

"This was the time that some of the diehards finally admitted that he was one hell of a horse," Harvey crowed happily. "He made believers out of all the skeptics."

The Star Pointer was raced on Monday night. On Saturday night of the same week he was right back in action at Yonkers, winning the $53,495 Lawrence B. Sheppard Pace in 2:02 over an off-track.

Nobody is near as Albatross and Harry Harvey win the L. B. Sheppard Pace at Yonkers in 2:02. (Yonkers Raceway photo)

It was a cool, damp night—the track had to be scraped—and driver Harvey was relieved when it was over. He had encountered problems getting Albatross away from the gate—the colt had bumped his head on a wing of the vehicle—and Harvey had harsh words for Yonkers starter Jean Hembach after the contest. Hembach "is the slowest in the world" in getting a field of class horses away, he said hotly. "I had to take Albatross back to avoid breaking."

The colt's pair of fleet triumphs within a six-night period won him some friends among members of the New York writing fraternity, many of whom had not seen him prior to his invasion of the metropolitan area. Louis Effrat of *The New York Times* was one of the writers hailing the young champion. Tapping out a piece for *The Harness Horse*, Effrat asked, "Can anyone possibly demur at the suggestion that in Albatross, Bert James of Pittsburgh via Windsor, Ont., has the 2-year-old pacer of 1970?"

No one, it seemed, was prepared to deny it.

Following the Sheppard Pace at Yonkers, another cavernous gap appeared in Albatross's racing slate. Delvin Miller, a sort of unofficial adviser to owner James, suggested that it be filled by shipping the colt to Lexington for a time trial over the Red Mile, harness racing's fastest track. The annual Fall Trots were under way in the Kentucky city and time trials have been an important tradition at the Red Mile for decades. In a time trial, a trotter or pacer, accompanied by one or more running horse prompters, races against the clock instead of other horses. The object is to earn a fast record for the horse.

Harry Harvey could see no sense to the move. Albatross already owned a hell of a record, the 1:57.4 race mark picked up in the Kerr Memorial at Vernon Downs. Yet he wasn't about to try and budge the James-Miller combination. Down to Lexington went Albatross.

"We hit nothing but bad weather—rain, cold and wind," Harry said, looking back at the period. "I went so far as to warm him up one day, but the track simply wasn't fast enough at the time and I didn't go with him. We just sat there waiting and never did get the chance to try. I wasn't too terribly disappointed even if we did waste five days sitting on our tails."

Back to Arden went Albatross. Officially, he had no more races on his stakes agenda. It was getting late in the season and only one major Grand Circuit event remained on the slate for two-year-old pacers—the $50,000-added Roosevelt Futurity at Roosevelt Raceway on October 31. Albatross wasn't eligible, although the luck of the Irish, Jewish, Welsh, Scottish and several other nationalities was working for him. The Roosevelt Futurity is one of a rare few major contests which allow for supplemental nominations. Owners willing to come up with $7,500 entry fees can make their two-year-olds eligible to the Futurity.

Harry Harvey and 2-year-old Albatross wait for the rich Roosevelt Futurity to begin. Super Bird was a supplemental entry in the stakes affair. (Roosevelt Raceway photo)

When Roosevelt racing secretary Larry Mallar opened the Futurity entry box on October 19, there was a pair of $7,500 checks mixed in with the entry blanks. One was signed by Bert V. James, making Albatross a starter. The other bore the signature of representatives of the Capital Hill Farm, the owner of Nansemond. Six other freshmen, entered via the more traditional route, brought the number of Futurity starters to eight and the purse to $92,360.

Albatross still had nearly two weeks to wait for the giant stake, so Harvey entered him in an overnight event at the same track on October 24. It was an A-1 Pace, open to any pacer in that class, and Harvey was promptly criticized for tossing his youngster into the ring against a field of race-wise veterans. He had a rugged time of it battling the seasoned, older opponents, but finally emerged with a neck victory in 2:01.1. While his $5,000 share of the purse was not to be ignored, the vicious match served a more important purpose. It made him tough and tight for the rich Futurity only a week away.

The winner of the Futurity stood to enrich his owner's bank account by $46,180, 50 percent of the total purse. The first leg up on the Roosevelt Founder's Plate was also on the line. The Plate is actually a series of three races over a three-year period. To win it, a pacer must win the Futurity at two years of age, the Messenger Stake at three and the Realization Pace at four. A bonus of $50,000, divided among the horse's owner, driver and breeder, goes to any pacer able to perform that minor miracle. The same offer is available to trotting horses, although different stakes are involved for obvious reasons. The Plate series honors George Morton Levy, the man who not only pioneered the founding of Roosevelt Raceway, but is also considered the godfather of modern Standardbred racing itself.

There was the usual grousing by horsemen over the fact that Albatross and Nansemond had landed in the Futurity field by way of supplementary nominations, but that was nothing new. Eddie Cobb, who had Veri Special in the race, probably represented the majority when he spoke against the policy and then added, "But I guess it's as fair for one as it is for another. I'd think supplementary payments were all right, too, if I had an Albatross."

Harry Harvey *had* an Albatross. He was uncharacteristically confident when he worked his colt for the last time on Wednesday, three days before the race. "He's as sharp as he's ever been," he told Tony Sisti of *Newsday* in an interview. "Any horse that beats him will have to set some kind of record."

It was a curious bunch lining up for the start of the Futurity. Albatross and Nansemond, the two freshmen who had to be supplemented, were the two morning line choices at 1 to 5 and 7 to 2 odds respectively. William (Bud) Gilmour was sulky sitting for Herve Filion behind Nansemond. Veri Special, Eddie Cobb's entry, was a respectable 8 to 1 in the figuring, while the balance of the field was out in left field at 20 to 1 or worse.

Bert James was both amazed and amused to learn that Pretty Boy was among the entries. Pretty Boy was the only one of the three colts he had taken to the Harrisburg sale in 1969 that he had been able to sell. The youngster had enjoyed a decent season of racing,

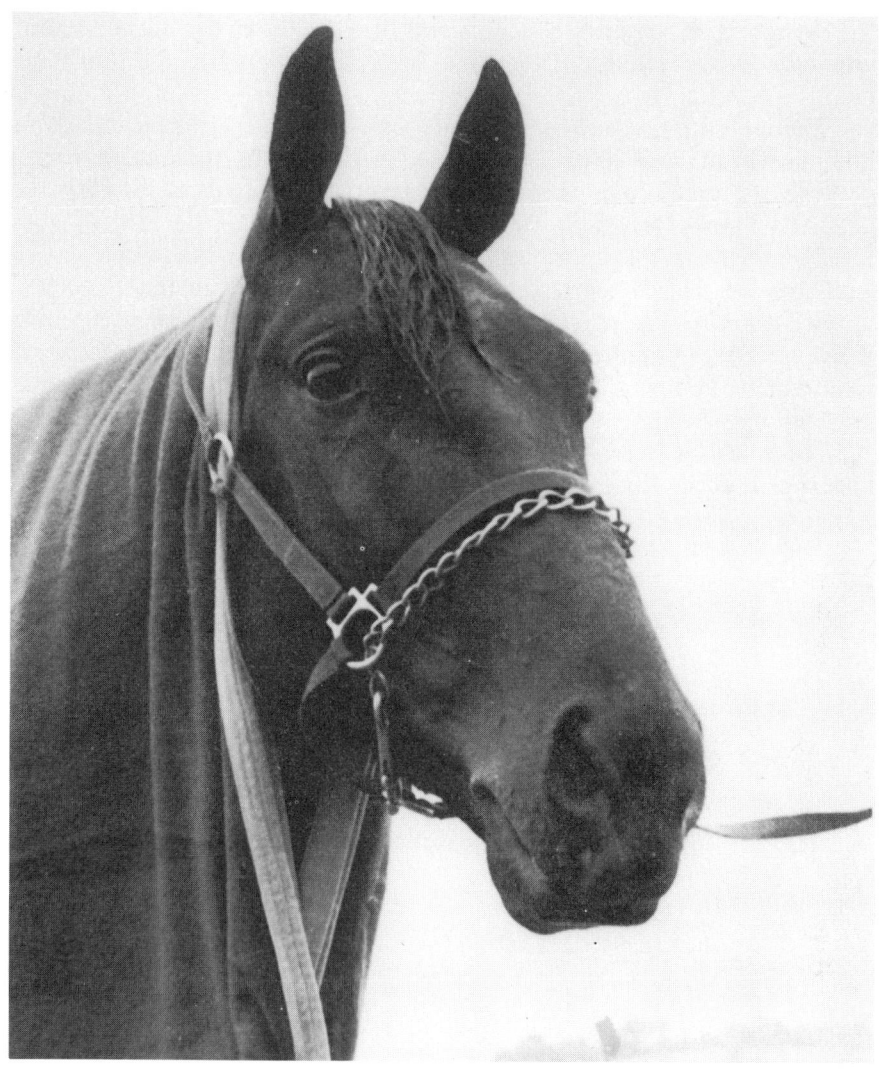

The race over, the champion cools out. (USTA photo)

taking a record of 2:04 and a tick, although he was hopelessly outclassed in the Futurity and destined to finish last.

The Futurity winner, of course, was Albatross. No one came close to him as he jiggy-jogged to victory in 2:00.4, cracking both the stake and track records for two-year-olds. He was parked out briefly, but zipped around the field in a single sweep to win going away by four lengths. Seton Hanover was second, with third money going to Nansemond.

Super Bird blotted out an eight-year-old stakes mark of 2:02.1 held by Steady Beau, and smashed the track record of 2:01.1 established by Rivaltime in 1964.

He returned a paltry $2.40, $2.40 and $2.10 at the three mutuel windows and presented the track with a $306 minus in the show pool.

Winding up the season, he had gone to post 17 times and come home with 14 wins, two seconds and a third. His seasonal earnings of $183,540 was a new standard for two-year-old pacers, besting the $180,864 figure turned in by Laverne Hanover in 1968.

Two-year-old Pacer of the Year honors were on the way.

Harry M. Harvey, grinning, laughing and joking in the Roosevelt winner's circle, was a happy man. The fates had been kind to him. What a perfectly glorious, unbelievable, fairy tale season it had been. Excitement. Drama. Recognition. Riches. And the future? Well, with a pacer like Albatross, the sky could only be the limit.

The sensitive, sincere horseman from Pennsylvania had no way of knowing that he had raced Albatross for the last time.

10

Not that Harry Harvey hadn't received a warning that he might one day lose Albatross. He had. On October 19, the same day that Bert James had anteed up $7,500 to make Albatross eligible for the Roosevelt Futurity.

Harvey and James were returning from the Empire Standardbred Sales at Madison Square Garden in New York City, where James had sold six yearlings from the first real crop turned out by his James Boys Farm. (James had touched all bases, selling strings of yearlings at *all four* major auctions in the fall of 1970). The owner and trainer were making small talk as they zoomed along the Garden State Parkway, en route to Philadelphia. Offering it conversationally, as though he were commenting on the parkway traffic, James remarked, "Alan Leavitt offered me a half-million for Albatross. What do you think?"

The message was delivered so casually, so routinely that Harvey found no cause for alarm in it. No bells rang, no sirens wailed. The trainer pondered the owner's question at length before responding. "I don't think it's enough. I think he's worth more, lots more. They couldn't beat him this year, and I don't believe they'll beat him next year. He's still growing, still fleshing out, and he's bound to be more rugged after a winter's rest."

Almost as an afterthought, he added, "What did you tell Leavitt?"

"I told him he wasn't even close," James said.

"Good," said Harvey. "And listen, Bert, if you do decide to sell the colt, I'd appreciate it if you'd give me a shot at him. I'll go to some people I know and see if they might be interested in syndicating him."

James and the trainer spent several minutes discussing the tax angles involved in a sale of that magnitude before the entire subject was dropped. Harvey barely gave it another thought. He went on and raced Albatross in the October 24 overnight event at Roosevelt, then wound up the colt's 1970 season with the big win in the Futurity. A day later he shipped the colt back to the Arden Fairground to begin the off-season.

The Pennsylvania horseman had never had a colt of Albatross's caliber in his stable before. How many horsemen had? Harvey was unsure of what route to follow with his young champion during the winter months: Let him down completely, or keep him occupied with light jogging and training.

He went to Frank Ervin for an opinion. Ervin had had a long list of trotting and pacing champions, the most recent of which was the incomparable Bret Hanover. "Keep him at the track and do a little something with him all through the winter," Ervin said flatly. "I've handled good horses both ways, but I've had more success with the keep-'em-moving routine."

"So we never let him down all the way," Harvey reported. "We jogged and trained him a little all through the winter. If we missed a session because of the weather, we didn't worry about it. Otherwise, he was out on the track doing something about every morning. He seemed to thrive on it, too. He was growing and putting on weight, although he never did get very fat. He was growing into his skin and his head. He was looking more like a race horse all the time."

The winter of 1970–71 was a frantically busy period for Harry Harvey. He scarcely had time to savor the success he had enjoyed during the racing campaign. It had been his best season by far. With Albatross making the largest contribution, Harry had reined horses to $298,621 worth of purses. He had won 92 heats and ended up with a .459 driving percentage, permitting him to repeat as the national champion among drivers with from 200 to 299 starts.

There was no time to rest on either his laurels or his duff. He was teaching the racing ropes to a whole new class of two-year-olds, including a half-dozen owned by Bert James. Unbelievably, James again had the stable leader among the freshmen . . . the most promising, most precocious baby in the bunch. Her name was Saucy Wave, a daughter of Shadow Wave-Sheena Hanover, and she was some kind of pacing miss. Barring injury or a sudden reversal of form, Harvey was ready to wager his stopwatch that Saucy Wave would be a force to be reckoned with in the filly ranks for 1971 and onward.

James, as usual, could do little wrong. The horseshoe, rabbit's foot, or whatever he used, was still producing spectacular results. He paid $15,500 for Saucy Wave at the Tattersalls Fall Sale in Lexington. She would win $42,816 in 1971 alone. At the same sale, he sold Jambo Andrea, the full sister to Albatross who had come to him as part of the Voodoo Hanover package. The filly, later renamed Doc's Fritzi, drew a high bid of $25,000 from Dr. and Mrs. George A. Smith, Jr. of Byram, Connecticut. Talented horseman Roland Beaulieu of Columbia George fame handled her, although a stubborn virus infection would cut short her racing career. In 1971 she would earn $395. As of the autumn of 1970, the three-horse parcel James had purchased from Tic Wilcutts and company for $11,000 had grossed him $208,540.

The weeks trotted by at a two-minute clip as Harvey hustled and bustled to mold his Standardbred recruits into polished performers for the new season. He jogged or trained Albatross most mornings and saw him every day. Yet James's remarks concerning the colt's possible sale, if not outright forgotten, were tucked away far back in the closets of Harvey's mind.

"For some reason, I sort of fell asleep during the winter and never did give it a thought," he said many months later. "James had plenty of time on his hands and was out to the track anywhere from three to five mornings a week, but he never brought it up again. We talked a lot about the horse—when to start him in 1971, his stakes schedule, things like that—but never said another thing about selling him.

"It got to be late March or early April, and Bert was still coming out to the track, but I began to notice that he was acting kind of funny around me. This went on for about two weeks until one morning he came to me and announced point-blank that he had sold the horse."

Harry Harvey, already plotting the season ahead, was thunderstruck. "Sold Albatross?" he stammered.

Sold Albatross, James repeated.

Stunned, Harvey had difficulty comprehending as the owner outlined details of the sale. Alan J. Leavitt, the short, slender, aggressive, boyish looking master of Lana Lobell Farms in Hanover, Pennsylvania, had assembled a syndicate to purchase the colt. The price was $1,250,000. In all, there were 10 shares in the horse. James was keeping two of them. The $11,000 Voodoo Hanover package had now yielded him $1,208,540—and he still owned 20 percent of Albatross (later increased to 25) and all of the mare who had borne him!

"It took me a while to come to my senses," Harvey recalled. "The horse was well along in his training; it was nearly time to take him back to the races. One would have thought the time for wheeling and dealing was well past. Finally I kind of muttered, 'Well, Bert, give me a chance to put something together. Let me have a shot at him.' 'No,' he said, 'I'm afraid it's too late for that. I've already sent Leavitt a telegram of acceptance.'

"I didn't know what to say to that. After a couple more minutes of just standing there, I asked him if he knew who would be training and racing the horse. He told me that it hadn't been decided yet. Then I asked him if I might have a chance at keeping and racing him, and he said it might be possible. That's the only bone that came my way that morning."

Why was James selling Albatross? Because he was a businessman, he told writer Terry Fraser in an interview in *Hoof Beats* magazine (when he was still granting interviews). "If I were a horseman, I never would have syndicated him. But I'm a businessman who is in the horse business and, after consulting with my lawyer, who is also in the horse business, I decided that I shouldn't keep Albatross.

Alan J. Leavitt, one of the dissidents who fired Stanley Dancer. (USTA photo)

"My lawyer gave me an easy rule of thumb to follow. He said that if I ever own something which is worth more than 10 percent of my total worth I should sell it.

"He asked me if I thought Albatross was worth $1,000,000 and I said yes. Then he said, 'If you are worth $10 million, keep him.'"

Bert James had made some pretty big coins moving Caddys and Chevys off his car lot in Canada, and harness horses had been most kind to him as well. But his bank account and holdings hadn't reached $10 million yet, so it was sales time in the Albatross corral.

Alan Leavitt had gained the inside track because he was the first man to knock on the door with a concrete offer. He had formed the Albatross Stable for the purpose of racing the horse in 1971 and 1972, then retiring him to stud service at his Lana Lobell Farms. Along with himself and James, the stable's membership included the Armstrong Brothers Ltd. (J. Elgin, C. Edwin and H. Charles Armstrong) of Brampton, Ontario; Leon Machiz of Great Neck, New York; Ira Helman of New York City; Mrs. Hilda Silverstein of New Hope, Pennsylvania; John W. Rollins of Wilmington, Delaware; and Mrs. Hazel D. Shriner of Taneytown, Maryland.

Harry Harvey, contemplating the loss of the colt, was in a state of shock for days. He performed his training chores in a kind of daze, his moods shifting alternately from dark and deep depression to bright and burning anger.

"I felt I had plenty to be angry about," he reported. "I realized he was perfectly within his rights to sell the horse; I wasn't disputing that. It was his horse. But I later found out the deal had been cooking for weeks, yet he never said a damn word to me about it.

"The thing that really had me sizzling, though, was the fact that I had asked him back in October for an opportunity to syndicate the colt if and when he decided to sell. Instead of that, he presented me with an accomplished fact. The horse had been sold and there was nothing I could do about it."

All Harry had to do to add fuel to the fire was jog his memory back some 18 months. Who had alerted James to the availability of Albatross, his dam and his full sister back in July of 1969? Alan Leavitt? Who had urged James to buy the three horses? Alan Leavitt? And who had taken the scrawny, mousy-looking, stall-kicking colt and fashioned him into history's richest two-year-old pacer, the horse of the year in his age and gait group? Alan Leavitt?

Harry Harvey had friends in high financial places, too, and might well have been able to round up enough of them to handle the sticker price on the sensational young horse. Yet Alan Leavitt had simply made an offer, and Alan Leavitt was walking off with the pacer.

All of this was eating at Harvey, costing him his sleep. But he passed none of it on to James. He swallowed a good deal of his pride along with some healthy helpings of crow.

"I realized that if I blew my stack, I'd not only lose the horse, but anything else I might get out of the transaction," he confessed. "Bert had told me I was to get a five percent commission on the sale. While it wasn't the 10 percent many trainers have gotten in similar situations, it was still a lot of money. And then he told me I'd have a chance to breed a mare to Albatross when he went to stud, which helped to make up for the missing five percent.

"At the same time, I had five or six of Bert's two-year-olds in my stable. Saucy Wave was one of them and I sure didn't want to lose her by shooting off my mouth. I was agitated as hell, but I kept pretty good control of myself."

Harvey managed to get his five percent sales commission into written form, although he and James were still squabbling over portions of the sum as late as 1973. The free breeding to Albatross was at the pleasure of Mr. James, according to Harvey, and got lost in the shuffle when the horse passed completely from James's hands in the noisy resyndication battle of 1972.

Harvey's tenure as trainer-driver of James's two-year-olds, including the classy Saucy Wave, lasted through most of the 1971 season. In August of that year, Joe Goldstein, the persuasive USTA publicist in the New York City office, prevailed upon Harry to sit for an interview with William F. Reed of *Sports Illustrated* magazine. When the story was published in the August 23 edition, it contained a couple of unflattering references to James (along with some flattering ones). Relations between the trainer and owner, strained before the piece appeared, snapped. The two-year-olds were soon missing from Harvey's barn, headed for Stanley Dancer's.

But these things were well in the future. In the spring of 1971, Harvey still had hopes of holding onto Albatross. Of continuing to be his trainer-driver through the 1971 and 1972 seasons.

"I kept asking James if the syndicate had settled on a trainer yet and he continued to tell me that no decision had been made," he stated. "I'm sure he was just trying to make me feel good.

"Bert continued to show up at the track every day, and though it bothered the hell out of me, I continued to go ahead and train the horse . . . pointing him toward a race at Rockingham Park on May 1. I was still hoping like hell the deal would backfire—I knew they had run into some legal snags—so that I would keep him for sure. Then one day James shows up and says, 'Stanley Dancer is coming down to try the horse for the syndicate.' He went on to say that it wasn't a hundred percent sure Stanley was going to get the horse, but again he was simply trying to make me feel a little better."

The globe-skipping Dancer, accompanied by his veterinarian adviser Dr. Edwin A. Churchill, flew in and worked Albatross over the fairground track. Dr. Churchill, a man equally experienced in pinpointing the pluses and minuses of both Standardbred and Thoroughbred horses, examined and probed the colt from nose to tail. Neither could fault him in any way. They talked briefly with Harvey, found him cooperative and helpful, and left as quickly as they had arrived, winging off for Stanley's farm at New Egypt, New Jersey.

Grimly, Harry continued to prep the horse for his seasonal debut. He vanned him the short hop over to The Meadows and worked him a 2:02.4 mile over the mutuel track's fast tartan surface. Then Stanley Dancer and Ed Churchill reappeared. Stanley again worked

The Jersey Rocket himself, Stanley F. Dancer. (James Ponter drawing)

the horse while Churchill hunted for physical flaws.

Harry Harvey did not need Bert James to tell him that Albatross was going to Stan Dancer.

It was midnight, April 22, when the Hutt nine-horse van pulled into the Arden Fairground. The big, flashy vehicle was there to pick up Albatross. Bert James was on hand to greet Joe Wideman, a Stanley Dancer caretaker, very possibly the top groom in all of harness racing. Randy Blackhurst, Albatross's groom under Harvey, was there, too. Blackhurst was to accompany the colt to Dancer's farm, where he would spend three days demonstrating the horse's rigging and discussing his feeding and habits.

Only one man was missing from the old Albatross team. Harry Harvey. He couldn't bear to see the horse leave. In fact, the hurt was so great that for more than a year he would refrain from mentioning the horse by name. And he would make it his business never to see Albatross race again.

11

It was a cool, raw morning for late February, the kind of day that makes the Broward County Chamber of Commerce in southeast Florida cringe. The rain had quit, but not before it made soggy, pink plaster out of the two tracks on the Pompano Park grounds. Training was suspended for the day—had never started, really—and Stanley F. Dancer was idly scanning the bookkeeper's report on the operation of his stable in 1970.

It had been one fine year, he had to admit, although expenses had gouged a massive hole in the $2,244,582 in purses he and other stable drivers had won for his owners. Running an 80-horse operation was an expensive proposition, however, and most of the costs seemed unavoidable as his eyes roamed down the list:

Training: $133,140.
Feed: $147,167.
Shoeing: $47,586.
Veterinary fees: $66,960.
Stakes: $270,903.
Grooms: $334,989.
Trucking: $100,007.
Supplies: $37,306.
Harness and Repairs: $47,373.
Stall Rent: $36,433.
Compensation Insurance: $24,900.
Bonuses: $44,000 . . .

It was all somehow depressing to see it there in black and white—thank God he had ended up with a profit of $827,451 for his owners—and it was a relief to set it aside when the phone rang.

"Stanley Dancer stable," he reported crisply.

"Stanley?" the voice said, mild surprise in it.

"Sure is."

"What are you doing answering the phone?"

"Happened to be sitting here in the office when it rang. The rain's knocked us out of the box this morning."

"This is Alan Leavitt. I didn't expect to reach you so quickly. Usually you're tougher to pin down than the President."

"What's going on, Alan?"

"Something big. Maybe. Listen, Stanley, how would you like to have Albatross?"

"Anybody'd love to have Albatross," Dancer answered cautiously. "What's the catch?"

"No catch," said Leavitt, going on to explain his plan for syndicating the great young pacer. The owner, Bert James, had a total price tag of $1,250,000 on him. Leavitt hoped to divide the total into 10 shares, two of which James would keep. Leavitt had some people interested in the deal and could probably sell three or four shares without any difficulty. If Stanley could persuade some of his wealthier patrons to purchase the rest, they could have Albatross. Stanley would race him through 1971 or 1972, then the horse would retire to Leavitt's farm, Lana Lobell, for stallion service. A single share would cost the purchaser $125,000, although it would be a spread-payment kind of thing—$25,000 a year for five years. Chances are, Albatross would win enough in purses over the next two seasons to reduce or even cancel out the need for payments the first two years. The outside stud fees the syndicate would receive from that point on might well take care of the future. If things worked out, the horse could be purchased without anyone having to come up with a dime in cash.

Dancer was interested. He was aware that young Leavitt possessed a shrewd mind, had manipulated the formation of other horse syndications with big money involved. In fact, Dancer was the trainer-driver of world champion trotter Noble Victory when Leavitt had syndicated the horse for a million dollars in 1966. Stanley had gone on and raced the trotter for the syndicate.

Would the Silversteins or some of Dancer's other good owners be interested, Leavitt asked.

"It's possible, Alan," Dancer replied. "I could sound them out. Of course, I'd want to check the horse out pretty good. Train him, have Dr. Churchill look him over, and all that. I'd have to convince myself that he was sound and healthy."

"No problem," Leavitt said readily. "Can you get back to me like pretty quick. I can't sit on this thing for long."

"Can do."

"Good," said Leavitt. "I'll be talking with you."

Stanley Dancer, as he laid the phone in its cradle, knew two things for sure. First, he would certainly like to handle Albatross, providing the syndicate took decent care of Harry Harvey, the man who had developed the pacer. Second, he would have no problem whatsoever selling shares to his patrons if the horse checked out all right.

Dancer, sitting there mulling the proposition, could feel the excitement mounting in him. Like a football player suiting up for the Super Bowl. Like a cub reporter sprinting back to the office with his first big story. It was a real grind handling the champion horses—living under pressure for months on end—and an immense relief when they retired. Yet there was nothing to match the thrill of being in charge of one. Of touring them from track to track. Winning the classic races, the giant purses. Setting the speed records. Hearing the thunder of the crowds pouring down out of the stands.

Big horses, world champions, had helped Stanley Dancer to make his mark in the industry. And what a mark it was for the slim, supple, high-voltage horseman who had fled junior high school in 1945 to sign on with the gaudy, raucous harness racing sport as a $45-a-week groom. The U.S. Trotting Association had it right when it sketched Dancer's biography in one of its bulky publications:

"Each sport has its super star. In football Joe Namath fills the bill, and in basketball Lew Alcindor is the best known. Stanley Dancer is harness racing's No. 1 personality, and with excellent reason. During his 25-year career the New Jersey horseman has become a legend in his own time . . ."

The "legend in his own time" had recently wound up the 1970 season with a truly "big horse"—Most Happy Fella. Happy Fella, owned by Stanley and his wife Rachel, ended his career with earnings of $419,033, a time trial record of 1:55 and the Triple Crown of Pacing under his harness. Then the Dancers had sold him to the Blue Chip Farms, Wallkill, New York, for a flat million dollars. A year earlier Stanley had put the finishing touches to Nevele Pride's spectacular career. And before that there had been Noble Victory, Henry T. Adios, Lehigh Hanover, Egyptian Candor, Cardigan Bay, Bonjour Hanover, Worth Seein, Su Mac Lad and a dozen other kings and queens of the trotting and pacing world.

With Most Happy Fella gone, hopefully to reproduce great performers like himself, Stanley had been wondering where he'd find his big star for 1971. He or she might well come from the string of 50-plus two and three-year-old colts and fillies he was training there at Pompano. Some of them, notably Super Bowl, Decorum, Star's Chip, Verna Rainbow, Queen's Blue Chip and Keystone Memento, looked like excellent prospects. He was also getting ready to spend $350,000 of his own and his clients' cash for Quick Pride, the sport's top two-year-old trotter in 1970.

But, like he'd told Alan Leavitt, no horseman in his right mind would turn away Albatross if the super colt were offered him. Stanley had handled two or more racing giants in his stable at the same time before, and would again if the opportunity presented itself. As long as he had his sleek and efficient Queen Air to zoom him from track to track.

If he landed Albatross, he would not be getting a stranger. Dancer had raced Jolly Roger against him and could not forget the night he had trailed the youngster when he stopped the clock in

1:57.4 at Vernon Downs. He was also familiar with Super Bird's family, especially the grandsire on his dam's side, Dancer Hanover.

Dancer Hanover was named for Stanley. It happened in 1957 while the New Jersey horseman was still climbing the racing peaks. He was visiting the Hanover Shoe Farms, checking their crop of yearlings, when the late Lawrence B. Sheppard invited him to lunch.

"You know, Stanley, we've never named a yearling after you," the peppery, outspoken squire of the Shoe Farms remarked over coffee.

"I know it. You can make amends by naming that new stud colt out of The Old Maid for me," Dancer replied brashly. He had chosen the farms' prima donna mare, the dam of Thorpe Hanover, Titus Hanover, Torpedo Hanover and other horses of that splendid ilk.

"We can't do that, Stanley," Sheppard said. "You know damn well that Hanover always takes the first letter from the dam's name and uses it as the first letter of the colt's name. You're going to have to let me pick a mare whose name starts with the letter D."

"No soap," said the trainer. "It's The Old Maid's colt or nobody."

When Dancer left him, Sheppard was still grumbling that he didn't see how the farms could violate tradition that way. But two weeks later Stanley received a letter from the venerable breeder telling him The Old Maid's new foal had been called Dancer Hanover. "You damn well better bid on him when he goes in the ring next year," Sheppard warned.

Indeed, Dancer did bid on him. He knew that Dancer Hanover would bring a horrendous price, sired by Adios and out of The Old Maid as he was, and he badgered a number of his owners to come up with a total of $60,000. Once in the ring, however, Dancer Hanover quickly exceeded that figure. Dancer was despondent until one of his owners, Marlin L. Shriner, instructed him to continue bidding. "If the other partners don't want to go that high, I'll buy him myself," Shriner said. Stanley jumped back in the bidding and eventually got the colt for $105,000. It was the highest price ever paid for a yearling at auction up to that time—1958.

Stanley had only limited success with Dancer Hanover. He had trouble getting him to pace. When Sheppard offered to buy him back for $200,000, Stanley urged the syndicate members to sell. Delvin Miller, with a big assist from Jimmy Arthur, had more luck with him later, picking up more than $87,000 in racing spoils and giving him a time trial mark of 1:56.4. Dancer Hanover's greatest impact on the sport, however, would come in the stud barn, where he would sire such offspring as Romeo Hanover, Romulus Hanover, Romalie Hanover, Betty Hanover and Dexter Hanover. To say nothing of Voodoo Hanover, Albatross's dam.

Stanley's ties with Albatross's family also included a brief relationship with the colt's sire, Meadow Skipper. Skipper was a two-year-old, camped at the Delaware County Fairground in Ohio at the time. It was 1962, and driver Del Miller had asked Dancer to give the youngster a good, stiff workout at Delaware. Stanley trained him in 2:02 and a tick, but was signally unimpressed with the colt. "He was terribly rough gaited around the turns, and I doubt that I'd have given very much for him on that particular day," he recalled.

Now, nine years later, Dancer had pretty well decided to take an active role in the purchase of Meadow Skipper's son for a cool $1,250,000.

He called some of his prime patrons, as Leavitt had suggested. He had no difficulty at all in enlisting Mrs. Hilda Silverstein, Mrs. Hazel D. Shriner and John W. Rollins. He explained the proposed syndication to them and emphasized that they would not be committed until he and Dr. Edwin Churchill thoroughly examined the horse. "More than likely he's all right," he commented, "but I'd feel a lot better about it if I had a chance to look him over and train him."

The Silversteins, Hilda and Louis, were typical of the faithful clientele Dancer has assembled over the years. "I can go to a sale, spend $25,000 or $30,000 for a horse, and call them up and say, 'Look, I just bought you a horse,'" Dancer once said. "In fact, I've done it on several occasions."

While his remark was essentially accurate, it was also unduly modest. Louis Silverstein placed it in better perspective when he volunteered: "If Stanley Dancer came to me and said, 'Look, I want to buy some horses which will cost $200,000, $300,000 or even $700,000,' I would give him a check with my name on it. Stanley could fill in the amount. That's the kind of faith I have in that man."

Mrs. Shriner, John Rollins and other Dancer patrons shared that trust. Other people in the industry would learn the degree of their loyalty before the Albatross story was ended.

Stanley made two winging trips to Harry Harvey's winter training base at the Arden Fairground. He flew commercially from Florida, met Dr. Edwin Churchill at Philadelphia, then zipped the rest of the way to Arden in his own aircraft—piloting it himself. En route the first time, he cautioned Dr. Churchill against being too critical of Albatross on aesthetic grounds. "He's not the best looking horse you've checked for me," he warned.

Heading back on the plane, Churchill passed his own judgment on to the trainer. "You know," he said, "it's a curious thing. While this colt is certainly not a big, handsome animal, I believe he impresses me more than any other horse I've examined for you. He doesn't have any real conformation faults at all. He's an all-around, well-made horse, and I can't remember seeing a better gaited pacer."

Dancer had already noticed the gait. He couldn't avoid it. He'd never sat behind a pacer who could cover the ground so effortlessly, including his own Cardigan Bay, Lehigh Hanover, Henry T. Adios

Louis Silverstein. (Frank Ross photo)

and Most Happy Fella, along with Frank Ervin's mighty Bret Hanover, whom he had trained several times during the Big Bum's three years at the races.

"I vote yes," Dancer told the veterinarian. "He's fantastic. I think we ought to get him."

"You won't get an argument from me," Churchill agreed.

The two returned to Arden nearly three weeks later. A couple of legal snarls had to be untangled before the contract for syndication could be completed. Time had slipped by. With such big money at stake, Dancer wanted to reassure himself that the colt was still sound. He had worked him in 2:20 the first time around. This time he trained him a mile in 2:09. He had all the proof he needed.

He noticed that Harry Harvey was very glum throughout his second visit. Harvey had obviously determined that he was to lose the horse and Stanley was to get him. Dancer himself had been the man in the middle of two major syndications—those of Noble Victory and

Mrs. Hilda Silverstein. (Frank Ross photo)

Nevele Pride. In both instances he had been assured the horses would remain with him, although that hadn't saved him from some anxious moments while negotiations were under way. He sympathized with the stricken Harvey and thought it strange that Bert James hadn't bothered to tell him outright that Albatross was leaving his stable.

Dancer and Harvey had been friendly for many years. Both were young and relatively raw racing recruits when they drove in the Hambletonian Stake for the first time at Goshen, New York, in 1953. It was Harvey's only start in the Hambo, but he made the most of it by winning the classic contest with Helicopter. Stanley finished far back with Newport Champ, a trotter Del Cameron asked him to drive. Later he would win it with both Nevele Pride and Super Bowl.

Dancer had—still has—high regard for Harvey's horsemanship. "Harry has never gotten the attention that people like Billy Haughton or myself have received. Working for Del Miller all those years, he was out of the public eye. But look at what he's accomplished with a small stable over a comparatively short period. Albatross, Saucy Wave, a dozen other fine colts and fillies. If he had been training and driving from the time he broke into the sport, he'd be one of the biggest names in the business."

In the future, Dancer would take great pains to credit Harvey with the development of Albatross. "Harry Harvey made Albatross, not me," he told the press. "I never sat behind him the year he came out. He was a great horse when I got him."

Stanley knew he was getting a great horse in Albatross. Now he needed a great groom to care for the champion. He had such a man in Joe Wideman, a 46-year-old native of Wilkes-Barre, Pennsylvania, who had spent 11 of his 25 years in the racing business with the Dancer stable. Wideman, tall, slender, friendly but rather taciturn, had rubbed some of Stanley's biggest winners—Cardigan Bay, Sly Yankee, Lucky Creed and First Lee. Doubtless, he could have had many of Dancer's top Grand Circuit horses as well but for his strong distaste for travel. Joe liked to be stationed at one track for long spells. Preferably a metropolitan track. Preferably Liberty Bell Park.

He was headquartered at Liberty Bell, grooming Stanley's swift but problem-plagued Adapter, when Dancer phoned him from Florida. "Joe," he said, "some people are syndicating Albatross and they want me to handle him. I'd sure appreciate it if you'd take care of him for me."

"Aww, Stanley," Wideman protested, "I'd like to oblige you, but you know me and traveling . . ."

"Well, I won't force you, Joe, though I do hope you'll at least think it over. You know what a heck of a horse he is and the kind of money he's likely to earn over the next two seasons."

Wideman later confessed that he knew little of Albatross's record and reputation when Dancer first approached him. "I'd heard some-

Albatross and faithful caretaker Joe Wideman. (Hollywood Park photo)

thing about him, but that was about it," he reported. "I really don't keep up on those Grand Circuit horses very much."

A week later Dancer turned up in person at Liberty Bell. Wideman was still reluctant to leave the Dancer string at Philadelphia and journey all over the country with Albatross. The boss, who goes to great lengths to keep his help happy, left without the commitment he was hoping for.

Back at Pompano, Stanley went up and down the roster of caretakers working for him searching for the right man to put on Albatross. Every time his finger ended up on Joe Wideman's name. A colt worth $1,250,000 deserved—*had to have*—a responsible caretaker. There was no more trustworthy groom in the Dancer organization than Joe Wideman.

"If they ran a poll on who is the greatest groom in harness racing, Joe Wideman would be the first to go into the Hall of Fame," Dancer once told an interviewer. "I can send Joe anywhere, absolutely anywhere, and know the horse he's grooming is all right. He's so devoted he's hardly ever away from the barn."

Stanley's mind was made up. He wanted Wideman for Albatross. When he returned to Liberty Bell the following week, he tried a new approach.

"Joe," he said flatly, "Huttie's truck will be here the evening of the 22nd. I want you to go up with the van and pick up that Albatross colt. And, Joe, I want you to rub him."

Wideman fidgeted some, shifting his weight from foot to foot, tugged his cap down a little further over his short-cropped grey hair, and nodded. "Okay, Stanley," he said, "if that's what you want."

So the heart of the new Albatross team was complete.

Ten new owners who called themselves the Albatross Stable.

Stanley Dancer.

Joe Wideman.

12

The final version of the syndication contract, hammered out only days before Albatross was due to open his 1971 racing season, established a four-member management committee to guide the colt's considerable destiny.

Named to the stewardship unit were Bert James, who had ended up with 25 percent of the syndicate; Alan Leavitt, a 15 percent shareholder; Dr. J. Glen Brown, super-sized emissary of the Armstrong Brothers and their 10 percent, and Stanley Dancer, the colt's trainer-driver elect. Leavitt had purchased 10 percent and had another five percent awarded him for forming the syndicate.

Dancer was wary of the four-way leadership from the beginning. The contract clearly stated that he was to train and drive Albatross so long as the horse raced, but it did not grant him decision-making powers in the areas of where, when, how often and how long the colt should compete. That was the realm of the committee, and he held but one of four votes.

It hadn't been that way with Nevele Pride. Ben J. and Julius Slutsky permitted him to call all the racing plays while they were sole owners of Pride. The situation did not change when Lou Resnick came up with a million dollars to become a co-owner early in Pride's three-year-old form. And Stan was still the man in complete charge of the trotter's schedule after the folks at Stoner Creek syndicated the trotter for $3,000,000. Dancer picked Nevele Pride's racing spots, time-trialed him when he determined the time was ripe, skipped a stake if he thought the horse needed a rest, and brought a halt to Pride's career when he felt further competition might cause serious injury to the champion.

Much the same had been true in the case of Noble Victory. In fact, he pretty well insisted that he have general control over the racing fortunes of all the Standardbreds he accepted in his stable. "You can't have two or three people making decisions where training and driving are involved," he told his owners, who were only too happy to acquiesce in the face of his remarkable record of success.

And now, in the syndication of Albatross, he was being asked to share that right with three others, one of them—James—a total stranger with very limited experience in the racing game. "You know, the

Dr. J. Glen Brown represented the Armstrong Brothers' interest in the Albatross Stable. (USTA photo)

seats on those jog carts and sulkies are built for one man, not four," he grumbled to Leavitt.

Dancer didn't have a thing to worry about, the young squire of Lana Lobell said soothingly. He wouldn't have any trouble with Leavitt. Glen Brown wouldn't be giving him any grief. And counting Dancer himself, that made three horsemen on the committee. What could go wrong? What could happen?

Plenty. But that would come later.

At the time, everything seemed relatively placid. The contract *had been* straightened out. He *had* trained a horse for Leavitt. He *did* know Dr. Brown—and was reasonably sure that Brown did not interfere with the efforts of the Armstrong Brothers' trainer, Joe O'Brien. And Harry Harvey *had* survived a year with Bert James. Perhaps he was making a lofty mountain out of a tiny molehill. Leavitt was probably right; everything would be fine.

Stanley tucked his grievance away—filed it, so to speak—and got on with the job of training Albatross. In eight days the colt was slated

The Big Bird looks mean, but was only getting used to the bit during a morning jog. (Brandywine Raceway photo)

to start in the $25,000 Romeo Hanover Pace at Rockingham Park, Salem, New Hampshire.

Randy Blackhurst, the Harvey groom who had accompanied Albatross back to Dancer's Egyptian Acres Farm, was gone, leaving Stanley and Joe Wideman to get acquainted with the pacer on their own. They quickly learned that Super Bird had a pleasant disposition, that he would invariably trot rather than pace during his jog miles, that he would duck if you drove him too close to machinery on the track, and that he had a penchant for sugar cubes and dandelion greens.

When Ronnie Dancer, who heads the New Egypt operation for his father, quizzed Wideman on how it felt to jog a million-dollar horse, the imperturbable groom shrugged at first. Then he said at length, "He's just another horse. Or, at least, that's the way I've got to treat him. If I thought about what he cost, why I'd be shaking every time I took him out on the track. I'd more than likely make him nervous, too."

Young Dancer, who had grown from childhood to manhood watching great veteran grooms like Joe at work, doubted that he would live long enough to witness Wideman losing his cool.

The senior Dancer, working Albatross over his half-mile farm track on April 24, offered a silent thank-you to Harry Harvey. Harvey had known—suspected, at the very least—that he was losing the colt. Yet he'd done an excellent job of conditioning the pacer. Dancer trained him three trips, the last in 2:03. Then he sent him on to Rockingham Park.

Since Albatross had won about everything that wasn't nailed down in 1970, his new trainer saw no reason to change his rigging. He instructed Wideman to dress him in a Kant-See-Back bridle, head poles on both sides, scalpers in the front, and a set of 56-inch hopples. The head poles, Harvey had told him, were designed to prevent the colt from getting his head around when leaving the gate.

Dancer would experiment with bridles along the way, although he would not alter the basic formula of Albatross's gear. Neither would he tamper much with the horse's shoeing, racing him in the same type of flat shoes in front and half-round, half-swedge in back that Harvey had campaigned him in.

Stanley flew into Rockingham on Wednesday to work the colt three easy miles. He had to borrow a stopwatch from trainer Leroy Copeland and caught the Bird in 2:17 in the last trip. Dancer whistled merrily throughout the leisurely tours. As though he had something to be happy about.

The United States Trotting Association's annual Experimental Championship Ratings did nothing to dampen his euphoria. Each year in late April or early May the USTA consults either a computer or a warlock in an effort to forecast how fast the nation's better sophomore trotters and pacers will go before the year is out. The projected speeds are based on the premise that ideal conditions will prevail as the colts race over a mile track.

The 1971 ratings, published about the time Dancer was preparing to open the colt's season, had Albatross leading the parade with a projected speed of 1:55 flat. It was a nice round figure, easy to remember. It was also a set of numbers that would have Bird equaling the world record for three-year-olds, which was set by Bret Hanover in 1965.

Rounding out the Top 10 behind Albatross were Seton Hanover, 1:55.4; Dexter Hanover, 1:56; Tarport Skipper, 1:56.1; Springfield, 1:56.3; Veri Special, 1:56.4; Keystone Memento, (a filly), 1:57; High Ideal, 1:57.1; Truthful Waverly (another filly), 1:57.2, and Jolly Roger, 1:57.

Interestingly, three members of the USTA's Top 10 speedsters on the pacing gait were all headquartered in the Stanley Dancer barn. In addition, the second swiftest sophomore trotter in the land—according to the Trotting Association's cloudy crystal ball—also called the Dancer barn home. That was Quick Pride, rated at 1:58 and trailing only Noble Gesture (1:57) on the list.

Small wonder Stanley was doing a lot of whistling during the late spring of 1971.

A crowd of 13,197 turned out on Saturday night, May 1, to bid a seasonal greeting to Albatross and his new pilot. Six fellow three-year-old pacers, headed by Del Miller's Tarport Skipper and Art Nason's Mountain Skipper, were also on hand to say hello.

They had to squeeze it in fast because Albatross whipped by them with a gigantic whoosh to win by 11 lengths in 2:01.3, establishing an early national season's record in the process. The two Skippers, Tarport and Mountain, finished second and third as expected.

Dancer was relieved the debut was over. More than two decades worth of experience had told him that Albatross was one hell of a colt. Yet there was no substitute for actual competition for a horseman to get a true reading on a race horse. He had that reading now, and it registered high, very high on his measuring stick. He was grinning broadly as he met the waiting Joe Wideman in the winner's circle. "He's something else, Joe," he whispered to the groom as they unchecked the horse. "He about took my breath away with that move on the clubhouse turn."

"He can go," Wideman agreed solemnly.

With no stakes affair in sight for nearly three weeks, Dancer brought Albatross home to New Egypt. He had a difficult decision to make. The Messenger Stake, the year's richest race for three-year-olds, was on the horizon. Stanley had to decide whether to keep his colt idle during the interim and hope for the best, or find him a start in an overnight event.

Harvey had not passed on the major discovery he had made: that Bird could go long stretches without a race and still remain as tight

Albatross and Stanley Dancer, a team for the very first time, win the $25,000 Romeo Hanover Pace at Rockingham Park in 1971. (Rockingham Park photo)

as a drum head. Or if he had, Dancer had forgotten it. In the end, he called Roosevelt Raceway racing secretary Larry Mallar and asked him to find a spot for Albatross in an overnight. Mallar assigned him to a Junior Free-For-All contest on May 8 despite Dancer's plea for a softer berth.

Stanley sent him in against five older rivals for a purse of $17,500 and the best the colt could earn was third money. Colonial, driven by Bill Popfinger, put a 2:01 timing on the board to win the match over an off-track. Carbine Hanover and reinsman Buddy Gilmour finished second.

The New York Times's Lou Effrat, for one, excused Albatross for his slip. Effrat wrote: "It was hardly a disgrace because Albatross started from the outside against older horses, had to travel four-wide through the stretch, and was beaten less than a length in an excellent clocking."

Effrat did not chide Dancer for starting him in such rugged company, but Dancer did. "A bad mistake," he commented. "I was afraid I'd goof up the Messenger if I didn't race him. But with only one start behind him, I never should have tackled those older horses who had been racing. It won't happen again."

When Albatross returned to his stall that night, there was a new face there to greet him. Joe Wideman was still the caretaker on the colt and would be through the end of his racing career. But a small, friendly, dark-haired man named Roger Pritchard had been added to the caretaking crew. Roger was the freshly assigned night watchman on Albatross. It was a sure sign that Stanley Dancer considered Super Bird a super horse, despite his loss to the older veterans.

Nearly all of Dancer's great horses, once they proved their greatness, earned themselves a night watchman. Noble Victory and Nevele Pride were but two of them. Night men such as Pritchard were expected to park their sleeping cots as near the horse's stall as possible to guard them from whatever evil might be lurking during the hours of darkness—fire in the barn, tampering by would-be race fixers, or accidental injury in the stall. The watchman was supposed to look in at his charge at intervals all night long.

Pritchard was one of the most trusted men in the Dancer aggregation. He was a former Dancer caretaker—$885,095-winner Su Mac Lad was one of the horses who had benefited from his care—who had injured his back and could only perform lighter chores. Equipped

Night watchman Roger Pritchard settles down for another evening of guarding the welfare of the famed pacer. (Hollywood Park photo)

with a comfortable chair, a cot, a portable television set and a radio, Roger would spend countless nights faithfully guarding the welfare of Albatross. He would also join Joe Wideman in the paddock on race nights, making Albatross one of the more pampered pacers in racing.

Having a pair of devoted individuals like Wideman and Pritchard on the job permitted Stanley Dancer to sleep a little sounder at night.

Bert James, who had been Harry Harvey's shadow when Harvey was racing Albatross, was quickly attaching himself to Dancer. Like a barnacle. James was in and out of the paddock for the races at both Rockingham and Roosevelt, and would be a visitor in the racing stockade for almost all of the pacer's remaining races. It was a new experience for Stanley; his owners rarely bothered him before a contest. He eyed the former Cadillac dealer with suspicion, but found that James was no real problem, that he was quiet, friendly, and offered no advice.

Dancer was also wondering what James's reaction might be to a defeat. He considered the Roosevelt loss as a kind of test, watching James closely to gauge his reaction. The owner passed with flying colors. He took the race results in stride. The colt had lost and that was that. It was best to look ahead.

The Messenger was next. Dancer dropped two entry blanks into the box for the super-rich affair at Roosevelt—one for Albatross, another for stablemate Jolly Roger. In all, 13 entries (and 13 $2,000 checks) turned up, forcing the Roosevelt management to schedule a pair of trial races on Tuesday night, May 18.

The four top finishers in each trial would win the right to start in the $114,977 Messenger four nights later. Stanley was not overjoyed at starting his horses twice within five nights—none of the trainers were—but it was the only route available to the Messenger gold.

The Tuesday trial had all the appearances of being a romp for Albatross until Flying Bret, handled as usual by Charlie Clark, turned the routine affair into a dramatic happening. Albatross was making his move past the pacesetting Bret Hanover son when Flying Bret strayed off the rail and hooked wheels with the Dancer colt. The two horses, with sulkies locked, veered toward the outside rail, causing the Roosevelt crowd of 24,000 to gasp. A whiff of disaster was in the crisp night air until Dancer, cooly, cleverly, maneuvered his horse free of the knot. Then he spurred him back to the front and went on to score easily over Nansemond and Springfield in the $12,000 test.

"If we hadn't slid over together, I might have ended up with a smashed wheel or something a whole lot worse," he offered in a paddock post-mortem to the incident. "That would have been a great way to be eliminated from the Messenger. It wasn't Charlie Clark's

Bird scores handily over Nansemond and friends in Messenger Stakes trial. (Roosevelt Raceway photo)

fault, but, you know, the same horse did the same thing to me last year when I was driving Jolly Roger. When something like that happens, it's like piloting a plane—you simply can't afford to panic."

At the very least, he would not have to worry about Flying Bret in the Messenger. The colt finished sixth in the trial and was eliminated from the big race.

Billy Haughton, who managed to qualify Seton Hanover for the stake despite a break in stride, earned a healthy new respect for Albatross after watching him rally from the mishap to win the trial. "It's hard to say how great he is, but some of these things are going to have to improve an awful lot in a few days to beat Albatross in the Messenger. This bunch should have done better after the way Albatross was parked out."

The second trial was won by Local Time and driver Ted Taylor, who scored a mild upset over odds-on choice Tarport Skipper. Tarport Skipper, however, paced most of the mile on a blown sulky tire, leading most observers to believe that he was the only pacer with a phantom's chance of sinking Super Bird in the big contest. Also qualifying in the second dash were Jolly Roger (driven by Dancer) and a pacer from the Midwest called Jake Jackson.

A field of eight, including Stanley's dynamic duo of Albatross and Jolly Roger, was set for the Messenger. The race was the first jewel in the Triple Crown of Pacing for 1971. The Cane Futurity at Yonkers Raceway and the Little Brown Jug at Delaware, Ohio, were the other two gems in the Crown.

Roosevelt Raceway was dropping the curtain on its 70-night spring season, and a thundering herd of 35,080 fans pushed its way through the turnstiles to help the Long Island harness headquarters close its campaign and to view the drama of the classic contest.

It was the largest house Albatross had ever played to.

While Stanley Dancer was doing his best to keep it from his mind, the huge, festive crowd was well aware that he was shooting for his third straight Messenger victory. Stanley had guided Jane Falley Galt's Bye Bye Sam to a 2:02.3 decision in 1969. In 1970 he had returned to win the big stakes affair with a mile in the same time by Most Happy Fella, a colt owned by him and wife Rachel. No one in the 15-year history of the contest had ever won it three years running.

The metropolitan press—*The New York Times, Daily News, Post, Mirror, Newsday, Long Island Press, Newark Star-Ledger* and others—had made no secret of the fact that the New Jersey reinsman was hoping to make a little more harness racing history with his third consecutive Messenger victory. It was hardly a case of a pitcher having a no-hitter going and everyone in the park studiously ignoring the fact for fear of jinxing the hurler.

The press and crowd were conceding the race to Albatross and Dancer, although Dancer was not about to count his third Messenger egg until Super Bird hatched it. He could not help but remember the 1962 edition of the same race. Adora's Dream, driven by Morris MacDonald, was the 3-to-10 favorite in that one. The favorite had the race virtually clinched until rank outsider Thor Hanover, guided by John Simpson Sr., came out of nowhere to wrest the win away with a blistering charge in the final seconds. Simpson, known as harness racing's "Iceman" because of his tendency to make his move at the last conceivable instant, had made a little Messenger history of his own. His horse had provided the stake with its highest mutuel payoff—a $144 return for win.

No outsider was going to win the 1971 edition of the rich affair, if Stanley Dancer had his way. He was out and moving with Albatross from the start, beating the unsung Jake Jackson to the lead with a quarter in 29.1. Once on top, he resolved to stay there, leading his seven opponents down to the half in 1:01 and the three quarters in 1:31.3.

Dancer was sure he was in no jeopardy at the third striped pole, but shook the lines at Albatross anyway for a touch of extra insurance. Super Bird responded with an eye-popping 28.4 rush to the wire to score by three and a half lengths over the Herve Filion-steered Nansemond.

Rounding the final turn, Albatross starts to draw off to a 3½-length decision in the $114,977 Messenger Stakes. (Roosevelt Raceway photo)

Hardly ruffled, the famed driver and horse pose after victory in the giant Messenger Stakes. (Roosevelt Raceway photo)

Tarport Skipper, the one colt who might have made a race of it, had fallen upon hard times again. He was struck by the breaking Seton Hanover in the heat of battle and did well to rally for third money behind an excellent drive by John Chapman.

Trailing the three leaders across the finish were Jolly Roger, catch-driven by Stanley's nephew Harold (Sonny) Dancer, Jake Jackson, Local Time, Springfield and the misbehaving Seton Hanover.

The 2:00.2 clocking, third best in Messenger competition, was easily the fastest mile of the year by a sophomore pacer over a half-mile track.

Dancer had his hat trick, Albatross had the first ruby in his bid for the Triple Crown, and the 10-member Albatross Syndicate had a horse who had bumped his career earnings to $261,628.

Raceway punters, given an opportunity to wager on the powerful two-horse Dancer entry, made the most of it. They bet the entry down to $2.60, $2.20 and $2.10 across the board, but left Roosevelt with only a small minus in the show pool. The track could stand it. The liberal throng presented it with a $2,813,000 evening on the mutuel front.

With Roosevelt dark, metropolitan area racing fans changed their allegiance to Yonkers Raceway. So did Albatross. His May 28 event was the $25,247 Westchester Pace, and Stanley opened the throttle some to let him pace a 1:59.3 mile to win by open lengths over Springfield and H. T. Luca.

It was his initial two-minute journey of the season and first since Harry Harvey had driven him a pair of miracle miles to capture the Fox Stake at Indianapolis back in September of 1970. It was, of course, another season's standard for sophomores over a twice-around oval.

Dancer was nursing a severely lacerated knee when he drove him in the Westchester. The gritty reinsman in blue and gold silks had suffered the slash in a mishap at Yonkers three nights earlier. He was finishing up a warm-up mile with three-year-old filly trotter Egyptian Jody when his sulky collided with the bike of a breaking horse being reined by Sacher Werner. Stanley was thrown to the turf, the impact opening up a four-inch gash on his knee. The filly, turning up lame as well, had to be scratched from the $26,000 Hudson Stake.

Painful wound and all, Dancer was in an exuberant mood after his sizzling triumph with Albatross in the Westchester. From the first moment the colt had landed in his stable, harness writers had been urging him to compare Albatross with other fine pacers of the recent past—notably his own Most Happy Fella and Frank Ervin's Bret Hanover. He had been ducking the question, but not because of false modesty.

"Anybody who knows me at all knows that I'm one of the first to sing the praises of my good horses," he said in defense of his fancy footwork to dodge the issue. "I've never been shy about calling one great if I know he is great. I think it's my duty. It creates interest in the sport. People like to read about it. It promotes racing, and I think more trainers should do the same thing.

"In the case of Albatross, however, the writers were asking me to compare him with some of history's best pacers after I'd only raced him once or twice. It was obvious he was a great horse—Harry Harvey had proven that the year before. But I wasn't prepared to say he was better than Most Happy Fella or better than Bret Hanover when I'd only handled him a couple of times. A fella could end up looking like a monkey doing that."

Following the Westchester, however, he softened his stand, began to voice his opinion. He was so impressed with the way Albatross had scooted around the small Yonkers track that he told the writers he fully expected the pacer to crack Bret Hanover's long-standing world record of 1:57 over a half-mile track before the Bird's career was ended.

"Mind you, I won't be shooting for any records this early in the season, but I think you'll be seeing some fast miles when we hit those five-eighths-mile tracks over the next few weeks. You might write that down and check later to see if I was right."

Right as rain.

13

Nearly everything that could go wrong did go wrong for Albatross in the $50,000 Battle of Brandywine Pace at Brandywine Raceway, Wilmington, Delaware, on June 5.

The gremlins were at work as early as three days before the race, when post positions were pulled and Dancer's pacer inherited the 11-post in an 11-horse dash.

They were certainly present on race night, when the Brandywine plant suffered an unprecedented power failure, losing its track, toteboard, clubhouse and parking lot lights for 36 minutes. More than 14,000 fans, along with Albatross and 79 other trotters and pacers, had to make the best of it in near darkness until harried electricians could make repairs. The intricate warm-up routines trainers follow with their horses went by the boards.

And the little invisible gentlemen who allegedly plagued airplane pilots during World War II were still on duty during the course of the race itself, looking on malevolently as Albatross was shuffled from traffic snarl to traffic snarl and did not manage to reach the rail until the contest was seven-eighths over.

There was one facet of the race which was apparently beyond the reach of the gremlins: The finish.

Albatross won the Battle of Brandywine.

By more than four lengths.

In 1:57.1.

The colt's astonishing tenacity surprised even his trainer.

"You can have the greatest horse in the world, yet you never really know if he'll have anything left when you call on him after a journey like that. It's frightening. You're thinking about the horse's reputation. You're thinking of your own reputation. You're worrying about the people who bet on him, and you're worrying about the owners. You know you've got to call on him, but you don't know if it will do any good.

"When I asked Albatross for a little something extra that night, I was surprised at the way he responded. He just seemed to pick himself up and fly past those horses, winning by open lengths. And in 1:57.1!"

Albatross and friend pose after morning workout at Brandywine Raceway. (Brandywine Raceway photo)

He was so pleased with the colt's performance that he engaged in a spot of gentle crowing after the race. "Is he as great as I said he was?" he asked the working press, knowing the answer. "It was really no contest."

The timing was a new personal record for Albatross, slicing three-fifths of a second off the old speed badge he had picked up at Vernon Downs as a two-year-old.

The swift sophomore hardly worked up a sweat in his next start. He raced in the first of two $20,000 divisions of the Joe Neville Memorial Stake at Hazel Park, Michigan, and strolled in 1:59.3 to

Dancer whistles contentedly as he puts Super Bird through his training paces. (Brandywine Raceway photo)

whip seven outclassed rivals. Chalk players putting their money on him would have done almost as well at the nearest savings bank. He paid the minimum $2.20 in all three pools, and left a sizable minus in his wake.

Still, his payoffs at Hazel Park were actually generous in comparison with the returns he offered in his next few starts. Racing at Blue Bonnets in Montreal on June 20, he paid $2.20 for win and $2.10 for place. Competing again at Blue Bonnets a week later, and then at Richelieu Raceway in Montreal, he returned only $2.10 in all pools. While almost any bank in Canada or the United States would pay five percent interest on savings accounts, none was prepared to offer it so quickly.

Investors had only to wait a minute, 57 and two-fifths seconds to earn their dividends at Blue Bonnets. Albatross won both the $75,000 Prix D'Été and the $35,060 Trans-Canada Pace in that timing. He captured the former by four and a half lengths over Dexter Hanover and Seton Hanover, and the latter by three and three-quarters over Rob Ron Tarios and Nansemond.

His identical clockings were but a single tick off the all-time Canadian speed record set by Romulus Hanover in 1967. Romulus's

Winner's circle ceremonies after Dancer-Albatross duo wins $75,000 Prix D'Été at Blue Bonnets Raceway, Montreal. With them are Michael Mac Cormac, track vice-president of racing, and Raymond Lemay, track president. (Blue Bonnets Raceway photo)

standard had come over the same Blue Bonnets five-eighths-mile track.

The Canadian record for three-year-olds over a half-mile track fell to Albatross on July 10. The event was the $34,400 Beaver Stakes at Richelieu Raceway, and Dancer had to push his horse a little in the last half to preserve the win.

Richelieu's largest crowd in three years—10,385—assembled to see the American pacer, who had reaped a multitude of media coverage for his speedy exploits across town at Richelieu's sister track, Blue Bonnets. Dancer sent him to the front early, coasted down to the half in 1:01.1, then shook him awake as he glanced back and read "upset" in the eyes of surprisingly tough High Ideal. Albatross paced home in 57.2—the fastest half ever recorded in Canadian harness history—to complete his mile in 1:58.3.

His invasion of Canada had resulted in three sizzling miles—1:57.2, 1:57.2, and 1:58.3—more than $72,000 in purses, and a new fur cap for his trainer-driver.

The hat, made from Canadian beaver furs, was an unexpected bonus for winning the Beaver Stakes. Dancer wore it with aplomb as he paraded Albatross past the grandstand on the way back to the paddock. It was one of a number of wild mementos that he has earned in Canada over the years. Another, a multicolor, hand-carved totem pole, is prominently displayed in his trophy-packed office at New Egypt.

Starting with the Westchester Pace at Yonkers, Albatross had now gone five straight miles in less than two minutes. Dancer, without really pushing Super Bird at any time, had delivered the fast miles he had predicted to the New York metropolitan press and fans. The trouble was, both began to expect miracle miles every time the colt went to post.

Take the $106,795 Cane Futurity, for instance.

The Cane was the next big one on the list after Albatross completed his fruitful foray into Canada. As if the $100,000-plus purse weren't enough, the second jewel in pacing's Triple Crown was also on the line in the Yonkers Raceway fixture on July 16. Stanley Dancer, for obvious reasons, wanted desperately to win it. Lose the Cane and his chance for two straight Triple Crowns on the pace—he had won it in 1970 with Most Happy Fella—was as dead as yesterday's blockbuster hit on the rock and roll charts.

He intended to win it with a smart, heady drive, which, translated, meant a cautious, conservative steer.

Only six rivals—High Ideal, Nansemond, H. T. Luca, Paulos Hanover, Winning Worthy and Dexter Hanover—chose to challenge Albatross in the Cane, but they were the best sophomores still around and healthy in the United States and Canada.

Missing from the field was one-time Albatross conqueror Seton Hanover. Seton had made his last start of the year in the Trans-Canada at Blue Bonnets. The young son of Dancer Hanover had contracted a rare equine disease called purpura hemorrhagica. He was nearer death than life when he was shipped up to a Standardbred boarding farm near Vernon Downs. For 20 months Dr. John R. Steele and his staff, assisted by farm manager Richard Decker, battled first to save his life, then to get him back to the races. About the time that Albatross was retiring in 1972, Seton Hanover was bouncing back. He had missed the majority of his three-year-old stakes, but he was piling victory upon victory in the better class events at the metropolitan New York tracks.

The Cane Pace might have offered a mite more conflict had Seton

Hanover been one of the entries. On the other hand . . .

Albatross left out of the seven-hole. Dancer had him digging in from the go signal and the race track belonged to him before the field hit the quarter-pole. Unpressed, with the six foes strung out behind him, Dancer offered his horse a breather. They reached the half in 1:01.3, with some of the vociferous throng of 23,227 letting the Albatross-Dancer team know that it was disappointed with those figures. Stanley could hear the scattered hoots as he rode past the grandstand, but he kept his mind on the task at hand: Winning the Cane.

With a fresh, well-rested Albatross at the end of his lines, the lithe reinsman in blue and gold was confident there wasn't a pacer racing in 1971—or possibly one that had ever raced—who could beat him home from that point. He eased his tight hold on the colt, however, to make sure. Super Bird, picking up momentum with almost every stride, paced the third quarter in 30 seconds flat, then flew the rest of the way to the wire in 28.2.

The fractions all added up to a mile in two minutes flat—no bad clocking for a three-year-old racing over a half-mile track. From the mood of the crowd, however, one would have thought he had paced the mile in three minutes. Or even four.

One writer, gazing down at the restless throng from his sanctimonious perch in the press box, observed that "some of the 23,227 fans were in favor of charging Albatross and Dancer with 'loitering.'" They were peeved, the scribe said, because the horse and man "did not fracture a record."

It was a very frustrating experience for Mr. Dancer. He had driven a faultless race, his horse had performed admirably, and the two of them had won one of harness racing's richest prizes in the splendid time of two minutes. Yet the crowd was grumbling.

Stanley tried to set the record straight in his post-race comments. While it was a strain, he managed to keep the bitterness out of his voice.

"I'd be foolish to be going for world records this time of the year," he lectured. "He has a long season ahead and I don't want to take any more out of him than is necessary.

"I'll start worrying about records this fall after he's completed most of his stakes commitments. Right now, I'm primarily concerned with winning as much money as I can for the syndicate which bought him for $1,250,000 last April. The way things are going, he's beginning to look like a bargain."

It wasn't a new experience for the Jersey horseman. Driving back to New Egypt that night, he remembered that he had gone through much the same thing with Nevele Pride, Cardigan Bay, Su Mac Lad and other big horses in his barn over the years. Harness fans and the journalists who covered the sport deserved a large helping of credit for making it a booming enterprise, and that was precisely

The Big Bird captures the $106,795 Cane Futurity at Yonkers in two minutes flat. Fans thought he should have gone faster. (Yonkers Raceway photo)

why Stanley Dancer went out of his way to oblige them whenever it was humanly possible. Yet, they could be unreasonable at times . . .

Stanley hoped his small sermon in the paddock might find its way into print. Albatross had a bevy of stakes remaining, and fans reading his message, understanding his situation, might not be so quick to jump on him if he raced the colt with a degree of prudence.

When he started the 1971 season with Albatross, he'd told Bert James, Alan Leavitt and other members of the syndicate that the horse, blessed with good luck and soundness, might win between

One of the fringe benefits of winning the rich Cane Futurity at Yonkers was a smooch from dancer Bobbi Dee. (Yonkers Raceway photo)

$400,000 and $500,000 before the year was out. Anything over $407,534 would make him the richest pacer ever in a single season. Anything over $427,440 would make him the wealthiest pacer *or trotter* ever over one campaign. Pacer Bret Hanover held the former record; trotter Nevele Pride the latter.

With 11 starts behind him as Albatross left Yonkers and headed back to Canada, Dancer was privately raising his estimates of what Super Bird might hope to win during the '71 campaign. With judicious handling—and that meant easy miles occasionally—and continued good health, Dancer figured Albatross might slip over the half-million mark.

A fast mile was out of the question at Greenwood Raceway, Toronto, on July 24. Rain was falling steadily, ruining the final night of Grand Circuit action at the Toronto track, when Dancer drove Albatross to a 2:00.4 decision over High Ideal and Springfield in the $24,800 Queen City Stake.

Stanley left Greenwood with his pockets full of Grand Circuit cash for his owners. He won the Queen City with Albatross, a $15,000 division of the Van Riddell Stake with Super Bowl, a $13,083 filly event with Decorum, and had Del Miller catch-drive Quick Pride to a big win in the $26,500 Greenwood Stake for three-year-old trotters. In addition, Dancer finished second in two other major affairs.

Harry Harvey, Albatross's old boss, was on the Greenwood grounds at the same time, racing Bert James's tough filly pacer Saucy Wave. But he neither asked Stanley about Albatross, nor went to see the colt. The paths of Harvey and Albatross had crossed in the past—and would again in the future—but the pattern never changed. Harry was still toting a hurt so big, so great that he stonily refused to

All four feet off the ground and looking happy about it. (USTA photo)

Huge Roosevelt Raceway crowd watches Albatross win $32,200 Commodore Pace by open lengths. (Roosevelt Raceway photo)

either discuss or see the colt he had helped mold into a champion.

Rain was also an unwanted companion a week later when Albatross saw action in the $15,900 Thomas P. Gaines Memorial at Vernon Downs. The wet stuff arrived early and stayed late, a misty drizzle on a hot and muggy night. It neither stopped a Grand Circuit gathering of 9,019 devotees from turning out, nor from registering their dissatisfaction when Stanley sent him a 2:00.3 trip to outclass Paulos Hanover, Pat Taylor and two other overly optimistic pacers. The Vernon patrons, like race followers across the land, were convinced that Albatross could not only walk on water, but pace through it in two minutes or better.

It was a dryer, better night for the $32,200 Commodore Pace at Roosevelt on August 6. In fact, the whole weekend was balmy and beautiful if your name happened to be Stanley Dancer.

On Friday night the squire of Egyptian Acres drove Albatross to an almost noncompetitive 1:59.4 decision in the Commodore, then returned on Saturday night to garner the $107,686 Dexter Cup classic with Quick Pride.

Dancer's two-night spree moved Leonard Cohen of the *New York*

Horse breeder Adolph Karl and track Vice-President S. Harvey Fosner present Commodore Pace trophy to Dancer and Mr. and Mrs. Bert V. James. (Roosevelt Raceway photo)

Post to write, "Mayor Lindsay may call it 'fun city' but as far as Stanley Dancer is concerned, New York is 'money city.'"

Albatross's win was so easy that it again prompted some writers to go to the experts in search of comparisons between him and Bret Hanover. Bret, as usual, was the yardstick in measuring pacing greatness. Red Foley of the *Daily News* tracked down Dr. John Steele, the same veterinarian who was working miracles with the ailing Seton Hanover, and picked up some interesting comments.

Steele was not quite ready to bracket Super Bird with Bret, but he professed an open mind. "We'll have to wait and see if he can stand up over the long haul," he told Foley. "But I'd have to guess that Albatross can, because he's just the right size and build."

The vet went on: "He's not so heavy as to put too much pressure on his legs. That should permit him to remain sound. Right now I'd say he has a build something like Overcall, who got better as he went along and was unbeaten in his final season."

The observations of Dr. Steele, one of the nation's most prominent harness racing healers, were of special interest because they closely paralleled those of Dr. Edwin Churchill, Albatross's medical specialist throughout his days in the Dancer stable. Churchill, asked at one time to pinpoint the physical attributes which contributed to Super Bird's success, applauded both his size and conformation.

"He's a medium-small horse put together without any conformation faults. He has a long neck which helps give him great balance. He's relatively long-barreled for his height, which permits him to go cleanly. He stands very well from his elbow down. He's just an all-around well-made horse. Looking at him, you know he's a horse that would stay sound, barring an accident. He's not hard on himself in any way."

Ironically, Albatross's small stature as a yearling, a factor which had kept dozens of horsemen from bidding on him at the Harrisburg auction, was working to his advantage in his racing career. He had picked up both inches and pounds, of course, but both in perfect proportion.

His build had helped to give him such a perfect gait that he could wear a set of shoes longer than any other horse in the Dancer barn. "He steps cleanly, lands flush on his feet, and gets over the ground very lightly," Dr. Churchill commented. "As a result, he's remarkably easy on shoes."

Albatross: as perfectly gaited a pacer as was ever foaled. (Lubitsh & Bungarz photo)

Easy on shoes, he was. Easy on track balance sheets, he wasn't. Albatross left Roosevelt holding the bag for $2,700 worth of uncovered place pool bets. The massive Long Island plant had sensibly denied show wagering on the Bird. Otherwise, it would have had to cough up many more thousands. Tracks with guts enough to permit betting on him were rapidly discovering that it could be an expensive show of bravado.

The Adios Stake at The Meadows was next. The Adios, named for the late Standardbred super sire, is a newish affair, but gaining in prestige with every passing season. In 1971 it was worth $88,800. It also offered the winner a stunning statuette of Adios, sculpted by the late Edward Marshall Boehm, an artist whose works are treasured throughout the world.

The living room of Stanley and Rachel Dancer's sprawling, comfortable ranch home in New Egypt already contained a Boehm Adios (won by the Dancers' Most Happy Fella), as well as a pair of the sculptor's incredibly beautiful porcelain birds. Stanley assumed that the 1971 statuette, should he win the stake with Albatross, would wind up in Bert James's parlor. Nonetheless, the fat purse, the prestige of the win, and the fact that Super Bird had a win streak of 12 going, were inducements enough to prime Mr. Dancer for a supreme effort.

Albatross, as usual, was the beneficiary of a horrendous post in the draw for positions. He was racing out of the 10-hole in an 11-colt lineup in the first heat. It seemed like the Los Angeles Freeway on a Friday afternoon as Dancer wove through traffic, settling him in ninth spot rather than risking the danger of being parked out most of the trip. At the half, still back in ninth and some eight or 10 lengths off the pace, Stanley made his move. He eased Albatross off the rail and took aim at the leaders. He was sixth on the outside at the six-furlong mark and second on the outside as the merry band turned for home.

Pete Powers, the Meadows's publicist in those days, remembered it as a barn-burning finish. "He was a length and a half behind H. T. Luca at the top of the stretch, and for a brief moment it appeared he might not catch the colt owned by Ruby's Sterling Farm of nearby Morgantown, West Virginia. But then Dancer tapped him a couple of times with the whip. Albatross got the message, caught H. T. Luca 30 yards from the wire, and was a length and a half to the good at the finish."

The Bird had paced his mile in 1:58.3, with heaven alone knowing his clocking for the final half. He had blistered the tartan track which had hosted his racing debut 15 months earlier. He had singed the same five-eighths-mile oval where he had lost to Seton Hanover exactly one year ago to the day.

His win in the first heat gave him the one-post in the second. Owning the rail removed all vestiges of drama from the outcome.

Dancer sent him into the lead early and simply sat there as Albatross paced in 1:59.3 on his own to score by three lengths and wrap up his Adios victory.

H. T. Luca finished second in both heats. Dexter Hanover was third in the first, while Paulos Hanover got up for third in the final dash.

The winner's circle looked like Grand Central Station with all the Jameses, who lived nearby, congregating with the Dancers and other dignitaries. Squarely in the middle of the crush was Delvin Miller, the Adios Stake host, whose red and white sportcoat, white pants and white boots were visible practically to Scranton.

With the fifth edition of the Adios Stake now history, the race contestants scattered to the winds. Several headed for Springfield, Illinois, and the annual Review Futurity. Others made tracks for Batavia Downs, Batavia, New York, and a $20,000-plus colt stake. Some, like Albatross, were not eligible to the affairs or simply deserved vacations. Super Bird headed back to New Egypt to recharge his batteries for the final third of his season—the toughest portion.

The Dancer plan was to reunite his pacing champion with the Grand Circuit at Du Quoin, Illinois, in time for the Geers Stake on September 2. Albatross would rest for two weeks, race in the Geers, then enjoy another 11-day breather before competing in the Little Brown Jug Trial at Scioto Downs, Columbus, Ohio. Stanley would then have a fresh but sharp horse for the bigger stakes ahead.

The plan broke down, utterly crumbled, when the Du Quoin Fairground was hit by rain, rain, and still more rain. Young Bill Hayes and the Hambletonian Society managed to race Du Quoin's premier contest on September 1 (Speedy Crown won the 1971 Hambletonian), but the balance of the fair's stakes was a shambles. For the first time in its 36-year history, the Geers Stake for three-year-old pacers had to be canceled; a victim of rain.

Stanley Dancer was morose. Albatross's carefully conceived, fiercely followed training-racing schedule was destroyed. Tossing the cancellation in, it meant 30 straight days without a race—and in the heart of the season. He had no alternative. He had to grin and bear it. Rather, scowl and bear it.

And when Albatross did return to competition, more rain and mud were there to greet him. The event was the $23,000 Jug Trial at Charley Hill's modern harness palace, Scioto Downs. Chuck Stokes, the Scioto publicity chief, was looking for a record crowd for Bird's appearance, but had to settle for 9,446 hardy folks when heavy showers arrived to spoil the evening. Albatross, despite a month's layoff, dashed through the mud to win easily in 2:03.3. Dancer was pleased with his horse's snap, but doubted that a trip in the muck had done much to improve his physical fitness.

With the Jug Trial behind him, Dancer began to concentrate on the Jug itself—the Little Brown Jug pacing classic at the tiny Dela-

Super pacer wears odd expression, while his trainer-driver squints in the sun. (Scioto Downs photo)

ware County Fairground at Delaware, Ohio. It was decision time in earnest again. Ten days separated the Jug Trial and the mighty Jug itself. Should he start Albatross in the interim or not? The $25,000 Matron Stake at Wolverine Raceway, Detroit, was the only contest available. But that stake fell only four days after the Jug Trial. Was it wise to start Bird twice within four days? Or would the pair of stakes so close together simply tighten the colt, help make up for the four weeks of inactivity?

Bird-Dancer team wins Little Brown Jug Trial at Scioto Downs. Below, Dancer wears silly grin in winner's circle ceremonies. Members of Bert James family and track officials are with him. (Scioto Downs photo)

The Wolverine management team—Fred Van Lennep, Dick Wilson, Bob Cox—was composed of good people who ran a fine track. They were counting on Albatross to draw them a healthy attendance. Stanley was in a quandary. For the first and last time that season he turned to Bert James for an opinion. James discussed the dilemma with him, but eventually tossed the ball back to him.

Dancer opted to race the colt. It was, he convinced himself, essentially the same situation he had faced in the Messenger Stake earlier in the season. He had raced Bird in the Messenger Trial on a Tuesday night, then in the big race on Saturday. And Albatross had been magnificent, winning both for fun.

The Matron at Detroit, however, turned out to be a horse race of another color. A pair of outsiders, Sly Heel (Gene Reigle) and Veri Special (Chris Boring), teamed up to park Albatross to the half in 57.4 over the mile-track. Dancer grimly went on with his horse, finally reaching the front end as the two challengers melted in the heat of the contest.

Then Winning Worthy (Glen Garnsey) and Springfield (Dale

The $25,000 Matron Stake at Wolverine Raceway falls to Albatross in 1:58.2. (Wolverine Raceway photo)

Bert James and family, along with driver Dancer, collect Matron Stake silver from USTA's Larry Evans (right). (Wolverine Raceway photo)

Dufty) mounted mild threats at him coming home. His margin at the wire was three lengths, a seemingly comfortable cushion. Yet Dancer knew it had been a rugged workout for his horse. Bird, on the wing for more than half the race, had covered the mile in 1:58.2. But Stanley had felt the fatigue in his champion as he labored the final quarter in 30.2 seconds.

Dancer was not at all happy with the way the race had cut, but he scoffed at reports that his driving rivals had ganged up on him in an effort to halt Albatross's long victory streak. "They were trying to beat him, sure, but they didn't gang up to do it," he said.

Wolverine had done well at the gate—12,417, the largest regular Friday night house in the track's history. Going game, however, it had to muster $13,589 to handle uncovered tickets on Bird. It was the grandest minus pool Albatross had ever created.

The next morning, September 18, the Meadow Skipper son was en route to Delaware. Joe Wideman, stretched out on several bales of hay, was riding along with him in the Hutt van. He was studying the colt's 1971 eligibility papers to help break up the monotony of the long ride.

Joe wasn't like some of the other Grand Circuit caretakers, who could recite their horse's records chapter and verse. He left that chore for Stanley. But reading Bird's papers now, he was pretty damn impressed.

His horse's 1971 earnings stood at $374,329. He had scored 11 triumphs in two minutes or less. Starting on May 1, Albatross had raced 18 heats, winning 17 of them and finishing second once. He had not been beaten since May 8, and that loss was to a four-year-old.

Albatross had never bowed to a three-year-old, and the way it was going, Joe figured, he never would. With that comforting thought in mind, Wideman closed his eyes and tried to doze.

Meanwhile, the big, streamlined horse trailer continued to roll along Ohio's Interstate 71.

Headed for Delaware.

14

Richard Downing, the late owner of Bret Hanover, was once asked to explain the mystique of the Little Brown Jug pacing classic. Downing, a gruffly articulate man who was rarely at a loss for words, took his best shot at the task.

"Let's put it this way: You buy a pacing colt, and you hope he makes it to the races. When he does, you hope he's good enough for the Grand Circuit. If he is, you automatically begin thinking of the Little Brown Jug—is he solid enough to start in the Jug? Could he win it? I don't know why, but the Brown Jug is the Hambletonian, the Kentucky Derby of the pacing gait."

Which was no explanation at all.

The late Mr. Downing is to be excused for fumbling the assignment. He was not alone. No one else has sufficiently explained why the Brown Jug has grown weedlike to such heights in the minds of harness people everywhere. It just has.

Harness racing's classic races are traditionally contested over a mile track. The Jug is raced over a half-mile oval located on a postage stamp-sized fairground in the southwest corner of Ohio. The Horseman Futurity for sophomore pacers at Indianapolis is 39 years older; the Messenger Stake some $75,000 richer on the average. Yet, when the U.S. Trotting Association sets out to prepare color films on the sport's headline events at each gait each year, it sends its cameras to Du Quoin, Illinois, for the Hambletonian, and Delaware, Ohio, for the Little Brown Jug. No questions asked; no arguments received.

Harness buffs from all over North America assemble at Delaware each September to see the continent's classiest three-year-olds strut their swift pacing stuff. They have roasted, nearly melted, in the bleachers, on rooftops and in trees to see Bullet Hanover win the 1960 edition; and they have shivered, almost turned blue, to witness Lehigh Hanover gaining victory in the 1962 contest. Broiling sun or frigid winds, they keep coming back for more.

As many as 40,000 have turned out on Jug Day, give or take some 10,000 or 20,000. There is no method known to man nor computer to accurately measure the Jug Day attendance, yet each year a firm figure is soberly released from the press box atop the grandstand. It is a charming put-on. *The Horseman & Fair World*, in its

"Down The Stretch" column, once revealed the formula used to gauge the house.

"... *You take the amount of the Jug purse, divide it by the number of Jug starters, and multiply by the number of flower beds in the infield. That gave us a base figure of 42,458. From this you subtract the number of people partying in the orchard who never saw the race, several thousand who couldn't tell a colt from a filly and thought they saw the Jug on Wednesday, and some more people who ate too many apples in the orchard. Now you add the number of legs and tails on the non-human guests at the Thomson pre-Jug party (a total of nine for Angel and Coon-Coon), and the number of people on the roof of the grandstand prior to the Jug first heat (they all fell off after the second heat), and then subtract one man from Adrian, Michigan, who called long distance to find out if the Jug was a trot or pace. That gives you 43,578. Honest.*"

The "official" attendance for the 1971 Brown Jug, duly reported by *The New York Times*, the newspaper of record, was 43,609—a record!

The actual attendance, whether it was 30,000 or 50,000, was not important. What was significant was the fact that all harness racing fans worth the title were there in spirit as Albatross & friends walked out of the backstretch paddock and began to limber up for Little Brown Jug number 26.

Records were expected to tumble before the afternoon was out, and Standardbred followers dearly love to sit in on the birth of racing milestones.

The 1971 Jug was virtually conceded to Albatross before the colt dropped a hoof on the very fast Delaware track.

The Ashtabula, Ohio, *Star Beacon* topped a United Press International story with this headline: "Jug Officials Nix Bets; Albatross Solid Choice." The UPI story went on to say that the Jug field "included such a heavy favorite that for the first time in the 26-year history of the event no pari-mutuel betting was allowed on the horse."

Ralph Morrow, executive sports editor of the *Dayton Daily News*, went quite a bit further. Morrow's story was headlined: "Albatross Regarded Shoo-In at Jug." The sports editor grabbed himself a perch far out on a limb by writing, "It matters not how many horses are entered in Thursday's Little Brown Jug. The winner will be Albatross."

Morrow's opinion wasn't far off that of a man who was considerably closer to the situation—Stanley Dancer. While Dancer was not in the habit of asking for the trophy before the running of a race, he was as confident of winning the Jug as he was of winning any of the thousands of racing battles he had engaged in up to that point.

Dancer and a horde of other knowledgeable racing figures were more than mildly surprised when 14 additional pacers were entered against his colt. "It's more than I expected, but that should make it more interesting," he commented when the number was announced.

The bulky field made for an abnormally rich Jug purse, $102,954—third best in the history of the classic. It also guaranteed a long afternoon for the horses, their reinsmen and the thousands upon thousands of spectators clogging the fairground facilities.

Splitting the entrants into a pair of divisions meant a minimum of three heats, since a horse must capture two heats to officially win the Jug. Eight colts were to go to post in the first division; seven in the second. The top four finishers from each would earn the right to compete in the third dash. And if a horse other than the two who had scored wins in the eliminations should take the third dash, then the three victors would come back for a race-off.

All the Albatross rivals still racing were present and accounted for in the Jug—H. T. Luca, Springfield, Dexter Hanover, Paulos Hanover, Veri Special, Winning Worthy, Nansemond and Local Time. Rounding out the big brood were a half-dozen horses whom Albatross had either raced infrequently or not at all—El Patron, Keystone Journal, Gamely, Ring Leader, Scottish Bret and Airy Way.

While none boasted the credentials of Albatross, some of the contestants were pretty fair country pacers by anyone's standards.

Gamely, owned by the L-Bar Farms Corporation of Goshen, New York, was not one of the better known entries, but was fresh off a 1:56.4 victory in the Horseman Futurity at Indianapolis. Herve Filion and Joe O'Brien would share the driving assignment behind the Airliner son.

H. T. Luca, handled by Del Insko, had not raced since the Adios Stake, but had been one of Super Bird's toughest rivals in all contests up to that time. He was sporting a win record of two minutes flat taken at Yonkers Raceway.

Dexter Hanover, a $125,000 purchase as a yearling in 1969, was a familiar Bird foe and brought a speed badge of 1:59.1 into the race. John Simpson Jr. was down to drive the colt, owned by Thomas and Mildred Dexter of Pearl River, New York, Arthur W. Dexter Jr. and Alice Schmidt of Nanuet, New York, and the Apache Stable of Orlando, Florida.

Paulos Hanover, the property of the Alnoff and Gargreve Stables of Hewlett, New York, boasted a record of 1:59.3 from the Hanover-Hempt Stake at Pocono Downs. Driven by Bob Camper, Paulos Hanover had finished near Albatross in a number of matches.

Local Time, steered by Ted Taylor, was coming into the Delaware race with seven wins on his ticket, including one in 1:59.1 at Vernon Downs. Ray and Earl Forsyth of Bloomfield Hills, Michigan, owned the speedster.

Winning Worthy, the pride of the classy Castleton Farms, was a 1:57.2 victor in the Review Futurity at Springfield, Illinois, and would not be hurt by the driving skills of young Glen Garnsey.

And Nansemond, owned by Fermer Perry of Suffolk, Virginia, William M. Camp Jr. of Franklin, Virginia, and the Capital Hill Farm of Montreal, could be tough, although he was only now bouncing back from a ligament injury suffered in the Cane Futurity on July 16. The Tar Heel son had returned to action with a pair of September starts at Liberty Bell Park, one a victory in two minutes flat.

The presence of Herve Filion in the sulky behind Nansemond would make the colt a threat if he were racing on but two legs. Filion would find a way to get him around the track even if it meant carrying the youngster on his back.

Filion, the hurrying, scurrying French-Canadian, was well on his way toward scoring a thundering 543 wins in 1971, a mark which would obliterate all existing records—Standardbred and Thoroughbred—for races won. (As it turned out, his 1971 feat was a mere prelude to 1972, when he brought home 605 winners).

Short, stocky, tireless, fearless and cool, Filion has built himself a vast and ardent racing public with his track heroics and his outgoing personality, the latter of which includes a marvelous sense of irreverent humor. Once, in accepting an important award, he broke up a Toronto audience with his short and pungent acceptance speech. "I want to thank my mother and my father for making it possible," he told all the folks in dinner jackets and evening gowns. "For making it possible that I was born."

Herve, a professional driver since age 13, was making his third start in the Little Brown Jug. He hadn't had a winner yet, but Stanley Dancer was not counting him nor his peppery pacer out. Ignoring Herve Filion in a race was like disregarding a black widow spider climbing up your arm.

The race meant much to Filion; more to Dancer. Stanley had driven three Jug winners—Henry T. Adios, Lehigh Hanover and Most Happy Fella—and needed one more to draw even with Billy Haughton. The Jug was the concluding leg up to Pacing's Triple Crown, and Albatross had to have a win if he were to wear the esteemed headpiece. And, then, Super Bird had a chain of 16 straight triumphs going, and it would be a bitter blow to see it ended.

Stanley had ample time to ponder all that, since Albatross had received a spot in the second division. So had Nansemond. Dancer watched from the paddock fence as the first heat went to post. Filion, with two horses entered in the classic, was out on the track with the first of the pair, Gamely.

It was a few minutes before 2 p.m. when the initial field of Jug combatants fled the starting gate. The weather, for a change, was favorable. A trifle too cool and windy to be classified as perfect, but several rungs above what the Brown Jug had been drawing in recent years.

World Champion driver Herve Filion, a winner of 605 dashes in 1972. (USTA photo)

Gamely was away first, bullying his way to the front and leading the group over to the quarter in 28.4. It was the Airliner son's only moment of glory in the heat. Before the eight horses reached the half-mile marker in front of the grandstand, H. T. Luca and El Patron had whipped past, and it was merely a question of which would prevail over the other. For the entire final tour of the half-mile oval the two rolled along as though they were racing in tandem.

At the wire it was the Del Insko-reined H. T. Luca by a head over El Patron and driver Buddy Gilmour.

The time of the heat was 1:58.3, with Keystone Journal finishing third and Gamely hanging on to qualify for the fourth spot in the third heat. The remaining four contestants in the dash were through racing for the day.

The Jug Day fans, 43,609 of them on the button, had enjoyed an appetizer in the first dash. Now it was time for the main course —Albatross, Nansemond and foes. The crowds around the oval pushed tighter to the fence. The souls in the grandstand and bleachers craned their necks. The hardy crews on the roofs stood up and shielded their eyes to the sun. The mobile gate picked up speed . . .

Filion, now handling the reins of his stronger Jug entry, had Nansemond boiling from the outset. The Tar Heel offspring was quickly in charge of the class, heading to the quarter-pole in 29.1 with Springfield and Dexter Hanover tucked in behind him. Dancer was content to sit in fourth spot, biding his time.

Nansemond was still the boss as the bunch rounded the second turn and headed past the bleachers, but the fireworks were beginning. Dancer made his move in front of the grandstand, ranging up alongside the Filion-handled colt. Albatross managed to poke his head out in front of his rival, but could not gain enough clearance to move cleanly over to the rail. The half was in 59.3, the three-quarters in 1:29.4.

Dancer's colt was still a head to the good going into the final bend, but lost the advantage on the turn. He drew even again as the pair straightened out for the dash down the stretch, and then it was anybody's race. Both drivers were working furiously on their pacers, although their shouting could not be heard over the collective clamor of the wild throng. Side by side they slammed under the finish line, with only Stanley Dancer, Herve Filion and the photo finish camera knowing the identity of the winner.

It was Albatross by inches. In 1:58.1, with the two incredible pacers covering the last quarter-mile in a withering 28.2.

Springfield (Jack Kopas) and Dexter Hanover (John Simpson Jr.) followed the leaders across the wire to gain access to the vital third heat.

Albatross backers—the Bert James family, Mr. and Mrs. John Rollins and others—were all visibly excited and delighted with the game performance of their champion. Stan Dancer, on the other hand, was curiously restrained as he guided the plodding colt around the grandstand turn and back to the paddock. Despite Bird's courageous win, a faint but unmistakable scent of disaster was in his nostrils.

"We may be in trouble," he told groom Joe Wideman when the last of the well-wishers had drifted away.

Wideman stared at him.

"He went a great mile, but he seems flat. And I don't think more racing this afternoon is going to help him. I'd give anything to win the next heat and wrap it up."

"You ought to be able to," Wideman offered loyally.

"Maybe," Dancer answered. "We'll know soon."

Fifty minutes later the eight survivors from the elimination dashes were parading past the grandstand. Still alive in the Jug were Albatross, H. T. Luca, Nansemond, El Patron, Springfield, Keystone Journal, Dexter Hanover and Gamely. If either Albatross or H. T. Luca, winners of the eliminations, finished first, the 1971 Little Brown Jug would be history and Hank Thomson and Curly Smart, the classic's impresarios, could start planning the 1972 edition. If another of the entries won, however, the Jug would stretch to a fourth heat.

No one was surprised when Filion chose to drive Nansemond and named cagey Joe O'Brien to handle stablemate Gamely.

A hush fell over the tense multitude as the eight pacers formed behind the wings of the gate, and the powerful convertible began to pick up speed. Suddenly heat number three of the Brown Jug was under way.

Nansemond and Albatross were both out and flying. Dancer, starting from the rail, was intent upon parking Filion and his horse for as long as possible. Half-convinced that Super Bird was not up to peak effort, he was straining to stretch his driving skills to the maximum to compensate.

Down to the quarter in 29 seconds flat, Nansemond had his snout out in front by several inches, but Filion sensed he could not make it all the way to the top. The canny Canadian backed his horse off and settled him in third along the rail. Albatross was on top, H. T. Luca in second, and Nansemond still third as the half-pole arrived in 59.1 and the three-quarters in 1:29.

Herve then made his bid. He was whipping, slashing, bellowing, shaking the lines, bouncing up and down in the sulky seat the rest of the way home. At first all his work was in vain. Albatross held his margin. But halfway down the stretch, the gap began to diminish. Nansemond was even with Albatross, and then he was past him. At the finish, he had a full length on Dancer's colt, the timer read 1:57.2, and the Brown Jug was headed for a race-off.

The Tar Heel colt, never sharper and showing no signs of his eight-week bout with lameness, had halted Albatross's win streak at 17. The vast Jug Day throng saluted him with a booming round of applause and whistles. Filion, driving his colt past the grandstand, was wearing a grin that stretched from one side of his helmet to the other.

Stanley Dancer, jumping off his bike, managed a smile as well. "How about that," he told the small crowd around him. "I thought we were home free at the head of the stretch. My horse felt good; he just got tired. That's the way it goes. That's why they call it racing."

Back in the paddock, however, he grew solemn as he watched Joe Wideman bathe down Albatross. His colt had paced a 1:57.3 mile—only three-fifths of a second off Bret Hanover's world record over a half-mile track—yet he was now positive the youngster was off form. And he was sure he knew the reason. Two races within four nights—the Jug Trial at Scioto and the Matron at Wolverine—had taken their toll. Albatross had slogged through the mud at Scioto, then gone a grueling trip at Wolverine. And he may have forfeited his Little Brown Jug victory and the Triple Crown in the process, Stanley feared.

The New Jersey horseman's spirits, near their zenith when the Jug commenced, were plunging by the minute. Instead of relishing the race-off and the chance to gain revenge and salvage the win, he began to dread it.

"I hated to go out on the race track with him knowing he wasn't himself," he said, looking back at the painful moment. "Still, I had no choice but to go to the end. Like a prizefighter, you can't quit because you know you've lost your punch. The worst part of it was, I had no one to blame but myself. It was my decision to race him in the Matron."

The three heat winners, Nansemond, Albatross and H. T. Luca, returned for the final heat. It is traditional in harness racing—almost the unwritten law—that very little racing is done in the first half or

Fierce rivals but good friends: Herve Filion and Stan Dancer, along with John Simpson Jr. (Lubitsh & Bungarz photo)

three-quarters of a race-off. After two or even three rugged heats, the horses are weary and the men who drive them are concerned for their health and soundness. The racing, when it comes, is almost always confined to the final quarter.

Nansemond, earning the rail post position with his win in the third heat, set the pace throughout the race-off mile. Filion drove conservatively, reaching the quarter in 31.2, the half in 1:03 and the three-quarters in 1:36.2. Before he actually arrived at the third striped pole, however, he was cranking up his pacer. Sure as death and taxes, both foes, Albatross in particular, would be coming.

Dancer came out with his horse on the final turn. Albatross was digging in, moving up, and for an instant, Stanley felt he might be able to bring it off. Super Bird moved up to Nansemond's wheels halfway down showdown alley. But the spark was not there. The extra sting which set him apart, made him king of the class, was missing. Nansemond, pacing the final panel in 28 seconds flat, held him off. The Filion colt was three-quarters of a length in front at the end.

The 1971 Little Brown Jug was over. The harness racing upset of the year had been perpetrated.

Fans who had traveled hundreds, even thousands of miles to see Albatross capture the Jug were disappointed. But the throng, *43,609 strong*, had no complaints. It had witnessed one of the most epic struggles in harness racing annals.

Herve Filion, surrounded by family, friends, owners, fair officials and Brown Jug beauty queens, was the center of attention as he happily hammed it up for photographers in the winner's circle. He patiently engaged in all the necessary amenities, then made a bee-line for the airport. He had horses to drive that night at Roosevelt Raceway.

Stanley Dancer wearily dismounted from his bike to an audience of two—caretaker Joe Wideman and night watchman Roger Pritchard. Wideman recalled, however, that Dancer appeared unruffled by the defeat . . . that his dignity was firmly in place . . . that his class was still showing. "You couldn't tell from his face whether he'd won or lost," the slim caretaker reported.

Bert James apparently read his countenance quite differently. James, still the largest shareholder in Albatross, caught up with Dancer at his fairground barn. "It must have looked to him like I was taking the loss pretty hard," Stanley remembered. "He told me to forget it, that the horse had raced fine and that I'd done a great job of driving him. James was very, very kind, and I really appreciated it."

At Delaware, Dancer saw James at his sympathetic, gentlemanly best. In a Philadelphia hospital some seven months later, he would see quite a different side of the former auto dealer.

15

While Albatross had most assuredly had his wings clipped by Nansemond, neither Stanley Dancer nor Herve Filion believed for an instant that the wing-shearing was a permanent affliction.

"Every horse goes a bad race now and then," Dancer said protectively. "It was Albatross's misfortune—as well as mine—that he had to be a little off for an important race like the Little Brown Jug." Then he added firmly, "He's still the greatest pacer ever foaled."

Filion, delighted to be adding a homely brown jug to his trophy collection under any circumstances, did not quibble with his rival's assessment. In fact, with typical candor, he reinforced it. "I don't think Albatross was 100 percent for that race. My horse, he was very, very sharp and he beat Stanley's horse. Nansemond is a great horse, the best I've ever driven. But people must understand, he is no Albatross. No way."

Dancer, popping-vest proud of his colt, anxious to have him reclaim his spot at the head of the sophomore pacing division, appreciated the jaunty Canadian's testimony. He considered it a noble gesture by a gracious winner. But he was hungering for more tangible evidence to present to the harness racing jury. He wanted a clear-cut victory over Nansemond to firm up his case.

The victory could not come at the next stop along the Grand Circuit's winding trail, Lexington's Big Red Mile. Nansemond, Dancer knew, would not be on hand for the $52,865 Tattersalls Pace.

With the Little Brown Jug winner temporarily back on the shelf, Stanley selected a swift clocking or two over the world's fastest harness track as another means of reestablishing Albatross's image of superiority. He did not necessarily have world records in mind, but if one or more turned up during the heat of battle, so much the better.

Nine days existed between the Brown Jug at Delaware and the Tattersalls affair at Lexington. Stung by giving his colt too much work prior to the Jug—two tough races within four days—Dancer followed the opposite course in preparing him for the Lexington fixture. He permitted him to loaf. He shipped Albatross to the Red Mile and practically laid him up for an entire week. At the end

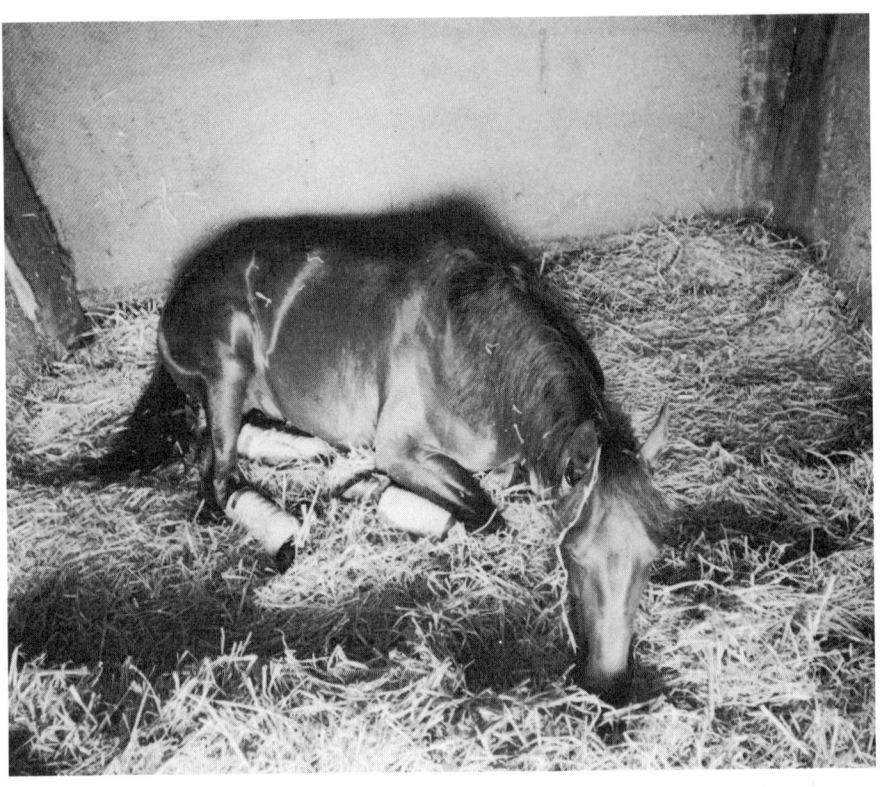

Even great world champions have to rest once in a while.

of the period, Dancer flew into the Kentucky city and worked the youngster a pair of lazy miles. The radical routine contained an element of risk, although Bird's trainer was prepared to accept the gamble. He wanted a fresh horse for the stake.

Albatross, bowing in the Jug, had proved himself mortal in the eyes of rival trainers. The champ could be had, they figured. Nansemond had beaten him, and their pacers might just beat him, too. Red Mile racing officials were happy to receive an even dozen entries for the Tattersalls.

Nansemond was not the only Brown Jug contestant missing from the field. H. T. Luca and El Patron, third and fourth in the race standings, were elsewhere as well. Most of the other Jug starters were primed for battle, however—Winning Worthy, Springfield, Dexter Hanover, Paulos Hanover, Veri Special, Gamely, Keystone Journal and Scottish Bret. Completing the small herd for the Lexington match were Spring's Pride, D. Judge and Steady Glow.

The Lexington mile, very wide and therefore very safe, is accustomed to entertaining large fields. The whole dozen was scheduled to leave the gate in the same wild charge, and Albatross had suffered his usual fate in the draw for posts. He had the 12-hole, placing him fourth from the rail in the second tier.

Hot, dry autumn weather and the devoted ministrations of track superintendent Joe Childs had brought the Red Mile to its height of speed. A steady flow of two-minute miles had been recorded during the first four afternoons of competition, including a show-stopping, history-making 1:52 journey by four-year-old Steady Star.

Steady Star, a Steady Beau son handled by Joe O'Brien for the Dave L. Brown Estate (namely Mr. and Mrs. Chester V. Ault), had set the record in a time trial on Friday, the day before Albatross and his pals were due to tangle. Costing only $5,000 as a yearling, Steady Star had gone the fastest mile in the history of Standardbred racing, easily beating the 1:53.3 standard hoisted by Bret Hanover over the same track in 1966.

Fans cramming the tiny Red Mile grandstand were still buzzing about the awesome mile when the 12 hopefuls in the Tattersalls Pace began to limber up on Saturday afternoon.

Dancer, convinced that the soft training schedule had worked wonders for his horse, was brimming with confidence as he jumped up behind Albatross to loosen him up for the pair of racing heats ahead. He hadn't gone 200 feet when the confidence suddenly turned to concern.

Something was wrong. Dead wrong. For the first time since Harry Harvey had taught him the rudiments of racing at the Arden Fairground, Albatross was showing a distinct fear of . . . unbelievably . . . *leaves!* Leaves from trees. Red, yellow, green, beige, brown leaves. Blowing slowly across the track or lying in bunches of four or five on the turf.

Babylike, Albatross was hopping, skipping and jumping sideways to avoid the dead foliage. Dancer had all he could do to control the colt, to keep him on his feet, to keep him from leaping into the paths of other horses jogging and working on the track.

He was mystified and shaken when he finally managed to complete the exercise mile. "I don't . . . can't understand it," he stammered to caretaker Joe Wideman. "He's never done that before. Leaves don't bother him. He's shied at other things, tractors and the like. But *leaves?* Why, we've never worn a shadow roll on him, have we?"

"Not to my recollection," the groom replied. "Like you say, he's been wary of track equipment from time to time. And a cigarette butt or piece of cotton from a bandage will make him take a funny step or two when he sees them once in a while. But, hell, you've always got leaves lying out on a track. He's paced through them hundreds of times."

"I'll tell you, Joe, if he acts like that in the race, I don't know how I'll get him around the track let alone win the thing. Yet we can't just throw a shadow roll on him if he's never worn one before . . ."

"If you keep him busy, he may be all right," Wideman suggested.

"That's about all I can do," Dancer said gravely. "That and hope for the best."

It was an edgy, cautious Stanley Dancer in the sulky as the field picked up speed in the first dash of the Tattersalls. He nursed his colt away from the gate and settled in 12th and last position in the early going. Up front, Keystone Journal and Dexter Hanover were sparring for the lead, taking the batch of pacers down to the quarter in 27.2—a fast and flashy first panel for even the speedy Red Mile.

Coming off the first turn and heading down the long backstretch, Glen Garnsey made a big, ripping move with Winning Worthy. He circled the leaders and ended up on top of the field, with the halfpole reached in a screeching 57.2. Dancer was still handling his horse with utmost caution, keeping him behind horses so that he had little or no chance to scour the track in search of his curious new enemy —autumn leaves. Albatross was pacing along in seventh behind Gamely at the half.

Going into the second and final turn, Winning Worthy continued to set the pace and was beginning to open up a bit of daylight on the pack behind him. Dancer knew he had to start his bid if he were to stand any chance at overhauling the leader. With trepidation he gently pulled Albatross three-wide from the rail, gave him his head, and headed for the front. This left his horse with no rival directly in front of him. The colt got his first real look at the track ahead, immediately spotted the enemy, and leaped in the air.

"He jumped so high that when he came down, I knew for certain we'd end up in a terrible heap," Dancer reported later. "There seemed to be no possible way he could land without falling down."

Yet, when Albatross's four legs were reunited with the earth, they were pacing. Like pistons. He hadn't missed a stroke. Not a beat. Dancer, with his heart in his mouth, went right on with him. He caught Dexter Hanover in third, flew past Springfield in second, and was drawing even with Winning Worthy in front.

Garnsey, purring along with Winning Worthy, wondering what had happened to Albatross, beginning to enjoy the thought of the smashing upset he had within his grasp, could not believe his eyes. "He looked like a locomotive," the Castleton Farms driver said of Dancer's horse. "I could almost see the steam coming out his ears."

Garnsey had only a split second to record his impressions for posterity. Albatross swooshed past him, still flying, and collected three lengths worth of sunshine over his colt in the rush to the finish.

The small grandstand, overflowing with serious, knowledgeable Standardbred students, was fairly swaying from the tumult. Albatross, autumn leaves ballet and all, had paced his mile in 1:54.4 to establish an all-time world mark for pacers of any age in a race! And since no trotter had ever come close to that timing, it figured

Reinsman Glen Garnsey, who drove Winning Worthy against the mighty Albatross. (USTA Photo)

out to be the fastest race mile in Standardbred history by a horse of any age at either gait.

Stricken from the record book was the 1:55 record that Adios Harry had set at Vernon Downs in 1955 and Bret Hanover had equaled at Indianapolis an even decade later. And, since Bret was a three-year-old when his standard was set, Albatross had picked up the world mark for sophomores as well.

To make the sweep complete, Super Bird had also set the Lexington track record for pacers in a race, dethroning, of all horses, his own sire, Meadow Skipper. Skipper had paced the pink track in 1:55.1 back in 1963. At the very least, Albatross had kept the Red Mile record in the family.

Dancer, beaming, was surrounded by well-wishers on the track and back in the nearby paddock. Uncharacteristically, Bert James even spent a smile on the occasion. James was probably remembering that fate and instinct had led him to keep 25 percent of the horse, rather than selling him outright. And Alan Leavitt, the master of Lana Lobell Farms, Albatross's eventual retirement home? Well, how would any breeder feel, knowing full well a horse like that was headed for his stud barn? Like rushing out and buying a new cash register? Like throwing a party to end all parties? Both?

Dancer confided to several observers that he had never had a faster ride in all his career than the one he had enjoyed coming home with Albatross. He searched in vain for some horseman or fan who might have had a clock on the colt during the last quarter. Then he consulted the timer built into his mind after 25 years of chauffeuring race horses and announced, "He had to have paced that last quarter in 26 seconds."

Truly, it was no time to stand around and ponder the case. That would have to come later. Stanley had more tough work ahead of him on the afternoon. He was also handling Queen's Blue Chip and Decorum in elimination heats of the $32,465 Almahurst Stake for two-year-old pacing fillies.

Queen's Blue Chip was a Bret Hanover daughter who was owned by the Kimbred Farms of Wallkill, New York. Dancer had driven her to a 2:00.3 triumph in the first of the three elimination dashes.

Decorum was a Meadow Skipper offspring who had been bred by Charles A. Kenney of Paris, Kentucky—the same Charlie Kenney who had been a co-breeder of Albatross and had advised his partners to sell the three-horse Albatross package. This time around, Kenney had leased Decorum to Rachel Dancer, Stanley's wife. It was a very good move for Mrs. Dancer.

In her attempt to gain a berth in the final dash of the Almahurst, Decorum had chased the reigning queen of the freshman pacing lasses, Romalie Hanover, to a world record 1:58 mile. Arthur Hult, sitting in for ailing trainer-driver Roland Beaulieu, had driven the Mitzi Stable star to the record, with Decorum finishing second.

The new mark barely lasted the hour out. In the finale, Dancer assigned Joe O'Brien to the sulky behind Queen's Blue Chip and drove Decorum himself. As always, he proved himself an impeccable judge of talent. Decorum toured the big oval in 1:57.1 to upset Romalie Hanover in the race and rob her of her hour-old world standard. The mile was so swift that it matched the time trial mark of Timely Beauty, set nine years earlier.

While it wasn't planned that way, it was turning out to be Stanley Dancer Day at the Lexington Trots. Dancer needed only one more victory to clinch the unofficial honor, but that loomed as a hairy assignment. He had to win the second heat of the Tattersalls Pace with touchy Albatross.

He was hoping the colt would conquer his strange aversion to leaves in the 80 minutes between heats, but it wasn't to be. Conditions were no better as he warmed up the Meadow Skipper son for the second and last heat of the stake.

It was late afternoon now, and a light breeze had foaled to deposit and scatter more and more of the foliage across the track. Albatross, seemingly obsessed, was still bucking and dancing to avoid the leaves, putting new furrows in his driver's brow. Super Bird had earned the rail post position with his triumph in the first dash, and Dancer knew there would be no horse in front of him to block the colt's view of the ground in the early going.

In desperation, he sent Joe Wideman scurrying off to the barn to grab a shadow roll. "I figured we'd put it on him while he was standing in the paddock and, with luck, he'd get used to it by race time," Stanley explained. "He was fine in the paddock, but when I scored him for the dash, he began to fight it. At the last second we pulled it off. I knew it wasn't going to work."

With Scottish Bret and Steady Glow withdrawn, 10 young pacers faced the starting gate for the last half of the Tattersalls. The "go" signal was scarcely out of starter Tom Eaton's mouth when Albatross spooked again. He leaped in the air and came down sort of half-pacing, half-staggering as Dancer worked the lines to steady him, to keep him from going down. All nine rivals sailed past as the driver struggled with the recalcitrant youngster. The crowd in the stands, yearning for more records, groaned its collective disappointment.

Seconds later, Dancer had him back on the pace. There were open lengths between him and the field up ahead. It looked hopeless, but Stanley decided to shoot the works. He tightened his grip on the handholds, settled a little firmer in the sulky seat, and growled at Albatross. The world pacing champion took it from there.

Albatross was eighth at the quarter, third at the half, and leading the field, pacing pretty, at the three quarters. Rounding the final bend, he was three lengths to the good of Winning Worthy and never surrendered any of that advantage in the drive to the wire.

A sharp, crisp roar, almost like the boom of a cannon, exploded out of the grandstand as the throng caught sight of the infield timer. It read 1:54.4 for the second time that afternoon.

Elizabeth Rorty, covering the event for *Horseman and Fair World* Magazine, had never seen an effort to match it. "The middle half of that mile was officially paced in 56.2, and what Albatross must have paced to move from eighth at the quarter to lead at the three quarters we leave to your imagination," the veteran harness scribe reported.

Dancer, occupied with keeping his horse pacing all the way, had no real appreciation of the mile his pacer had turned in when they slammed across the finish. He knew it was a quick journey, but little more. "It was inconceivable that any horse could pace that kind of a mile after a start like that," he said wonderingly.

He also had to revise his thinking. The brush coming home in the first heat was no longer the fastest ride of his career. The midportion of the later dash, probably the second quarter, had topped it.

Albatross, of course, had matched the all-time world marks he had posted in the initial heat. Larry Evans, the U.S. Trotting Association's keeper-of-the-records, was hard at work in the minuscule Red Mile press box, straining to add up the championship standards Super Bird had netted on the afternoon. Breathlessly, Evans reported that they totaled six.

Albatross was now the fastest pacer *of any age* in a race (1:54.4), replacing Adios Harry and Bret Hanover (both 1:55) in the record book.

He was the fastest *three-year-old* ever in a race (1:54.4), erasing Bret Hanover's (1:55) name in that category.

He was the swiftest pacer *of any age* going two heats combined (3:49.3), snapping a record held by Adios Harry (3:51.3).

He was the swiftest *three-year-old* going two heats combined (3:49.3), removing the name of Columbia George (3:52) from that section.

He was the speediest pacer *of any age* going the first heat of a two-heat race (1:54.4), supplanting Adios Harry and Bret Hanover (1:55) in the book.

And he was the speediest pacer *of any age* going the second heat of a two-heat contest (1:54.4), robbing Rum Customer and Columbia George (1:56) of that honor.

Lexington's ancient Red Mile itself had enjoyed one of its most productive days ever. Counting time trials sprinkled through the day's program, the track had hosted 14 two-minute miles and eight world records. No one, anywhere could ever remember a day to match it.

Stanley Dancer, shedding his blue and gold silks back at his barn, had personally accounted for all seven of the marks which would go into the USTA's *Trotting and Pacing Guide*. The eighth, Romalie Hanover's 1:58 mile, had been beaten by Dancer and Decorum and would not make the guide.

Hurrying to change clothes for the journey out to the airport, he engaged in the same game that was occupying hundreds of Lexington fans as they streamed out of the track. "How fast do you think Albatross would have paced if it weren't for those skips?" he asked caretaker Joe Wideman.

Wideman was cooling out the colt, walking him slowly up and down the length of the barn. Dead serious as always, he hesitated before answering, letting his mind do a little quiet calculating. "I'd say 1:53, or maybe a tick better."

Dancer nodded. "You got it about right, Joe," he said.

John Simpson Sr., the boss of the Hanover Shoe Farms, was playing the same mental game as he and other Hanover personnel headed for their rental car in the parking lot. Independently, he had arrived at the same figure mentioned by Wideman and Dancer. "I've seen a lot of great performances in my day, but I can't remember a greater one than we saw today," he directed at Murray Brown, Hanover's public relations director.

"And to think that horse is going to wind up with Alan Leavitt at Lana Lobell," Brown said bitterly.

"You know, Murray, you could have gone all day without reminding me of that," Simpson scolded lightly.

"Sorry, John. Sure would be nice if something happened and he ended up in the Hanover stud barn instead."

"Sure would," Simpson agreed. "But you know Leavitt. He's not about to let an Albatross get away from him. Not when he's got him signed, sealed and practically delivered."

"You're telling me," the slender publicist murmured, aiming a foot at a pebble on the ground and sending it sailing.

16

Stanley Dancer's blue and gold-trimmed Beech Queen Air fled the runway at Lexington, climbed smoothly and settled down for the long flight back to Robbinsville Airport near the Dancer farm in New Jersey. Stanley, a licensed pilot, was at the controls. Staff pilot Paul F. Morton II was seated beside him in the cockpit. Back in the cabin Rachel Dancer discussed the Tattersalls Yearling Auction with the Dancers' flying companions.

It was Monday night, October 4, two days after Stanley's great victories at Lexington, and the party was headed home after attending a session of the Tattersalls sale. The Dancers, Stanley and Rachel, had bid $205,000 on a Meadow Skipper yearling called Good Humor Man, a full brother to their Triple Crown winner Most Happy Fella. Unbelievably, they had not landed him. Vernon Gochneaur, an Aurora, Ohio, women's cosmetics manufacturer, had bought him for $210,000—a record price for a Standardbred yearling.

Stanley, weary and drained from the pressure of the sale, but boyishly excited as always to be flying his sleek aircraft, reached over to activate the ship's transponder—the transmitter that automatically bounces radar signals back to the ground. It was a simple matter, the mere turning of a switch. But he couldn't manage it. He couldn't perform the routine chore. There was no strength, practically no feeling at all, in his right hand.

Paul Morton watched Dancer's quiet struggle out the corner of his eye. He remained silent for some 10 seconds, not wanting to embarrass his friend and part-time employer. Finally he inquired, more curious than alarmed, "Something wrong, Stanley?"

"I'm afraid so," Dancer answered slowly, meekly. "For some reason, I can't seem to get my hand to work. It's almost like it's paralyzed."

"You want me to take over?"

"I guess you'd better, Paul. I don't feel so good."

It was the start of a long and disheartening series of physical problems for the famous horseman, most of them stemming from injuries to his cervixes, vertebrae and intervertebral disks—his neck and back. Subsequent testing and x-rays would indicate the current

Stan Dancer likes nothing better than to take the controls of his handsome airplane. (Bill Taylor photo)

trouble was the result of a calcium build-up from damage suffered in a racing accident at Yonkers Raceway in 1952. In that one, he was driving a horse called Hal Oaks, who went down, spilling him out of the sulky. Five trailing horses then rumbled over him, innocently battering him with hoofs and sulky wheels. Two decades later he was still feeling the effects of the beating.

The powerless hand was only part of it. Soon he was experiencing throbbing pain, starting at the base of his neck and extending down into his back. He was in near-agony by the time the plane had reached the skies over West Virginia, and Rachel Dancer was instructing pilot Morton to alter his course. "We've got to get him to the hospital," she said.

The hospital, Morton knew, was the University of Pennsylvania Hospital in Philadelphia. Dancer has been in and out of that institution so many times over the years that he is considered the staff's resident harness driver.

Dr. Erwin R. Schmidt, hardly a stranger to the Dancer spinal column, was there to greet Stanley and Rachel as they arrived at the huge and busy health complex. "You'll be with us for a while," Dr. Schmidt warned after a lengthy examination.

"Traction?" Stanley asked.

"Traction," the doctor answered.

"Let's get one thing clear before I check in," Dancer announced. "I've got to drive Albatross at Liberty Bell Saturday night . . ."

"We'll see," the doctor said noncommittally.

"I mean it. It'll be the first time we've met Nansemond since we lost to him in the Little Brown Jug. And my horse is as sharp as he's ever been. Set six world records at Lexington . . ."

"We'll talk about it later," Dr. Schmidt interrupted. "It's more important that we get the treatment started."

"Saturday night," Dancer insisted.

"Maybe a furlough," Schmidt said.

The good doctor was not only familiar with his patient's tender vertebrae, but his tigerish tenacity as well. It was a waste of time and breath to order Stanley Dancer confined to bed when there was a horse he felt he had to drive. Dr. Schmidt had been around in 1968 when Dancer had limped in with torn ankle ligaments and deep scrapes, burns and bruises on his hip and buttocks after a nasty spill at the Syracuse, New York, Fairground. And he was there the next day when Dancer limped out, bound for Indianapolis, where he drove Nevele Pride to a 1:56.3 world race record. Dancer had to be helped into and out of the sulky, but he drove nine heats on the afternoon card and won six of them.

Having made his point with Dr. Schmidt, the ailing driver surrendered to the hospital bed and the Rube Goldberg-looking contraption of weights, ropes and pulleys designed to ease the pressure on his aching neck and back.

For four days he directed his vast racing empire from the hospital room. On Saturday afternoon, October 9, one week after he had driven Albatross to his collection of records at Lexington, he demanded and received a temporary release from the medical center and was driven crosstown to Liberty Bell Park to drive his pacer in the track's $25,000 Super Mile. A steady rain did little to improve his health.

A night earlier he had entrusted his son Ronnie to handle his fine three-year-old trotter—Quick Pride—in the Liberty Bell feature race (and Ronnie had obliged with a 2:02 win), but Quick Pride was not Albatross. And Quick Pride did not have a score to settle with Nansemond and Herve Filion. Albatross and Stanley Dancer did, and that was reason enough to foresake his sick bed.

Albatross, as hale and hearty as his driver was weak and ailing, barely worked up a lather as he paced the damp five-eighths-mile track in 1:58.3 to score by a length and three quarters over his one-time conquerors.

Aside from the obvious pleasure his victory over Nansemond and

Dr. Erwin Schmidt of the University of Pennsylvania Hospital poses with one of his most famous patients, Stanley Dancer. (Lubitsh & Bungarz photo)

Filion gave him, the race had even more significance for the Jersey reinsman. The winner's share of the $25,000 purse pushed Albatross's 1971 earnings to $437,526. He had now won more money in a single season than any harness horse—trotter or pacer—before him. Bret Hanover had earned $407,534 on the pace in 1966; Nevele Pride $427,440 on the trot in 1968. Albatross was the new king and still had a goodly portion of his season remaining.

Satisfied that revenge and the money title belonged to his horse, Dancer returned to the hospital, his bed and the traction apparatus. As always, he had to rerun the race for many of the doctors, nurses and other personnel on his floor—standard operating procedure when the resident harness driver was indeed in residence.

All things considered, Stanley felt he had come through the test in reasonably good shape. His neck and back had not bothered him as badly as he had expected, although his hand was a continuing cause for concern. It was still without appreciable strength. A harness driver with only one hand in working order is at a great disadvantage and could literally be a menace on the track if an emergency should arise.

It still had not come around 12 days later, but Dancer had had it with the invalid's role. He checked out of the hospital on Thursday night, October 21, and journeyed over to Liberty Bell to watch his brother Vernon drive and win with Super Bowl. After the races, he went home to his farm at New Egypt.

The next morning he was up bright and early, anxious to check the progress of the colts he had purchased at a variety of auctions before he had entered the hospital. Ronnie Dancer, assisted by Jean-Guy Lemarre, Walter Welch, Jack Smith and other Dancer aides, had been in charge of breaking and training the youngsters during Stanley's absence.

It was Dancer's intention to merely watch the colts jog, simply hang over the fence and look them over as they passed by. Within minutes he was up behind one, sitting there contentedly as the young horse circled the meticulously cared for Dancer farm track. Before the morning was out, he had driven 25 of the youngsters—each a half-mile or more. Then he drove into town for a haircut. Then he returned to the farm, picked up Rachel, drove to the Philadelphia Airport and boarded a plane for California.

Albatross was starting in a $15,000 invitational pace at Hollywood Park, Los Angeles, the next night, and he intended to drive him.

The mammoth TWA 747 was about two hours out of Philly when Dancer collapsed.

It started with nausea. Rachel Dancer could see the distress in his face. "Stanley, are you all right?" she demanded.

"No," he said. "I feel terrible."

"What's wrong?"

"I don't know. I'm awful short of breath and I just feel terrible."

Mrs. Dancer, watching the color fade from his face as he answered, immediately summoned a stewardess. "My husband's ill," she said desperately. "Would there be a doctor on board?"

"I'll check right away," the girl said, hurrying off.

Minutes later she was back, a physician with her. The doctor quickly examined him as best he could under the circumstances. He raised an eyebrow when he checked the driver's pulse. It counted 42, hardly more than half the normal rate. "He's got to lie down," the doctor said. "And he needs oxygen."

Dancer was helped, half carried, to a seat up near the front of the airplane where he could stretch out. His clothes were loosened, and the aircraft's emergency oxygen system was tapped to help him breathe. It was the last he remembered until he awoke outside the plane. When he came around, he was on a stretcher, about to be placed in an ambulance which had been summoned by the plane's radio.

He was rushed to a Los Angeles hospital, where a team of doctors went to work on him, suspecting cardiac problems. For three hours Dancer underwent a barrage of tests—cardiograms, x-rays, blood tests, urine checks, probes of all kinds. The medical men, however, could find nothing wrong with him. They had to settle on exhaustion, especially after Rachel Dancer described his stay in the University of Pennsylvania Hospital and his foolhardy schedule since his discharge 24 hours earlier.

The doctor in charge of his case could only prescribe rest for the headstrong patient.

"He thinks he's going to drive a horse tonight," Rachel informed the doctor. "Would you please tell him differently?"

"I'll be okay," Dancer protested. "I feel better already."

"He's in no condition to race a horse," Mrs. Dancer argued. "Please make him understand that, Doctor."

It was a classic skirmish between wife and husband, with the doctor serving as an unhappy, unfortunate buffer. Finally, with Rachel out of the room, Dancer told the physician flatly that he was going to take Albatross to post at Hollywood Park.

"If you insist on leaving, there's not much we can do about it," the doctor admitted. "But frankly, Mr. Dancer, your wife is right. If I were you, I'd certainly leave the driving to someone else. Or I'd take the horse out of the race."

"If I don't feel right when I'm warming him up, I'll take myself down and put somebody else up," Stanley promised. "I wouldn't want to endanger any other driver or any of the horses in the race. I'm not that stubborn."

A smoldering Rachel Dancer looked on that night as her husband drove Albatross to a 1:57 victory at the spacious Inglewood racing palace. Dancer, weak and trying to ignore an aching neck and hand, had to work hard on his pacer to preserve the victory over the Bruce Nickells-driven Kentucky.

It was the first time since early spring that Super Bird had faced older rivals, and both he and his driver may have forgotten how tough more experienced horses could be. Four-year-old Kentucky actually headed the sophomore champion with only 50 yards remaining in the contest. Only Dancer's frantic efforts to reawaken his colt saved the win.

The flush of victory—Stanley thought he was going to lose it until the final strides—helped to shroud his physical ailments, although the warm glow could not assist him in pulling up his horse when the race was over. Hampered without the use of his hand, he had to steer Albatross to the fence to stop him. Then he had to sit there and wait until groom Joe Wideman could run out on the track and lead his horse back to the winner's circle.

The indignity of having to be led down the track was the final straw. Dancer was fed up with pain, with his physical handicaps, with the necessity of bouncing in and out of hospitals. He resolved to find a cure for his ills. With the aid of Pres Jenuine, vice president

The cheesecake was trotted out, but Super Bird preferred a flower in pre-race publicity at Hollywood Park. (Hollywood Park photo)

and general manager of Hollywood Park, he and Rachel remained in the Los Angeles area and sought the opinions of two top men specializing in his problem—one a surgeon who had worked on famous sports figures like jockey Bill Shoemaker and former pitcher Sandy Koufax.

Surgery was the prescription, as Dancer had feared. He was told that traction and butazoldin, a powerful pain-killer, could keep him going, but nothing was going to cure him except a surgeon's scalpel.

The operation recommended would involve removing bone from his hip and using it to build fusions in the back of his neck.

It all sounded "pretty involved and pretty scary" to Dancer. And it would lay him low, put him out of action, for a long period. He told the surgeon he would think about it. Depressed, he headed back

Stan and Rachel Dancer, along with interested fan, pose after victory in the $51,000 Western Pace at Hollywood Park. Dancer is nursing ailing arm and hand. (Hollywood Park photo)

East for additional treatment at the University of Pennsylvania Hospital, hopping out of traction only long enough to drive Albatross.

He raced Albatross at Hollywood Park again on October 29, winning the $100,000 L. K. Shapiro Stakes for three-year-olds with a mile in 1:58.2. He had regained some of the strength in his right hand, and the timing was highly propitious. He had to use the hand to rap his champion a lick or two in the stretch drive. As it turned out, he crossed the finish with three quarters of a length over Winning Worthy and old friend Nansemond.

George Sholty, guest-chauffeuring Winning Worthy for regular driver Glen Garnsey, entertained notions of winning the contest in the late stages. "If Billy (Haughton) could have stayed up with Paulos Hanover around the turn, I think I would have won it," Sholty informed the press. "But he couldn't keep up and I was stuck behind him. But even at that, I think we'd have won it in a couple of more strides."

Dancer couldn't agree, however. "Albatross was going comfortably at the end and I didn't know we were being pressed," he said, dousing Sholty's theory with cold water.

Albatross had found a home in California. He had raced there twice in succession. He had only two more races on his schedule for 1971, and both of those were in the Golden State. He seemed to thrive on the balmy weather and the splendor of the tree and flower bedecked stable area of Hollywood Park. His brief morning exercise out of the way, he was free to hang his head out of the stall door and enjoy the scenery around him or stare fixedly at the morning game shows on Roger Pritchard's television set. He was also free to nap when he chose, and he selected that alternative frequently. Most of the great horses before him, the Bret Hanovers and the Nevele Prides, had been accomplished and devoted dozers, and he was no exception.

His next start was the $51,072 Western Pace on Friday night, November 5, and track publicist Bob Wellman was billing it as a grudge match for the Bruce Nickells-handled Kentucky, the Quaker City Stable four-year-old who had come within a slender whisker of upsetting the sophomore champ in their last meeting.

Trainer-driver Dancer, back East recuperating and overseeing the schooling of his sizable crop of yearlings from his hospital bed, had all kinds of respect for Kentucky, but was not concentrating all his concern on the one horse. Other veteran free-for-allers were in the Western, including one of the toughest customers of all-time, Rum Customer.

Rum Customer, trained and reined by Bill Haughton for the Kennilworth Farms of Kingspoint and Louis and Connie Mancuso of Deer Park, New York, owned a speed badge of 1:56 flat and was closing in on the million-dollar mark in purses won. Customer was only a few thousand greenbacks away from becoming the second pacer in history to hit the million milestone. Revered New Zealand import Cardigan Bay, guided by Stanley Dancer through his most fruitful money-harvesting seasons, was the first pacer *or trotter* to reach that lofty height.

Horton Hanover, 1:56.3, Isle of Wight, 1:56.2, Ozzie Hanover, 1:58, and Keystone Andy, 1:58.3, were a few of the other upper classmen in the line-up for the Western. In all, there were 11 pacers slated to vie, with Albatross and Nansemond the only three-year-olds among them. Taken as a whole, the 11 had earned $3,768,344 on their careers, making it one of the richest fields ever assembled.

It was probably the sternest test Super Bird had faced in his 44 lifetime journeys to post. So rugged, in fact, that when he won—and he did win, flying away from his foes at the end—he returned the next thing to a king's ransom. His mutuels were $3.40, $2.80 and $2.40, the grandest figures he had yielded since the midpoint in his two-year-old form.

Dancer had to weave him through some sticky congestion in the first half of the race, but once clear of the bottleneck, Super Bird flew away to score by three and a half lengths in 1:57.4. Horton Hanover and Rum Customer trailed him through the electronic beam. Kentucky, the pacer with an alleged score to settle, the side-wheeler expected to put up the most fight, was a victim of traffic troubles and finished 11th and last in the affair.

Bert James, his wife and J. Elgin Armstrong were on hand in the winner's circle to collect the silver for the Albatross Stable. Presenting the Western Pace trophy was Hollywood actor Adam West, who had portrayed Batman in the very popular television series of the same name back in the mid-1960s. Hunch bettors had a real field day when a horse called Batman turned up a winner in the very next race on the Hollywood racing card. Batman, the horse, was worth $5.20 at the win windows.

Swapping his racing silks for mufti in the track's auditorium-sized driver's lounge, Dancer engaged in some quick arithmetic. The victor's portion of the purse had boosted Albatross's 1971 earnings to $513,009, he figured. It was comforting, made him proud, to look back and know he had been in the sulky all the way as the first Standardbred ever reached a half million in earnings in a single season. It was almost like receiving a shot or two of Novocaine for his aching neck and hand.

One event remained on Albatross's dance card for 1971—the $100,000 American Pacing Classic at the Inglewood plant on Friday night, October 12. Seven of the best pacers he had met the week before—they had aggregate career earnings of more than $2.5 million —were in the Classic, but none was likely to have improved that much in a week's time to change the results.

The Southern California track drew 27,647 fans, an all-time high for a harness racing card there, to help celebrate Albatross's seasonal swan song. The happy horde was not only present to say farewell to the young champion, but to try its luck in an unusual "Share the Purse" promotion as well. The names of eight fortunate fans were drawn from the multitude of entries. Then, in a second drawing, each was assigned a horse going postward in the Classic. The auxiliary "owners" were to receive 10 percent of whatever purse money their horse won in the race.

Mrs. Jackie Resnick of Palms, California, shrieked with delight when she plucked the name of Albatross out of the pot. Nobody had to explain to Mrs. Resnick that her horse was the likely winner of the last major pacing stake of the year. She would stand to gain $4,500, a tenth of what Bird would pick up if he triumphed as expected.

The American Pacing Classic is at a mile-and-an-eighth distance. It was the first time Albatross was scheduled to travel beyond a mile in a race, although that did not disturb his trainer-driver in the least. "If your horse is a true champion," Dancer said later, "it really doesn't matter what distance he has to go." Much the same is true with tracks and track conditions, he pointed out. "A great horse doesn't have to carry his track around with him. If he's truly great, he's great over a mile, half-mile or five-eighths-mile track. And he'll be just as tough over a muddy track as a fast track."

Albatross was a great horse, and he had no difficulty going the extra eighth-mile. Dancer kept him in third spot until the pack headed into the backstretch, then made one big move to land on top of the field. From that point on, it was a case of catch-me-if-you-can. Nobody could, and Albatross paced the nine furlongs in a fast but not sensational 2:13.4 to wind up his 1971 season with a win. Kentucky, remaining clear of road trouble, was a length and three quarters back in second. Rum Customer finished third.

Mrs. Resnick had her $4,500; Albatross his $45,000.

The 1971 racing season was ended for both Albatross and Stanley Dancer. Albatross, at the very peak of his powers, could easily have gone on, raced further had there been more days and more races remaining on the calendar. But Stanley Dancer? He could only feel relief that it was over. The last six weeks had been a nightmare for him. Full of hospital emergency wards, hospital rooms, hospital beds, x-rays, doctors punching and probing him, torturous traction machines, limp and powerless hands, and persistent, nagging pain.

With the '71 campaign over, he was in no hurry to return to the hospital in Philadelphia. And he had decided after weeks of vacillating that he would not undergo surgery. When Pres Jenuine asked him and Rachel to be his house guests for a time, he accepted with gratitude. The warm sunshine of Southern California would feel good on his aching neck.

So the Dancers camped at Jenuine's handsome, pleasant home, doing little but relaxing in the sun. One day, with nothing else

Track officials and members of the Albatross Stable gather for trophy ceremonies following Super Bird's breezy victory in the American Pacing Classic in 1971. (Hollywood Park photo)

planned, Stanley visited a nearby spa and health club. He found a different kind of traction table there and tried it. It seemed to give him relief. He was back the next day and the next. He was there nearly every day through the rest of his California stay, strapping his neck to the weird looking table, adjusting the "pull" and turning on the heating pad. He seemed to improve with every visit.

Stanley was not so naive as to believe the magic machine was the lone factor in his apparent improvement; the University of Pennsylvania Hospital and the efforts of its staff were due their share of the credit as well. But then he wasn't selling the new table short, either. Before heading home—back to New Egypt—he made arrangements to buy one. When it arrived, he installed it in a spare room and used it religiously. Within weeks, the pain was gone. The strength returned to his arm and hand. He was, he felt, at least temporarily cured. And without surgery.

17

Albatross was back home lounging in an Egyptian Acres paddock while votes were being counted in the annual contest for Harness Horse of the Year honors. Running—rather *pacing*—on his record, he looked like a shoo-in.

First off, he had paced 18 two-minute miles in 1971, three more than former record-holder Columbia George had mustered in 1970, and five more than Bret Hanover had collected in any one of his three seasons at the races.

On the money front, he had ended the campaign with $558,009 on his card, exceeding his trainer's most optimistic predictions and eclipsing Nevele Pride's Standardbred single-season mark by more than $130,000. Super Bird's two-year bankroll was $741,549, easily topping his trotting rival's total of $649,683.

His racing record on the year reflected 25 wins, two seconds and a third in 28 contests, providing him with a two-year total of 39 firsts, four seconds and two thirds in 45 starts.

And, while his trainer-driver had sent him after no world records during the season, he had wound up with six of them nonetheless—all coming in a single afternoon of competition. He was history's fastest Standardbred in a race with a mark of 1:54.4.

The U.S. Trotting Association, handling the coast-to-coast balloting in conjunction with the U.S. Harness Writers Association, likes to send out the voting results in bits and pieces, hopefully gaining three or four national publicity shots for the harness sport instead of one. The USTA will announce the Two-Year-Old Trotter and Pacer of the Year one day and the Three-Year-Old Trotter and Pacer a few days later. Four-year-old and aged trotters and pacers have their moment in the spotlight, too, but the grand finale is always reserved for vote tallies in the race for Harness Horse of the Year.

The element of suspense was conspicuous by its absence when the association revealed the name of its Three-Year-Old Pacer of the Year. Albatross received 188 of the 189 votes cast by the harness writers. Nansemond ran second with the lone remaining ballot.

The contest for Harness Horse of the Year was closer, but not by much. Albatross won the title in 1971 with 141 votes. Trailing him in the standings were Steady Star, 34; Fresh Yankee, 8; Speedy Crown, 4; and Gunner, Isle Of Wight, Rum Customer and Super Bowl, 1 each.

It marked the fifth time that Stanley Franklin Dancer had harnessed the nation's finest Standardbred of the year. Dancer had trained and driven Su Mac Lad to the honor in 1962 and Nevele Pride in 1967, 1968 and 1969.

The Albatross Stable, the multimember group which owned the pacing champion, did not wait for Albatross's crowning before heaping praise and gifts upon Stan Dancer and others for their roles in the colt's incredible success in 1971.

The stable's four-member management committee—Bert James, Alan Leavitt, Dr. Glen Brown and Dancer—met in New York City on November 22, 1971. It was a pleasant parley, full of warmth, cordiality, camaraderie, congratulations, happy news and plans on a grand scale. Stable member Leon Machiz was the host.

The syndicate's original plan was to retire Albatross at the end of the 1971 season, but Dancer had argued against it and Super Bird's performance during the year had made the trainer's case look good. The committee, at the New York meeting, put the early retirement plan to rest.

Bert James, acting as secretary, said in his minutes of the meeting: "It was decided to race Albatross in 1972, with Stanley Dancer preparing Albatross for a possible race or two prior to The American National scheduled for April 15th. As soon as the Stake and Invitational Racing schedule is available a schedule will be worked out for 1972. It is considered that there will be available to race for, purses totaling slightly over one million dollars . . ."

In view of the firm decision to race the champion another year, the committee also voted to delay a test breeding of Albatross to determine his fertility until the conclusion of his racing career.

James, in his minutes, had some rosy financial news for the syndicate members. "Your share payment of $25,000 plus interest will be made from the trust funds you will have on deposit, so you will have no cash outlay in 1972 for the first payment of your share in Albatross."

He also tossed in a spot of income tax advice. "The 1971 net income of approximately $45,000 per share will be charged to you and as such should be handled to suit your personal situation. It was suggested that your tax advisor should be contacted as some, on a cash basis of accounting may not need to include this in 1971 income. As the receipt of the actual funds has not been transacted in 1971 there are many accounting possibilities in this rather unique situation . . ."

The syndication, Stanley Dancer noted with satisfaction, was working out well for the three owners he had helped to enlist—Mrs. Hilda Silverstein, Mrs. Hazel Shriner and John Rollins. The three, each owning 10 percent of the horse, were not scheduled to make the first of five $25,000 payments until 1972, and that installment was already in the bank, courtesy of Albatross. In fact, the colt had done so well, earned so much in 1971, that $20,000 of their 1973 premium was already provided by the colt.

Alan Leavitt had predicted that shares in the horse might be purchased without ever having to come up with any cash, and Leavitt's forecast was holding up.

The syndicate's members were delighted with the job Stanley and his assistants had done with Albatross during the season and were anxious to prove it in a material way. According to James's minutes, "The Syndicate members agreed that bonuses will be paid to: Mr. Stanley Dancer—two annual nominations to Albatross when in stud service. These nominations shall be nonassignable and nontransferrable. Joseph Wideman, groom—be granted a bonus of $2,500. Roger Pritchard, night watchman—be granted a bonus of $500 . . ."

In Dancer's case, the bonus could have amounted to $200,000 or more, had the Albatross Syndicate kept the horse. When Super Bird eventually entered stud service, his initial fee was set at $5,000. A pair of breedings would have amounted to $10,000 a year without taking into consideration the fact that his fee might double or even triple over the years. While no one can predict the life span of a given horse, it is reasonable to assume that Albatross will be in his twenties when he passes on to the great race track in the sky.

The bountiful bonus, of course, was in addition to the $55,000 Stanley had gained from his driver's percentage of Albatross's purses. Collecting the standard 10 percent of the horse's earnings, he had probably earned more money from a single horse in a single season than any harness reinsman in history.

The syndicate had been very generous and he was most grateful. Leaving the New York meeting, where he had represented the interests of his three owners, Dancer was wondering how he could have ever feared and fought the idea of a four-man management committee guiding the destiny of Albatross.

Back in April, when Leavitt broke the news to him, he had balked at the plan, nearly turned his back on the proposal that he train and drive the horse. Dancer wasn't used to that course. He had been his own man too long, serving as a one-man management committee to plan and carry out the racing schedules of all horses placed in his care.

Only the persuasiveness of Alan Leavitt had saved the day. You don't have a thing to worry about, Leavitt had reassured him.

And Leavitt had again been right. Nothing had gone wrong. Nothing had happened. And even committee member Bert James, the novice, had been nothing short of fine. Friendly and cooperative from the start of the season to its conclusion.

Dancer had not seen much of Leavitt or Dr. Brown during the

racing year. They were on hand for an occasional race, but most of his contact with the two men had been by telephone. James, on the other hand, had barely missed a contest. Practically as regular and as faithful as the sunset. The former auto dealer was prone to visit Albatross's barn before each race, visit Dancer and the horse in the paddock, and visit the horse back at the barn after the race. He and members of his family were also frequent visitors to the winner's circle since Albatross and Dancer had given them 25 opportunities to turn up there during the campaign.

Stanley was the first to admit that the syndicate and its management committee had not interfered in the least with his handling of Albatross in 1971. "They didn't bother me at all that first year," he confessed much later. "I went through the whole season without trouble. I couldn't have had a better relationship with anybody. I was never asked what I was going to do; I simply notified them when the horse was going to race.

"Mr. James himself couldn't have been more cooperative. To my recollection, he saw every one of Albatross's races. If I was not going to race the horse, I'd call Mr. James and tell him where I was going to train him. He never tried to second-guess me. He never tried to urge me to do this or persuade me to do that.

"We had absolutely no problems of any kind. It was a very happy, friendly year all around. And at the end of it, the syndicate voted me two free breedings to Albatross for the life of the horse. That told me that they were pleased with the job I had done. How else could I interpret a generous gesture like that?"

Stanley Dancer, with his health improving with every passing day, was a happy man. He had not only trained and driven the nation's top three-year-old pacer and Harness Horse of the Year—Albatross—but the country's leading two-year-old trotting colt as well. Super Bowl, co-owned by his wife Rachel and by Mrs. Silverstein, was a runaway winner of freshman trotting honors, picking up 144 votes to Songcan's 19.

Dancer was the Grand Circuit's leading driver by a country mile in 1971, rounding up $462,694 in purses to runner-up Billy Haughton's $193,590. In all, he had personally piloted trotters and pacers to $1,208,453 worth of purses. His stable as a whole had gathered up $2,356,906 on the year.

Stanley had gone to post 321 times and had come ripping home with 93 wins, 66 seconds and 39 thirds for a Universal Driver Rating System batting average of .444. Only Dick Buxton (.483) and Gene Riegle (.461) had finished ahead of him.

Driving 25 miracle journeys on the year, he had slipped past Frank Ervin to take over second place on the USTA's list of Leading Drivers of Two-Minute Horses. Joe O'Brien led the roster with 169, with Dancer closing the gap at 131.

While his trainer-driver was scurrying around, picking up this

Picking them up and laying them down during a brisk morning jaunt. (USTA photo)

award and that trophy, Albatross was enjoying 31 days of leisure at the Dancer headquarters in New Jersey. His vacation was interrupted twice—once when he was given a required VEE (Venezuelan Equine Encephalomyelitis) shot, and another time when Dr. Edwin Churchill gave him his monthly physical examination. He ran a brief temperature after the shot, but passed the exhaustive exam with flying colors.

Albatross was loaded on a van on December 15 and shipped to

Pompano Park, Florida, arriving there two days later. He was jogged for two weeks before being turned the right way of the track. On January 3, 1972, he was trained a mile in 2:47. He was on his way back to the races.

Dancer and his family spent Christmas at the New Jersey farm, then followed Albatross and the majority of the trainer's younger horses to Florida.

Stanley was soon immersed in his regular off-season routine—training his vast colony of young horses, and spending his spare hours with Rachel and their friends, cruising along the canals and coastline in their plush powerboat.

His freshman colts and fillies were training well, Super Bowl was looking like the million-dollar colt he turned out to be, and Albatross . . . well . . . he was Albatross.

Dancer was free of pain. He was healthy, happy and feeling great.

He was sitting on top of the world.

On a perch about as solid as Humpty Dumpty's.

18

It was 10:30 on a warm, shimmering morning at the Pompano Park race track. The date was Friday, March 17, 1972, and Stanley Dancer was seated on the top rail of the track fence, reveling in the sunshine while waiting for the next set of his freshman colts to arrive for their training miles.

Dancer could see Dr. Raymond M. Galt approaching, half-jogging and vigorously waving a friendly hello as he drew nearer. Dr. Galt, a Chicago area physician, is a patron of the Dancer Stable, and a close friend of the trainer. He was fresh off an airplane from Chicago and anxious to see the young horses he co-owned with his wife put through their training paces.

The doctor, ebullient to be in Florida, delighted to see Dancer, immediately began to climb the fence, intending to throw an arm around the shoulders of the trainer in an effusive greeting. He was settling himself on the top rail when the upper portion of the wooden barricade shattered with a sharp crack. Both men tumbled backward, hitting the ground in a tangle of bodies and shattered wood.

Dr. Galt was up instantly, unhurt. Dancer was on the ground, writhing with pain. A broken rail had caught him in the tail of his spine.

A crowd quickly gathered. Dancer aides Walter Welch and Jack Smith came running up, followed by Bill Haughton and George Sholty. A dozen other horsemen, trainers, owners and caretakers, were also on the scene within moments. Dancer had made it to his knees, was crawling about, moaning. Somebody suggested an ambulance, was about to run off and call one when Stanley protested. "No ambulance," he insisted weakly. "I'll be all right."

While he was far from being "all right," he was up and on his feet within minutes, supporting himself on a part of the fence that had remained whole. Soon he was walking gingerly, rubbing his tailbone, urging the crowd to disperse and trying to reassure the embarrassed Dr. Galt that he was not seriously injured.

The pain was intense, but he tried to shake it off. He had a horse—Quick Pride—to drive at Yonkers Raceway that night, and he wanted to make the assignment. He decided to test himself. He waited 20 minutes, hoping for the pain to subside, then trained one of his colts. It hurt like hell, but he managed to complete the mile. He foolishly decided to keep his driving date in New York.

A chagrined Dr. Galt supplied him with pain pills. Later in the day, Dancer drove himself to the Miami Airport, boarded a jet and flew to New York. Arriving at Yonkers Raceway, he discovered he was down to drive three horses, not one. He accepted the news stoically.

Drugs and all, the tip of his spine was aching fiercely. Before the races began, he phoned his faithful doctor—Erwin Schmidt—at the familiar University of Pennsylvania Hospital in Philadelphia. Schmidt was hardly surprised to hear from him; Dancer was one of his regulars. He could very nearly build a private practice around the injury-prone horseman, if he chose.

The physician made his usual pitch—don't drive; get right over here for x-rays—with the usual results. Dancer was determined to handle the three horses and would report to the hospital in the morning. Going to post, he wished he had accepted the doctor's advice. The pain was almost unbearable as he bounced up and down on the sulky seat and stretched to tattoo the horses' saddle cloths with his whip. He won with two of the horses (Quick Pride included), however, and finished third with the other.

Then he rented a car, gulped more pain pills, and started the fairly long drive from Yonkers to his farm in central New Jersey. He had left the New Jersey Turnpike and was rolling along one of the back roads to the farm in the small hours of the morning when he blacked out, either falling asleep or falling victim to the pain-killing pills he had been taking since mid-morning of the previous day. His rental car plunged off the road.

Mother Fortune, for a change, was with him. The car suffered heavy damage, but he escaped without apparent injury—other than aggravating his already painful spine. Two teen-age boys in a jalopy came along to give him a ride the rest of the way to his Egyptian Acres.

All in all, it was one of the blackest, most depressing days Stanley Dancer had ever experienced.

He managed only two or three hours of fitful sleep before his son-in-law, Gene Phelps, arrived to drive him to the hospital. He dozed as Phelps drove the car along the country roads and wove it through Saturday morning traffic in Philadelphia.

Dr. Schmidt was waiting for Dancer. With scarcely a word being spoken, he hustled him off to the x-ray suite. Dancer was with him when he read the still-wet negatives. Dr. Schmidt whistled softly. "When you do a job, you do it right," he reported ominously.

"What do you mean?" the trainer asked with growing alarm.

"You see that?" the physician queried, jabbing a finger at a spot on the x-ray. And Dancer could. The problem was obvious to even his untrained eyes. The negative clearly indicated that he had fractured the very tip of his spine—the L-1 in medical parlance.

Tears began to stream down Stanley's face.

"What's that all about?" Dr. Schmidt asked in amazement.

"I'm supposed to drive Albatross in Canada tomorrow."

"On Sunday?"

"Yes."

"Well," said the doctor, sighing, "knowing you, you'll probably do it."

It was Dancer's turn to be amazed. "Are you telling me I can drive?"

"That's not what I said," Schmidt pointed out. "I don't want you to drive a horse, and I'm advising you not to. But you've never listened to me before and I doubt you're going to listen this time. Even if it means you run the risk of crippling yourself. Now pull yourself together. We've got to get you upstairs and into a cast."

The spinal injury was Dancer's second major setback in March. The first had occurred six nights earlier when Albatross had been defeated in his 1972 debut. The event was the $20,000 Milestone Pace at Liberty Bell Park, and Albatross had finished third behind Isle Of Wight and Miss Conna Adios. Ironically, it was Super Bird's first defeat since he had lost the Little Brown Jug to Isle Of Wight's younger brother, Nansemond.

The brothers were sons of Tar Heel-Adios Scarlet and were both named after counties in the State of Virginia. Isle Of Wight, pacing like a champion with a screw in his ankle to help hold a broken sesamoid bone together, was six years old, two years older than his Brown Jug-winning relative. The senior brother was owned by Ben Babb, Fermer Perry and William M. Camp Jr., all of Virginia.

Dancer was smarting from the Liberty Bell loss. He felt he should have won the affair and couldn't really put his finger on the reason he hadn't. True, Isle Of Wight had been racing through most of the winter and was at mid-season form. On the other hand, Stanley had a nagging suspicion that he might have asked his horse for too strenuous a mile in a workout under the lights at Yonkers on March 4. Albatross had paced in 2:01.4 on a cold, raw, drizzly evening.

The Philadelphia race had been rugged—Albatross was on the limb more than half the mile and still paced in 2:00.2—and his losing margin was only a slender nose. But a loss was a loss. He didn't want it to happen again.

Stanley had that race—and the next one—in mind as he rode the elevator up to the floor where he had drawn a room. Dr. Schmidt was not far behind. The doctor gave him a shot of morphine in the hip to ease the pain, then set to work to immobilize the ailing tailbone by placing him in a body cast.

"I'll never be able to drive in this," Dancer complained.

"I'll look in on you tonight," Schmidt promised. "I think you'll come to your senses by then and be content to stay here. But if you're still insisting that you go to Canada and drive that horse, then I'll whip up something that will be a bit more mobile."

Stanley nodded his approval.

Dr. Schmidt was back that evening. If he expected the Jersey horseman to change his mind, he was disappointed. Dancer was adamant. He was going to Canada in the morning. He was going to race Albatross in the $50,000 Provincial Cup at Windsor Raceway. Nothing the physician said could change his mind.

"I'll be back in the morning," Schmidt said grimly.

"Could you make it early?" Stanley asked.

"Would 6:30 suit you?" the doctor said, half facetiously.

"Fine."

At 6:30 a.m. Sunday, March 19, while most of the nation remained warm and comfortable in its collective bed, Dr. Erwin Schmidt was fashioning a lighter, "traveling cast" around Stanley Dancer's midsection. Dancer was seated backwards in a chair, his feet up on the bed. He was trying to simulate the position he would have in a sulky seat. Dr. Schmidt worked skillfully but silently, as though he had something on his mind. Something like the Hippocratic oath he had taken years before. It had said something about his duties and obligations to the sick, lame and halt. To his recollection, it had not mentioned his responsibilities toward a stubborn, half-crippled harness horse driver who seemed bent upon self-destruction.

An ambulance carried Stanley Dancer out to Philadelphia's National Airport. Rachel Dancer, hardly enthusiastic over her husband's hard-headed decision to drive, was with him. Dancer's Queen Air was waiting. Pilot Paul Morton was there. So was Vernon Dancer. Vernon was going along to warm up Albatross. And if worst came to worst, which seemed highly possible, he would drive the champion in the Provincial Cup.

Stanley was well aware that Vernon would give Albatross a fine, professional steer if he were called on. Vernon, taller and heavier, had often sat in for his younger brother when other assignments had made it necessary for Stanley to be elsewhere. In fact, it had been Vernon Dancer in the bike at Yonkers in 1964 when ageless Cardigan Bay had set a world record of 1:58.1 for aged pacers over a half-mile track.

Still, no one but Stanley had raced Albatross since the mighty Meadow Skipper son arrived in his stable and some curious, altruistic mechanism within him made him duty bound to keep it that way. Even at the peril of limb and life.

Stanley was helped aboard the aircraft. He stretched out on the plane's couch and remained in that position all the way to Canada. Needing all his wits about him for the race that afternoon, he had to keep his medication to a minimum. By the time the Queen Air touched ground in Canada, his tailbone was aching viciously.

The Dancers and pilot Morton had lunch in Windsor Raceway's luxurious Canadian Club. Dining at a table directly across the aisle from them were Bert James and Alan Leavitt. At still another table nearby was a party which included Fran Smith, the track's lively, inquisitive director of public relations.

Smith vividly remembers the afternoon. "The Dancers seemed rather subdued. They were talking quietly among themselves. Stanley was in obvious pain, and his brown business suit bulged in the midriff from the body cast which the doctors had insisted he wear to prevent further damage to his injured vertebrae.

"James and Leavitt, on the other hand, were quite talkative. They kept their voices low, but they were busy discussing something. At one point, someone came up to James and asked him if he thought Stanley would be able to drive the horse. 'I feel sure he believes he can drive him and win, but we'd feel better if he let Vernon drive,' James told the man.

"Vernon Dancer eventually left his table to go down and warm up Albatross. During his absence, James and Leavitt conferred privately at their table, then moved across the aisle to speak with Stanley. It was obvious they were talking to Stan about his physical condition.

"Later, following the crushing defeat at the hands of Herve Filion and Isle Of Wight, James and Leavitt were observed in animated conversation . . . and the seeds of discontent that had bloomed in the previous week's loss to Isle Of Wight at Liberty Bell . . . were obviously in full flower."

The Windsor public relations chief, sensing that a touch of history was being made right there in the track's dining room, was aware of the James, Leavitt, & Co. insurrection before Stanley Dancer really caught wind of it.

Dancer, feeling he was up to it, raced Albatross in the Windsor race as planned, and felt the horse went a good, solid trip. Unfortunately, he bowed again to Isle Of Wight. This time around, Stanley raced him on the front end. Albatross led the field all the way, flashing past the quarter-poles in 28.1, 59.1 and 1:28.4. The afternoon was cool, the track anything but lively, and the fast early fractions took their toll as the champion came home. Isle Of Wight, with Herve Filion up, collared him halfway down the stretch and pulled off for a length victory in 1:59.4.

It was Albatross's second start of the young season and he was still without a triumph. The seeds of discontent that publicist Smith had mentioned were indeed in full flower.

Dancer was back in the University of Pennsylvania Hospital on Monday, stretched out on a hospital bed, encased in a new and heavier body cast, when the phone at his bedside rang.

"It was Bert James," Dancer told an interviewer later, "and he

Dancer, bulky in body cast and winter silks, works The Bird prior to losing start in the Provincial Cup Pace at Windsor Raceway. (Windsor Raceway photo)

asked me when he might see me. 'How about Saturday night?' I suggested. 'I'll be back at Liberty Bell racing Albatross and we can talk then.'

"'No, that won't do,' he told me. 'You won't be racing Albatross at Liberty Bell.'

"'What?' I asked, thinking maybe I had misunderstood him.

"'I said you won't be racing Albatross at Liberty Bell,' he said very clearly. 'In fact, you may not be racing him anymore at all until we're sure he can win.'

"I was stunned, really shocked. I couldn't believe my ears. Finally I said to him, 'You know, Mr. James, I've been driving horses practically all my life and I've never driven a single one that I was absolutely sure I could win with. If you're going to wait until it's positive he's going to win, you might never race him again.'

"'Well,' he said, 'that might be all right, too. I do know that we're not going to let you cheapen that horse anymore by losing with him.'

Heading into the stretch, Albatross had the lead, but Isle Of Wight roared up from fourth to nip him in the Provincial Cup at Windsor Raceway. (Windsor Raceway photo)

Isle Of Wight (3) upsets Albatross (7) for the second straight time, and the battle over the pacing champion was under way. (Windsor Raceway photo)

"In all my years in the horse business, I don't think anybody ever said anything like that to me. I really couldn't believe I was hearing that from the same man who'd been so great during the 1971 season. I was lying there, uncomfortable in that cast, hurting, feeling bad enough about the loss at Windsor, and this guy was saying things like that. I lost my cool. 'I'm racing Albatross at Liberty Bell on Saturday night,' I told him flatly. 'I'm entering him.'

"'I'll take him out,' he threatened.

"'If I were you, I wouldn't do that,' I said. 'He's going to race.'

"'We'll see about that later,' he told me. Then he hung up."

Stanley Franklin Dancer, harness racing's "legend in his own time," winner of 2,808 races, winner of $15 million in purses, member of the sport's Living Hall of Fame, trainer-driver of the Harness Horse of the Year five times, the nation's leading percentage driver five times, was shaken. Nothing like this had ever happened to him before. Nobody had ever treated him that way. People in harness racing—and he knew most of them, owners and trainers—simply didn't act like that.

Dancer, stewing and fuming, wondered how widespread the Albatross revolt was. His owners—Mrs. Silverstein, Mrs. Shriner and John Rollins—would have no part in it, he was sure. But how about Alan Leavitt? And Dr. Glen Brown? Was James speaking for himself, or for Leavitt and Brown as well?

He didn't have long to wait to learn the answer. James called back. Could Leavitt, Brown, Ira Helman, Leon Machiz and himself meet with Dancer in his hospital room Tuesday afternoon? They wanted to discuss the Liberty Bell race. In fact, they wanted to discuss the future of Albatross in general.

"If it's absolutely necessary," said Dancer. "Of course, I'll want to have some of my people here as well. Lou Silverstein at the very least."

James agreed. The meeting was scheduled.

Dancer immediately called Silverstein. The Philadelphia industrialist-philanthropist, well into his seventies but as scrappy as a tough kid in a school yard, was horrified. "You mean they're bothering you with a thing like this while you're flat on your back in a hospital?" he roared.

"They sure are," Stanley said.

"Count on me to be there," Silverstein growled. "I'll be representing the interests of my wife, Mrs. Shriner and probably John Rollins, too. And you know I'll be in your corner all the way. I don't know what these guys are trying to do, but if it's a fight they want, they're going to get one."

Dancer felt better. Lou Silverstein was some kind of man to have in your corner. Someone to truly count on. A real fighter. Stanley had known him many years, had admired him throughout that period. But then, anyone who knew Silverstein, was familiar with his background, had to admire him.

He was born in South Philadelphia, the son of Russian immigrants who made their living operating general stores in the Philly area. As a young man, Silverstein was stricken with a serious intestinal malady which necessitated an ileostomy operation. His physical condition was precarious for years until he met Dr. I. S. Ravdin, a staff member of the University of Pennsylvania Hospital, who guided him back to health. Silverstein was so grateful that he vowed to devote a major portion of his life to improving the health of all people —whether by the thousands or as individuals.

Owning boundless energy and a talent for business, he amassed a fortune after co-founding the Camden Fibre Company, which manufactured filling for furniture, mattresses and other products. In 1970 his firm merged with the Celanese Corporation. He was also a substantial investor in successful enterprises like the Camden Trust Company, the Connelly Container Corporation and Crown Cork and Seal.

When the future of him and his wife, the former Hilda Lieberman, was secure, he began to spend less time and effort in business affairs, more in the good works he had vowed. Contributing his own money and badgering friends for the rest, he raised more than a million dollars for a new surgical building at the hospital. When it was completed in 1962, it was named for his friend and early benefactor, Dr. Ravdin.

Silverstein did not stop there. He involved himself in countless other charities, most of them aimed at improving the facilities at his beloved University Hospital. When Dancer phoned him about Bert James, he knew the silver-haired philanthropist would not have far to go to attend the meeting in his hospital room. Silverstein had an office at the hospital. He made daily visits there to supervise construction of the Silverstein Pavilion, a multifloor structure designed to provide ambulatory surgical care and cancer research facilities. The giant, modern building, due for completion in 1974, had a price tag of $5 million. Silverstein had pledged to raise the entire sum himself, planning to donate the bulk of the funds personally and again turning to his friends for the balance.

His fetish with health is not confined to projects on the grand scale. He has plunged into the physical problems of countless individuals, helping them to select the right doctor, paving the way for examinations, arranging hospital rooms, pushing and probing them into seeking help. He frets over the health of his friends, friends of his friends, and on into infinity. And when you're as close to him as Stanley Dancer is, his concern knows no bounds. The bare fact that someone—*anyone*—was attacking Dancer as he lay in a hospital bed was enough to send him into orbit.

Silverstein was the first person to arrive for the Tuesday, March 21, meeting in Dancer's room. There was fire in his piercing blue eyes as he waited for the James gang to march in. It promised to be a long, heated session.

19

Seven men crowded into the small hospital room that afternoon—Bert V. James, Alan J. Leavitt, Dr. J. Glen Brown, Ira Helman, Leon Machiz, Louis Silverstein, and Silverstein's attorney, S. Jay Cooke. An eighth—Dancer—was already there, flat on his back with the head of his bed cranked up so that he could face his accusers.

James, when he walked in, was carrying a pad and pencil. Silverstein spotted them. "What the hell are you going to make notes for?" he demanded.

To keep a record, James indicated.

"That's criminal," Silverstein growled. "What is this, a trial? A court-martial? You going to hang this boy after its over?"

Silverstein's remarks set the tone for the meeting. No time was wasted on false pleasantries. The disgruntled syndicate members, headed by unsmiling Bert James and massive Glen Brown, were on the attack from the outset. Brown owned no shares in Albatross, but was there to represent the Armstrong Brothers' investment. Brown was the Armstrongs' general harness racing adviser and manager of their horse enterprises.

Dancer and Silverstein were aggressive defenders . . . defenders of Dancer's record with Albatross.

The mood of the parley was in such contrast to the genial gathering in New York in November, when a grateful syndicate had conferred two free lifetime Albatross bookings upon Dancer, that the casual observer would not have believed the same men were involved. The transition was great enough to give an observer a case of the bends.

James, covering much the same ground that he had in his telephone conversation with Dancer, stated the dissidents' case: The majority of the syndicate's membership did not want Dancer to start Albatross at Liberty Bell that coming Saturday night. What's more, the champion was not to be raced in the $80,000 American-National Maturity at Chicago, the first major stake of the year, unless Dancer could assure them that the horse would win. The syndicate, James continued, was sick of having Dancer cheapen the horse, hurting his eventual worth as a sire, by losing races with him.

The trainer, struggling to hold his temper—and losing—repeated his earlier message to James. "You know better than that, every one of you. How can anyone guarantee a horse will win? It's impossible. The only race I ever felt absolutely sure of winning was last year's Little Brown Jug, and you know what happened there. I can't tell you for sure he's going to win at Liberty Bell . . . or at Chicago. But I can tell you one thing, there's no chance of him winning at Chicago if he doesn't start at Liberty Bell. He needs that race."

Under those circumstances, it would be better if he didn't race at all, James said stubbornly.

"Well, he's going to race," Dancer replied with equal tenacity.

The syndicate owned the horse, James reminded him.

"And I'm the trainer," Dancer said, opening up a brand new can of worms.

Noisily, heatedly, they argued the question of who actually managed the horse. The initial contract had indicated Dancer; the amended document had said the four-member management committee. "But where was the management committee last year?" Dancer asked. "Who actually managed the horse? Planned his schedule? Picked his spots? Made all the decisions that led him to more than $550,000 worth of earnings?"

That was last year, James interjected.

"But both contracts read that Stanley Dancer would train and drive the horse so long as he raced," Silverstein pointed out. "Why else would my wife, Mrs. Shriner and John Rollins join you guys in a syndicate? Who needs you? We're Stanley Dancer people, and we wouldn't be in the thing if Stanley weren't the actual manager."

Nonetheless, the amended contract stated that a four-man committee would control the horse, James persisted. And Dancer was but one member of the committee.

Dr. Brown joined the fray. If Dancer had properly prepared Albatross for the current season, if he had driven him a little better in the first two starts, all the present squabbling might have been avoided, Brown pointed out.

Dancer was angry before; now he was sizzling. "Of all the men in this room, you're the only one who's really been involved with horses for any real period of time," he shot at the veterinarian. "You've been associated with the Armstrongs for many years, and that means you've been associated with Joe O'Brien, too. Have you ever questioned Joe's ability to train a horse? To drive a horse? To plan when and where to race a horse? Would you dare to criticize Joe's work?"

Brown did not answer.

"Awww, come on, doctor . . . I'm lying here hurting like hell. Would you be good enough to give me a yes or no answer? Did you ever tell Joe O'Brien how to handle a horse?"

No, admitted the veterinarian.

"Would you ever?"

Doubtful, admitted the veterinarian.

"What the devil gives you the right to criticize me, then?" Dancer asked heatedly. "Where do you come off telling me I didn't have Albatross ready to race? I'm not knocking Joe O'Brien, but I've got a pretty decent record in this sport, too. I know how to get a horse ready for the races."

Well, then, said Brown, maybe there was something wrong with Albatross.

"There's nothing wrong with Albatross," Dancer shot back. "He lost to tough, aged horses that have been racing right along; it's that simple. He went good trips in both races, but probably needed a couple of starts to get real tight. You can train 'em from now to doomsday, but there's no substitute for a couple of races to get them really sharp. Bret Hanover lost to Cardigan Bay and me early in his four-year-old form, you know."

James jumped back into the action. Dancer should not have driven Albatross at Windsor Raceway, considering his physical condition. No one in that much pain, hampered by a body cast, with reflexes dulled by medication, could drive a horse the way he should be driven.

Silverstein fielded that one. "You didn't have any complaints last fall when he drove the horse to four wins out in California. Ask him and he'll tell you . . . he was hurting more in those races than he was up in Windsor. He was a great guy then, a real hero to you birds, because he was winning. But let him lose a race and he's too sick to drive . . ."

All the rhetoric aside, James commented, Albatross had lost his first two starts of the year, and the defeats were costing the syndicate money. The horse's prestige was falling, and that would be felt in the pocketbook when he was retired to stud.

"That's where you started," Silverstein pointed out. "We're getting nowhere."

The meeting had gone on too long. It was hot and stuffy in the compact room, and Dancer was beginning to feel the effects of the long and tense session. His back was aching severely. A doctor had poked his head in the door at one stage and asked, "What the hell's going on here?" Told that a meeting was in progress, he snapped, "Well, break it up. This is a sickroom and that man is sick." He nodded toward Dancer.

"Look," Silverstein said at length, trying the role of peacemaker on for size, "the syndicate should be thankful that it has someone as dedicated as Stanley Dancer handling Albatross. I don't have to tell you he's willing to risk his health for the horse, you've all seen that. Time after time. Why won't you give him a chance? Why won't you let him race the horse Saturday?"

It was very quiet in the room. Dancer broke the silence. "You want to win the American-National at Sportsman's Park. I'm telling you he can't win it if he doesn't start Saturday at Liberty Bell. He's in to race Saturday; I've entered him. Now leave us alone and let us do our job."

Grudgingly . . . very grudgingly . . . the dissidents relented. Actually, James and Brown relented, since Leavitt and his two associates, Machiz and Helman, had contributed little to the parley. Silent partners, as it were.

Dancer, in accepting the reluctant surrender, had no illusions about the peace terms. Lose with Albatross on Saturday night, he knew, and the war was likely to resume with increased ferocity. Dancer was grim-faced as the sullen majority filed out of the room. Silverstein remained.

"It's unbelievable," Stanley commented to his patron. "Can those be the same guys I worked for last year? They were great then; never bothered me at all. They gave me two bookings to Albatross in November and never fought me at all when I said the horse should race another year. They were perfectly agreeable when I planned the schedule for this year. What's gotten into them? What's made them change so much?"

"Greed," snorted Silverstein. "Greed and ignorance."

"Well, I can understand James's reaction a little," Stanley commented. "He's a businessman, a car salesman, not a horseman. He hasn't been in the sport long enough to know much about it. But Brown and Leavitt . . . that's a different story. It was Leavitt, you know, who warned me about James. Leavitt told me he wasn't sure how we'd get along with James because James had been such a tough customer when the contract was being drawn up. Leavitt almost backed out at the last minute because James wanted some things in the contract that didn't belong.

"And Brown? He's the one who really mystifies me. He knows better. He's been in the horse business a long time. He's a veterinarian and ought to be able to tell that Albatross is sound and good. And he ought to know that a tough old free-for-aller like Isle Of Wight, who has been racing much of the winter, is a rugged opponent for a horse coming back to the races after a long layoff. How do you figure a guy like that?"

"I don't figure him," Silverstein admitted. "In fact, I don't understand any of them. After the great year you had for them, after all the money you made with the horse, to come barging into this room and say those things to a guy who's lying flat on his back in great pain . . . I think it's criminal."

"I know one thing for sure," Dancer offered. "If Albatross loses Saturday night, I'm in big trouble."

"What do you suppose they'd do?"

"I don't know. Take the horse away from me, I suppose."

"Well, now," Silverstein vowed, "they won't be doing that without a battle they'll remember for a long time."

"I'll just win with him Saturday and it'll all be academic. Everything'll smooth over, be forgotten," Dancer said, mustering a weak smile.

"You got more faith in those birds than I do," the Philadelphia philanthropist reported.

Early Saturday night Stanley Dancer was driven crosstown to Liberty Bell Park. He was still encased in a body cast and the pain in the tip of his spine was so great that he asked brother Vernon to warm up Albatross. A crowd of 18,858, largest of the Liberty Bell winter season, turned out to witness the renewal of the Isle Of Wight-Albatross feud. Few of the throng were aware of the extra bit of drama involving Stanley Dancer. The majority knew only that Dancer, sitting stiffly, awkwardly in the sulky seat, was trying desperately to gain the first win of the year for Albatross. And most of them believed that he would do just that. They made his horse the 1 to 2 favorite in the field of eight.

Joining Albatross and Isle Of Wight at the starting gate for the $40,000 James Clark Memorial were Bye Bye Max, Keystone Andy, Royal Count N, Claridge, Keystone Pat and Miss Conna Adios. Doubtless, they were the eight finest aged pacers active in North America.

Vernon Crank was back up behind Isle Of Wight after having yielded the reins to Herve Filion in the Windsor race. The gritty Isle Of Wight, hunting his sixth win in seven 1972 tries, had luckily drawn the rail post position. Albatross had the five-post and would have to start well outside his arch rival.

Stanley was convinced, however, that his horse was finally at peak form, a fact that Vernon Dancer confirmed after warming up the champion. His two starts—at Liberty Bell earlier and at Windsor—had tightened him as only actual competition can. The off-season rust was gone; the oil was back in his muscles. Dancer was not overly concerned with his less advantageous post. It was diffcult to imagine that traffic could become a major problem in an eight-horse field.

Isle Of Wight benefited from a classic racing journey, the kind Del Miller described in his famous *Sports Illustrated* feature on driving strategy. Veteran reinsman Crank took his horse away fast, settled him along the rail, and looked on with satisfaction as three eager foes dashed past to give him cover. The pace was swift—29.1 to the quarter and 59.3 to the half—and Crank was positive the three leaders would be well softened up by the time his pacer made his move.

Albatross, on the other hand, was in trouble throughout the mile. Dancer, anxious to avoid the pitfall of being parked outside that dazzling pack, had to settle for the seven-hole along the wood. He didn't intend to spend much time there. When the eight pacers were set in their positions, pretty well strung out, he pulled Super Bird off the rail. He was launching one of Albatross's patented sweeps which would land him on top of all seven foes. As he left the wood, however, Royal Count N, driven by Allan Cantor, pulled out ahead of him nearly cutting the legs out from under his pacer. Dancer, hooting at the rival driver, yanked back on the lines and brought the planned move to a sudden halt. Then, surprised, he watched as Cantor did the same thing, tucking his horse back in the hole he'd left.

The Jersey reinsman, warier this time, tried again between the half and three quarters. "Coming out!" he yelled at the top of his lungs as he nursed Albatross to the outside for the second time, easing his hold and encouraging his pacer to go on. To his everlasting consternation, Royal Count N and driver Cantor again bounced out in front of him. Dancer is not much of a one for foul language, but he stepped out of character long enough to hurl a word or two of invective into the night air. At the same time, he tugged on Super Bird's right line to carry him wide of a possible collision.

He was far on the outside now, about four horses deep from the rail, but there was nothing to do but head for the front. His pacer was the Albatross of old, at the height of his powers, and he was in full blown motion. Coming the last quarter, Albatross caught and passed five horses. There was only one he could not reach—Isle Of Wight—although he closed a huge gap to a length and a half at the conclusion of the mile.

Isle Of Wight was under the wire in 1:59.1; Albatross right behind him in 1:59.2. It was the fastest harness racing mile of the young 1972 season.

Stanley, riding back to the hospital, was smoldering over the way his horse had lost, yet hopeful that his battle with James, Brown, Leavitt and the rest of the revolutionaries was ended. Albatross had bowed, sure, but even the greenest of greenhorns could tell that the champion had come all the way back, was absolutely primed to resume his mastery over any and all horses on the pacing gait. Even the most untrained of eyes would have noticed the interference the horse had suffered in the race.

James and his associates might be a bit opinionated, he granted, but they certainly weren't blind.

20

The Dump Dancer Movement was picking up steam about the time Stanley was being chauffeured back to the University of Pennsylvania Hospital. By Sunday afternoon it was rolling along like one of Amtrak's finest.

The James gang sent telegrams to all the Albatross Stable members, calling for an emergency meeting at the Hampshire House, New York City, on Monday morning.

Everyone received a wire with the exception of one minor functionary connected with the horse—Stanley Dancer. While Dancer held no actual shares in the horse, he was a member of the syndicate's management committee. It made no difference. He wasn't invited.

Hilda Silverstein, receiving her copy of the message, turned to her husband for an explanation. "What's it all about, Lou?"

"What's it about? Why, I don't really know, Hilda. It just says 'emergency meeting'. But I tell you honestly, I wouldn't put it past that James bunch to try and fire Stanley."

Mrs. Silverstein, a gentle, refined woman with no experience in the rough-and-tumble world of ruthless plots and intrigues, had been thoroughly shocked by the dissidents' lack of decorum and taste in badgering an ailing Dancer in his hospital room. Now she was horrified, aghast at the possibility her husband raised. "That can't be," she protested. "It would be totally unfair. Why, it would be horrible, insulting and degrading. If that is what the meeting's about, we simply cannot let it happen."

"Maybe it's something else," Silverstein said. "I certainly hope so. But if they do try to can Stanley, I'm going to do everything in my power to prevent it. I'll have Mrs. Shriner's and John Rollins's proxies, although those other guys still got 70 percent control of the syndicate."

Louis Silverstein, accompanied by attorney S. Jay Cooke, attended the meeting in Manhattan. His worst fears became realities. Silverstein remembers it as one of the most frustrating experiences of his long life. He was still smoldering about it a full year later.

"They invited us Dancer people, but they were genuinely surprised that any of us bothered to show up. Their minds were made up, and there was nothing we could do about it. They were getting rid of Stanley. In fact, while I was there they were busy on the phone, making arrangements to switch the horse over to someone else. It was all cut and dried.

"I tried to persuade them to postpone their action. 'Wait a month and everything will change,' I told them. 'Albatross will win the American-National and you'll feel differently.' It was like talking to a brick wall. 'Nothing doing,' they said. 'We made our decision Saturday night. Stanley Dancer has driven that horse for the last time. He's cost us enough money already.'

"'Think of what he did with Albatross last year,' I argued. 'A bunch of world records, more than $550,000 in earnings, Horse of the Year honors . . .' 'That was last year,' they told me. 'All he's done this year is lose three straight races with him. He's probably cost the horse a couple of million dollars in prestige.'

"'That's nonsense,' I told them, but then just about everything they were saying was nonsense. That Bert James, he looks me in the eye and says, 'Now why in hell did Dancer take Albatross down to Florida? What did he ever accomplish by taking horses all the way down there?' 'Mr. James,' I said, 'did you ever hear of Nevele Pride, Most Happy Fella and Decorum? That's what he accomplished down in Florida.'

"'You know,' I reminded them, 'you're just about going to kill that Stanley Dancer fella by taking that horse away from him. You're going to hurt his reputation, and you're just about going to kill him mentally.' 'That's his tough luck,' they said to me. 'We've got to worry about our own mental health.'

"'What's going to happen to the horse?' I asked them. 'What can I tell my wife, Rollins and Mrs. Shriner?' 'Oh, he's going to be in good hands,' they said. 'We're making arrangements to pick him up tomorrow, and we're trying to line up Lee Broglio as his trainer. We'll find a good driver for him later, since Broglio doesn't drive,'

"Actually, I learned that they had called trucker George Hutt on Sunday, asking him to send a van to Liberty Bell on Monday. And I also learned that they had made arrangements with Lee Broglio to train the horse and Herve Filion to drive him well before the meeting on Monday. They were just going through the motions."

Silverstein, taking all he could stand, finally signaled attorney Cooke. The two men left in a hurry. During the taxi ride to Pennsylvania Station, Silverstein decided to seek an injunction in an effort to keep Albatross in the Stanley Dancer Stable. On the train ride back to Philadelphia, he definitely decided to buy the horse himself —whatever the price—if it became necessary. There was no way that Stanley Dancer was going to lose Albatross.

While the angry meeting was transpiring, Dancer fretted away the hours in his hospital bed. He knew the syndicate was gathering

Amicable Stable star gets a bath from groom Joe Wideman. (Greenwood Raceway photo)

in New York—Silverstein had alerted him—but he had no idea of what had gone on until he received a phone call from Joe Wideman, Albatross's caretaker, late in the afternoon.

"Stanley," Joe said, as excited as Dancer had ever heard him, "there's some guys from the Lee Broglio Stable here and a horse van on the way. They say they're here to pick up Albatross. What's it all about? What'll I do?"

Dancer felt like he'd been struck in the forehead by a sledgehammer. While he wasn't expecting good news from the New York parley, neither was he expecting anything so drastic. Hadn't the James gang seen Saturday night's race? Were they blind after all? "Joe," he said, his mind racing at a two-minute clip, "you've got to stall. Don't go anywhere, don't do anything until you hear from Mr. Silverstein or myself. And whatever you do, don't release that horse!"

The next hour was a blur. Dancer had trouble locating Silverstein. Silverstein was in attorney Cooke's office. The two were hard at work preparing legal papers aimed at seeking the injunction to freeze Albatross in the Dancer Stable. Finally, Silverstein reached

Stanley. He was told that a crew was out at Liberty Bell, trying to pick up the horse. "Don't worry," he told the hospital-bound trainer. "I'll take care of everything."

Then Silverstein phoned Wideman in the stable area. "The horse doesn't go anywhere, Joe," he instructed the groom. "We're in the process of getting a court injunction, and he sits tight until we get this thing settled. If you have any trouble, you call me and we'll get the State Police out there."

"Right," said Wideman.

And so began a curious, awkward week for Joe Wideman and Roger Pritchard, the two Dancer aides in charge of Albatross. Eligio L. (Lee) Broglio, a tall, slender, 46-year-old New Yorker, was the newly designated trainer of Albatross. When he received the happy word from the James gang, he hustled two men—an assistant trainer and a groom—to Liberty Bell to fetch the horse. And then the plan broke down. Wideman refused to release the horse and Silverstein's injunction was soon in effect.

For a solid week the two sides—Dancer's two aides here; Broglio's assistants there—hovered around the horse. The Dancer people were armed with the injunction, the Broglio camp was equipped with a countersuit, aimed at wresting the horse away from Dancer. It was a standoff. The horse could not be removed from Liberty Bell, pending the action of the court.

"It really wasn't as bad as it sounded," Joe Wideman recalled. "The two guys hung around for a week while the negotiating and the court stuff was going on. Hell, they were all right about it. They had a job to do and so did I. We had cordial relations. They never interfered with Albatross's training. He was jogged every day and worked when it was necessary. I'd call Stanley from time to time and they were on the phone to Broglio at Yonkers. It was a kind of screwy situation, but it wasn't so bad."

Both sides were anxious that Albatross's training schedule not be interrupted. *Somebody* was going to race Super Bird in the American-National at Sportsman's Park, Chicago, on April 10. It was merely a question of *who*.

Beginning with the ugly, angry meeting in New York City, action became hot and heavy, fast and furious in the Albatross affair. The presence of a Chris Schenkel or a Curt Gowdy was needed to call the play-by-play.

It was Monday night when Stanley Dancer finally received a telegram from the James gang. It wasn't a belated invitation to the Monday morning meeting, but rather a notification that he had been relieved as the trainer-driver of the world champion pacer. He knew he was getting the axe because of his phone conversations with Lou Silverstein and Joe Wideman. Still, when the official notice of discharge arrived, it rankled, hurt and burned him.

"It's a real bad scene," he told his wife that night. "I'm in a rotten spot. My reputation's going to take a terrible beating, and I'm innocent. There's absolutely nothing wrong with that horse. He's 100 percent. Yet I'm going to lose him. The next guy, Broglio, gets him and doesn't do a damn thing with him. Just races him, with someone like Filion driving him. Since the horse is perfect in the first place, he reels off victory after victory. Maybe goes the rest of the season undefeated. Then people say, 'See, James and Leavitt were right; they took that horse away from Dancer and look what he's done!'"

"Mr. Silverstein knows that and is working on it," Rachel pointed out.

"Yes, and bless him," Stanley said with feeling.

On Tuesday morning Silverstein and attorney Cooke walked into Common Pleas Court in Philadelphia and obtained an injunction from Judge Ned L. Hirsh. The injunction, officially sought by Mrs. Silverstein and Mrs. Hazel Shriner, was based on the ground that the Albatross Stable's legal agreement provided that Dancer would remain as trainer-driver of the champion so long as the horse raced. The Silversteins' legal maneuver temporarily halted the dismissal of Dancer pending arguments before Judge Hirsh a week later.

By now the Albatross imbroglio had reached the ears of the press and Mrs. Silverstein found herself explaining the suit to reporters. "They (James & Co.) voided that part of the agreement without Stanley's consent. They didn't invite him to the meeting in New York Monday when they voted to take the horse away from him. I think I owe it to Stanley to put up a contest for him. What they did to him is insulting and degrading to one of the finest and most ethical horsemen in the country."

Bert James, through attorney Gordon W. Gerber, filed a counter-suit in the same court later in the day. James was seeking an injunction against Liberty Bell Park, Stanley Dancer and Joe Wideman, charging them with interfering with the removal of the horse from Dancer's stable at the track.

Judge Hirsh indicated that he would hear arguments in the James suit a week later as well. The judge hinted rather strongly to both sides that a practical solution to all problems might well be for one side to buy out the other.

Meanwhile, up in New York the press was getting to Herve Filion, pushing him for his views on the Albatross battle. Lee Broglio, the Albatross-less new trainer of Albatross, had announced that Filion would drive Super Bird in the American-National once he, Broglio, managed to pry the horse loose from Dancer.

"I feel very bad for Stanley," Filion commented to newsmen. "He managed the horse real good. He's a great man, he's done much for the business and he's my friend. But driving is my business. If I wasn't asked to drive Albatross, somebody else would do it."

Dancer harbored no ill will for Herve. He held nothing against

Broglio, either, although he felt the New York trainer might have given him the courtesy of a phone call to express at least a token of pseudosympathy.

Bert James was another ball game. Dancer was up to his hairline in ill will toward James. He was about to call James to tell the former car dealer to get his two classy pacing fillies, Saucy Wave and Jambo Belle, out of the Dancer Stable in Florida, when James beat him to the punch. Vernon Dancer had trained Saucy Wave that morning—Tuesday—and was about to work Jambo Belle when a van showed up and whisked both fillies away. The bills were all paid on the two pacers and Vernon Dancer had no choice but to surrender them.

Stanley had inherited the fillies when James pulled them away from Harry Harvey after Harvey had made a couple of unfriendly remarks in the *Sports Illustrated* story.

Harvey, reading of Dancer's troubles in the Pittsburgh newspapers, couldn't help but sympathize with the man who had succeeded him as Albatross's trainer. He wondered if James would put Stanley through the same wringer. When the James horses had left his stable, James had asked for a complete accounting of all the equipment and supplies purchased for his horses over the months—right down to bars of soap. When Harvey was unable to account for every single item, he was forced to cut his final training bill to satisfy the owner.

On Wednesday, Stanley Dancer received some good news, the first in several days. The fractured vertebrae at the tip of his spine was healing nicely and he was free to leave the hospital. The heavy cast was removed and replaced by a brace that he was to wear for 90 days. At first he planned to head for his winter home in Florida, but he quickly changed his mind after talking with Louis Silverstein.

Silverstein was bent upon buying Albatross and wanted Stanley to assist him. Would Stanley help in the effort to find a major investor, preferably a breeding farm, to share the purchase of the horse?

"Absolutely," said Dancer.

Silverstein made it very plain that he was going to buy the horse whether or not the big investor was found.

"My wife and I wanted to do it for Stanley," Silverstein explained a year later. "We knew how much he loved Albatross, and we knew the great mental harm it would do him to lose him. We were determined to save the horse for Stanley.

"I was sure it would take a great deal of money to buy out James and his gang, but I never worried about it. I knew that if we couldn't find someone to take a large share of the horse right away, we would eventually. With Albatross racing the way he could race, why, the breeding farms would be ringing our phone off the hook later in the season. The only way we could lose on the deal was if the horse fell down and broke a leg, and that wasn't likely to happen."

"We weren't thinking of the money at the time," Hilda Silverstein confirmed. "We were only interested in helping Stanley Dancer. He was being treated so horribly."

Silverstein, through his lawyers, Jay Cooke and Philip Hammett, began to dicker with the James-Leavitt side.

It was Wednesday afternoon when Dancer took to the telephone. He knew precisely whom to contact. It required only one call to turn up a serious candidate for the lion's share of Albatross. "Damn right I'm interested," the man said. "Keep me posted."

Did the man represent a breeding farm? Did he ever!

Negotiations took a full week, although a basic agreement was reached by Sunday, April 2. Jay Cooke's law office was the headquarters for the Silverstein-Dancer team during the long sessions. Attorneys Cooke and Hammett handled the actual negotiations, communicating by phone with the James crew's attorney, Gordon Gerber, who was headquartered in his office a couple of blocks away in downtown Philadelphia.

Performing a good deal of the legwork in the intricate relations was Delvin Miller, harness racing's Mr. Everything, who was recruited because he commanded the trust and respect of both sides.

The figure $2,500,000 cropped up early in the bargaining and held up all the way. That is, the two and a half million was the top figure, the total value of the horse. For Silverstein & Co. to buy out the 70 percent interest of James, Leavitt, et. al, he would have to come up with $1,750,000. For James and his group to pick up the 30 percent interest of Mrs. Silverstein, Mrs. Shriner, and John Rollins, $750,000 was needed.

"Negotiations broke down at one stage," Louis Silverstein reported. "My lawyers told me, 'They won't let you have the horse at $2,500,000.' 'Fine,' I said. 'Tell them they can *buy us out* on the basis of $2,500,000. Tell them all they have to do is come up with $750,000 and they've got the horse.'

"I didn't mean it at all. I was simply trying to smoke them out, and it worked. They said, 'All right, we'll sell.' But they wanted a half-million dollars right away and the balance by Thursday, April 6. They were insistent; so I had to round up all that money."

The transaction was virtually completed by the time the two sides were to appear back in Common Pleas Court for hearings on their legal suits. The court action was postponed when the two factions told Judge Hirsh they were very close to resolving the issue privately. Later, the suits were withdrawn.

The sale was officially consummated on Thursday. Louis Silverstein paid $1,725,000 for 70 percent of Albatross. Bert James's long association with the pacing champion was ended. The same was true of Alan Leavitt, Ira Helman, Leon Machiz and the Armstrong Brothers, along with the Armstrongs' representative, Dr. Glen Brown.

Stanley Dancer would keep Albatross. He would train and drive him with love, skill and great success throughout 1972. Right up to the moment the incredible pacing champion ended his racing career and headed for the stud barn.

"It was funny," Lou Silverstein said in retrospect. "When we started negotiating, those fellas (the James group) wanted to know what I was going to do with the horse. They knew I had no breeding farm and was probably too old to start something like that.

"'Don't worry about me,' I told them. 'Until I get something definite, a farm or proper home, I'll just tell my wife to clear the furniture out of the living room, and we'll have to keep him there.'

"They thought it was funny. They didn't know who the eventual owner was to be until four o'clock Thursday, the day we signed the papers. Then they didn't think it was so funny."

21

There is no larger, no busier, no more successful horse breeding establishment in the world than the Hanover Shoe Farms of Hanover, Pennsylvania—33 separate farms, 4,000 lush acres, 1,700 horses at the peak of the season, more than a dozen of the finest stallions available, annual yearling sales of $2,500,000-plus, and hundreds of thousands more in service fees paid by broodmare owners each year.

Hanover bills itself as "The Greatest Name in Harness Racing." It is not boasting, but merely stating a fact. In 1972 alone, Hanover-bred trotters and pacers won 1,347 dashes and $4,389,576 in purses.

One of its sires, the regal Star's Pride, is easily the most successful trotting sire of all time. His get had won nearly $18 million through 1972. He has also produced the winners of eight Hambletonians and enough other major stakes to challenge the capabilities of a computer.

On the pacing side, the Shoe Farms is the proud owner of Tar Heel, the leading living sire of two-minute performers. He was the first stallion of any breed to produce the winners of more than $2 million in a single year, with his offspring coming home with $2,092,970 in racing spoils in 1969, then surpassing that figure in subsequent years.

While Star's Pride and Tar Heel are clearly the stars of the Hanover show, the supporting cast is on the potent side, too. Hickory Smoke, Best of All, Bullet Hanover, Dancer Hanover, Ayres, Knight Dream, Gamecock, Lehigh Hanover and Speedy Count have all turned out their share of stakes winners, while newcomers Columbia George and Steady Star will doubtless be contributing their share as well.

Hanover Shoe Farms—big, bold and booming.

This equine conglomerate, the epitome of Standardbred breeding at its best, was the major investor that Stanley Dancer secured for Albatross . . . the name that Louis Silverstein sprang upon the James-Leavitt faction as he was affixing his name to the purchase agreement.

There would be no need for Hilda Silverstein to clear the furniture from her parlor. No need at all. Albatross had a future home, thank you.

When Dancer approached the Shoe Farms about its possible participation in the resyndication of Albatross, he brought it to the attention of John F. Simpson Sr., a tall, scholarly looking man, whose soft voice still contains traces of his South Carolina origin. Simpson, the late Lawrence B. Sheppard's hand-picked successor as the man at the helm of Hanover, was hardly a stranger to the New Jersey horseman. The two have been friendly since 1945, when Simpson was returning to racing after wartime duty as an Army officer and Dancer was an ambitious farm boy trying to break into the sport.

"I bothered a lot of people for advice in those days," Dancer said, "but probably no one more often than John Simpson. Even then John was one of the best and smartest trainers and drivers in the business."

Simpson got an early start in racing. His father and uncle raced horses at the fairs, and by the time he was 12 or 13, he was accompanying them around the circuit as a caretaker. He drove his first race at 17 and was marked for life, although his family had other plans at the time. He was urged to study animal husbandry, with livestock dealing and farming as his goal, and entered Clemson College. He lasted two years. The race track was too strong a lure. The livestock business was dying anyway—tractors were replacing mules and draft horses—and farming could hardly match the glamor of racing.

At the age of 22 he became the youngest man in history to drive a two-minute mile, earning the distinction with a horse called My Birthday in the old New England Pacing Derby at Old Orchard, Maine. From that point on, he heaped success upon success. He was the nation's leading money winning driver in 1951 and the country's top dash winner in both 1950 and 1951. With 90 two-minute drives behind him in 1973, he has won virtually every major stakes race worth winning, including the Hambletonian, the Little Brown Jug, the Messenger, the Kentucky Futurity and the Fox. Several, in fact, have fallen to him twice or even three times.

In 1971, with most of his driving heroics behind him as he plunged ever deeper into the affairs of the Shoe Farms, the sport of harness racing conferred its highest honor upon him—election to its Living Hall of Fame.

But most of those deeds and laurels were still in the future when salty and sage Lawrence Sheppard first sized him up in 1949 and decided he might be Hanover material. Sheppard, who single-handedly turned the Shoe Farms into a prolific producer of majestically bred Standardbreds, was an outspoken man who appreciated the same trait in others. In 1949 he recognized that quality in Simpson.

Sheppard's prize colt of that year was Imperial Hanover, and he was looking for the yearling to set a sales record. Top horsemen of the day like Ben White, Sep Palin and Fred Egan were all interested in the youngster, but one of Simpson's early owners, J. J. McIntyre of Hollins, Virginia, somehow ended up with him on a bid of $72,000. Then Simpson balked at training the colt. He didn't like him.

Sheppard, with injured pride, called the young trainer into his office. "Son," he said, "that colt is a full brother to Rodney and Egan Hanover. White, Palin, Egan and other famous horsemen think he's a great individual; yet you don't like him and you don't want to train him for Mr. McIntyre. Why?"

Simpson hemmed and hawed, not wanting to hurt the older man's feelings and doing his level best to escape his well-known wrath as well. But pressed by the determined Sheppard, Simpson finally confessed that he didn't care for the way Imperial Hanover stood.

"Go on," Sheppard demanded.

"Well, both his legs seem to come out of the same hole, and when he begins to trot at any speed at all, he's bound to hit his knees. I'm sorry, Mr. Sheppard. I hope I'm wrong, but you asked me, and that's the way I view the colt."

"We'll see about that," the master of Hanover said, dismissing the young trainer.

Simpson, quaking a bit in his horsemen's boots, left the office believing he had made an enemy out of one of the most important men in the sport. Yet, a week later, Sheppard was on the phone to him. "You run a public stable?" the peppery breeder asked. When Simpson answered in the affirmative, Sheppard sent him six horses to train.

For the next 19 years, until his death in 1968, Sheppard enjoyed telling the story of his association with Simpson. "That goddamn kid . . ." he'd say fondly . . ."those old-time trainers looked at that colt and said he was so great, and that goddamn kid looked at him and said he was no account."

Simpson, of course, had been right. Imperial Hanover did hit his knees and never amounted to much as a result. Sheppard, impressed with both the trainer's frankness and his obvious talent for judging horseflesh, gradually worked him into the Hanover operation—first as a trainer-driver, later as manager of the giant breeding operation itself. Simpson was a reluctant farm manager, preferring to spend most of his time training and driving colts. Finally, in 1964, Sheppard laid down the law. "If you don't come up here and get busy running this damn place, I'm going to put it in my will that it's to be sold," he said. Simpson reacted. He moved to Hanover— Sheppard had taken it upon himself to find the Simpsons a home on the farm grounds—and began to extract himself from the racing side.

Over the years he gradually turned the training and the driving reins over to his eldest son, John Simpson Jr. Young John, a softspoken redhead with both poise and skill, quickly proved that bloodlines are important in horsemen as well as horses. By 1970 he was winning his own Hambletonians and Kentucky Futurities, earning headlines and stature at the ripe old age of 27.

On March 29, 1972, when a troubled, maligned Stanley Dancer phoned about Albatross, John Simpson Sr. was the president and general manager of the Hanover Shoe Farms. Mrs. Charlotte B. Sheppard, widow of the co-founder, was still the titular head of the farms—chairman of the board—but she was perfectly content to let Simpson run the vast and complicated operation.

Dancer's message, when it came, shocked Simpson. The Hanover president found it difficult to believe that Dancer was being relieved as trainer of the champion pacer. "Stanley's a great kidder, you know, and I thought he was pulling my leg. Why, in all my years in the business, I'd never heard of a great horseman like Stanley being replaced under such circumstances."

Simpson was equally surprised to learn that an opportunity still existed for Hanover to add Albatross to its stallion barn. "We had given up on the horse for obvious reasons," John said. "What the hell, he was contracted to go to Lana Lobell. While we weren't happy about it, it seemed to be a fact of life. We had accepted it."

Dancer quickly sketched the situation. He had lost three straight with Albatross and the James gang had fired him. The horse was perfectly sound, ready to start winning big, and Louis Silverstein was purchasing him. The price tag was liable to range between $2½ and $3 million, and Silverstein was anxious to find a substantial party, preferably a breeding farm, to assume a major portion of the horse. Was Hanover interested?

Indeed it was, Simpson answered readily: "Keep me posted. Let me know precisely how much money they're talking. Meanwhile, I'll get things rolling at this end."

Simpson felt obliged to discuss a move of that magnitude with his "cabinet"—Paul E. Spears, executive vice president and treasurer, and Horace E. Smith, the farms' secretary and attorney. And he also wanted to consult with Mrs. Sheppard, although he knew her answer in advance: "If you think we should have him, John, let's get him."

Barring some astronomical figure, the Hanover president was positive the farms should jump in. There was no doubt in his mind that Lawrence Sheppard would do just that, were he alive. "Mr. Sheppard believed in going first class and realized that you've got to have great stallions if you're going to stay on top of the breeding industry," Simpson explained later. "Price never stopped him if he felt he was dealing for the best horse around."

Simpson's prime reason for recommending Hanover's involvement in the resyndication of Albatross was, of course, economic. Albatross was more than simply "the best horse around"; it was highly possible he was history's finest Standardbred to date. His breeding was impeccable (and Hanover had a flock of classy mares to perfectly complement his bloodlines). His conformation was as near to perfect as you can get. And he possessed the third ingredient

Super Bird at the Hanover Shoe Farms. With him are Stan Dancer and John Simpson Sr. (USTA photo)

which Simpson considers essential in a great stallion—burning speed on a race track. It made far more sense to have a horse like that residing in your stud barn than in the barn of your competitor on the other side of town.

It was icing on the cake that Simpson and Hanover could come to the aid of a beleagured Stanley Dancer at the same time. It was a genuine affront to Simpson's sense of justice to learn of Dancer's treatment at the hands of the dissidents. "For a great horseman, a master horseman like Stanley Dancer to be treated that way, to be degraded that way, by people who don't know a damn thing about horses . . . is just unbelievable," he said at the time. Ten months later, at the U.S. Harness Writers annual banquet at Liberty Bell Park, he said essentially the same thing in front of 700 of the most influential people in the harness sport.

The Hanover president was acquainted with Alan Leavitt; had helped him to get his start in Standardbred breeding, in fact. At the urging of Lawrence Sheppard, Simpson had assisted Leavitt in putting together the vanguard of his broodmare band.

John Simpson Jr., the youngest man to win the Hambletonian Stake, was one of a rare few who had the opportunity to work Albatross. Simpson's father is president of the Hanover Shoe Farms. (James Ponter drawing)

He had also met Bert James on a few occasions. James had sent mares to the Shoe Farms to be bred. Simpson had found the Canadian car dealer to be a close man with a dollar at times. James occasionally complained about his mare's feet being trimmed too often. In one instance he had scratched a blacksmith's charge off his bill from Hanover. It was a four-dollar item.

While Simpson did not classify Leavitt and James—nor Dr. Glen Brown—as close friends, he had gotten along with them tolerably well over the years. Right up to the moment that Stanley Dancer had called him and began to describe his recent problems with the trio. Then John Simpson became a hawk. A pro-Dancer, anti-Leavitt, James and Brown hawk.

When Stanley Dancer phoned a second time with a firm figure on Albatross—$2,500,000—Simpson told him to count Hanover in. The Shoe Farms, naturally, would want to buy controlling interest in the horse as a matter of policy.

"No problem," said a happy Dancer.

"And Stanley," Simpson added, "there's one other condition that we have to insist on if we're to join your people in the new syndicate."

"What's that?"

"That you train and drive Albatross until the day he retires."

Dancer enjoyed his first belly laugh in weeks.

The new syndication contract divided the ownership into 50 shares. Twenty-seven were purchased by the Hanover Shoe Farms. Hilda Silverstein increased her holdings to eight shares. Five each were retained by Mrs. Hazel Shriner and John W. Rollins. Dancer and Simpson bought two each, with the final share being picked up by Hal S. Jones, general superintendent of the Shoe Farms.

Although Dancer had not driven Albatross a solitary time for the new alliance, he was still assigned two additional free bookings to the champion for life. Stanley had a hunch he'd collect them this time around.

The contract named Dancer as the trainer-driver of Albatross; Hanover Shoe Farms (Simpson) as the manager of the horse in stud. Simpson, after considerable thought, set the number of mares to be bred to him the first year at 110, a figure high enough to fulfill the contractual obligations to the shareholders and still leave a few slots for outside mares.

Hanover itself would give the young pacer every conceivable advantage when he retired to stud. Simpson, Murray Brown, Hal Jones and the rest of the Shoe Farms brain trust worked hard and long at preparing the list of farm-owned mares to be mated with him. On it were three names—Romola Hanover, Brenna Hanover and Lavish Hanover—which showed the harness racing world what Hanover thought of Albatross.

Romola Hanover is conceded to be the greatest producing broodmare in the sport's history. Her sons and daughters have won more than $1,900,000 through 1972. She is the dam of six two-minute pacers, including the champions Romeo Hanover, Romulus Hanover and Romalie Hanover.

Brenna Hanover is the dam of three in 1:58 and four in two-minutes, including world champions Bret Hanover and Bonjour Hanover. Lavish Hanover's offspring includes world champion and Little Brown Jug winner Laverne Hanover. The offspring of each mare have already exceeded a million dollars in earnings.

Simpson was also charged with establishing the stud fee for Albatross. Although Super Bird could logically command a much higher figure, the Hanover president set it at $5,000. "I discussed it thoroughly with Stanley and decided that $5,000 was reasonable and right," John reported. "It gave us the opportunity to select the quality mares from all those applying, although I imagine we would have been able to do that had we started him at $10,000."

Murray Brown, Hanover's public relations director, can get an advertisement into the harness racing journals as fast as any man alive. The ink was barely dry on the new contract when the ads began to appear. "Albatross, 3, 1:54.4, Will Stand His First Season At Stud In 1973 at Hanover Shoe Farms," they read. Broodmare owners reading them were already too late; Super Bird's book was full and closed for '73.

The new syndicate consisted of five kindred individuals and one giant horse farm, all rallying around one great horse and one great horseman. Friendship, good cheer and trust abounded within the new group. A name was needed for the syndicate. *The Amicable Stable* was chosen. It seemed appropriate, accurately describing the harmony of the new people and contrasting vividly with the discord of the old.

"Now, let's get on with it," Louis Silverstein said in launching the stable. "Let's win some races and show that old bunch what they gave up."

"Amen," said Dancer.

The $80,425 American-National Maturity for four-year-olds at Sportsman's Park, Chicago, loomed as the big test. It was Bird's first major stake of the year, the race that Dancer was pointing him toward when the James gang cut him off at the pass. It went without saying that Stanley Dancer was rather anxious to win it.

Not that Stanley wasn't confident. He was. So was John Simpson, who flew out to witness the Monday night, April 10, contest. So were the 13,649 racing connoisseurs who invaded the track; they bet the Meadow Skipper son down to 1 to 5 odds. The only skeptics around anywhere were apparently back in their lairs, counting the profit they had made on the sale of Albatross.

Albatross got away fast, heading right for the top. He owned the front end by the quarter-pole, reached in 29.2. Then Dancer backed him off, permitted him to loaf down to the half in 1:01.3. H. T. Luca tried him at the five-eighths mark, but Dancer pressed the accelerator. Farewell H. T. Luca. Albatross, precisely as sound and as sharp as Stanley promised, simply paced away from his eight foes. He had three open lengths on all of them when the mile ended.

The Amicable Stable star had won in two minutes flat, the last half in 58.2 seconds. He had his first victory in 1972. He was on his way.

Stanley Bergstein, executive secretary of the Harness Tracks of

By the time he was four, Super Bird was a good-sized pacer—with power to burn. (USTA photo)

America and the U.S. Trotting Association's public relations chief, was in the winner's circle with a microphone. Bergstein was running a bit of a risk in interviewing the driver over the public address system. Dancer was still hot enough to roast the gentlemen who had unceremoniously dumped him. Instead, he chose the high road. "I knew all along Albatross was a great horse," he told the crowd. "His defeats were honorable. The last one was the result of tough racing luck. He proved tonight how great he is."

Simpson followed his example. The words were pleasant, but his message was clear. "We had faith in Dancer and really never considered any other trainer or driver. Tonight was the proof of our faith."

Later, when they met privately, Dancer told Simpson he could have gone much faster with the pacer. "He's absolutely perfect, John," he said.

"I never doubted it for a moment," the Hanover chief replied.

22

Albatross was suddenly flying again. Soaring higher than ever. Starting with the American-National, he ripped off 10 straight triumphs, crushing track marks, rubbing out stakes standards and battering world records as he went. It was the most eye-popping display of sustained speed paraded before the harness racing public since the days of the gaudy Dan Patch exhibitions.

The man—Dancer—had the hot flames of revenge licking at him, pressing him to scale lofty new mountains in a determined drive to repair Albatross's slightly damaged halo. The horse could not be credited with such heady inspiration, although he seemed to revel in the fact that his driver was taking off the wraps, was letting him ramble more and more.

The victory spree began at Sportsman's Park on April 10, but the speed carnival did not get on the road until April 29 at Liberty Bell Park. In between was an unsatisfactory slog through the mud at Maywood Park, Chicago, in which Albatross barely hung on to preserve a skinny win over a pair of little known mud lovers called Hail to All and Cafine Kid. The purse was $25,000, the time 2:07.4 and the margin a neck.

At Liberty Bell, Super Bird's event was the $40,000 Daniel C. Parish Memorial, a more crucial affair for both man and horse. Albatross and his driver were to meet Isle Of Wight for the first time since the tough-as-nails campaigner had hung the last of three straight defeats on them. Herve Filion was flying in to handle Isle Of Wight, making the match even more interesting.

It was a busy day for Filion. A Paramount Studios crew was tagging along with him, shooting thousands of feet of film as the frenetic Canadian drove six horses at Freehold Raceway, New Jersey, in the afternoon, jetted up to Greenwood Raceway in Toronto to steer a horse in the World Driving Championship, then shot down to Liberty Bell to handle Isle Of Wight in the eighth race at the Philadelphia track.

The shooting script had him driving horses at three different tracks in two different countries, hopefully winning at all three to give the film a typical Hollywood ending. The cameramen were de-

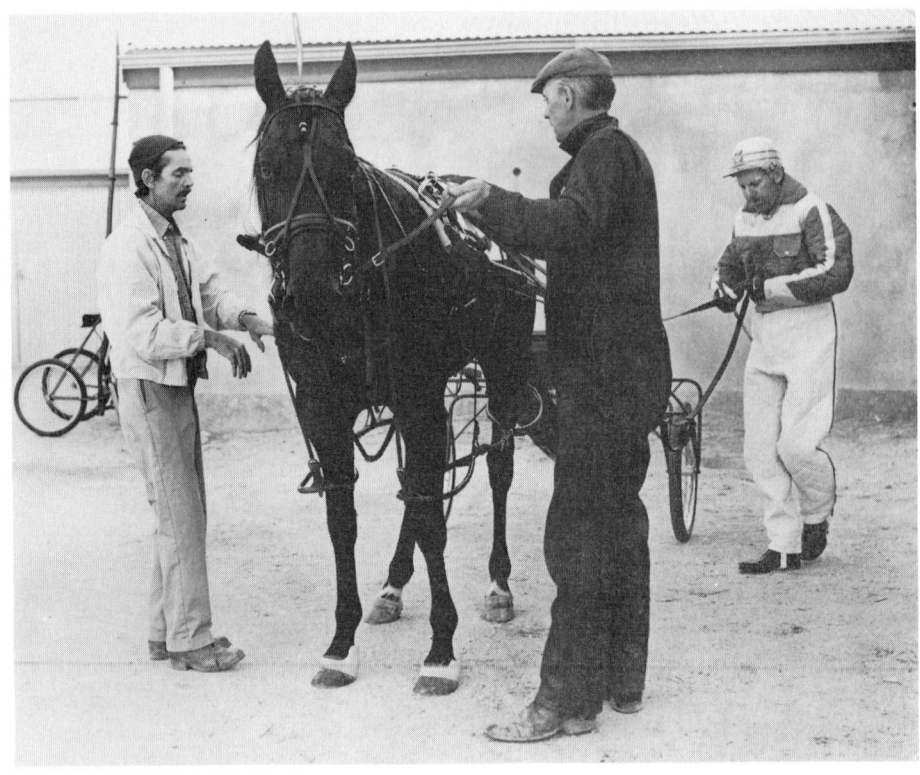

The Albatross team getting ready for battle: night watchman Roger Pritchard, caretaker Joe Wideman, trainer-driver Stanley Dancer. (Maywood Park photo)

lighted with the cooperation they were getting from Herve. He had won two races at Freehold, captured his lone start at Greenwood with a 22 to 1-shot, and needed only a decision in the Parish Memorial to provide a tidy finish to the sequence.

Isle Of Wight, tracking his eighth straight win, played his role to near perfection. He paced a 1:57.2 mile in the Parish, an incredible effort since it was a mere fifth of a second off the track record. Unfortunately for him, reinsman Filion and the Hollywood film makers, he finished fourth.

To quote Jack Kiser, the caustic *Philadelphia Daily News* racing columnist, "Albatross, with Stanley Dancer beaming in the sulky, won it with an unbelievable 1:56.2 clocking and made Isle Of Wight and Herve Filion look like raw amateurs in the process."

Filion and his horse got caught with their hand and hoof in the cookie jar. They tried to sneak past the pacesetting Albatross between the quarter and half-poles. Dancer looked to his right, spotted them coming and slapped the lines against his horse. The challenger and

What appears to be a snarl is merely Albatross adjusting his mouth to the bit. (Maywood Park photo)

his famous driver were suspended in the slipstream as Albatross zoomed away. They never recovered, finishing fourth behind Super Bird, Bye Bye Max (Jack Bailey) and Kentucky (Bruce Nickells).

Taking nothing away from Isle Of Wight, a fleet and stouthearted pacer by anybody's standards, he had finally met the real Albatross. It was an experience he would just as well have forgone.

Albatross had swept the Liberty Bell track record, the stakes mark and the world standard for four-year-olds over a five-eighths track.

Surprisingly, Super Bird was hard pressed to beat little known rivals in the mud at Maywood Park. (Maywood Park photo)

Neither rain, nor snow, nor . . . kept this pacer from his appointed rounds in the winner's circle. (Maywood Park photo)

The film crew had to resume their shooting. They were still at it out in California in December. The picture, when it finally made it into the nation's movie houses, was called simply *Filion*. It got excellent reviews.

Dancer, who had starred in a nationally released film a couple of years earlier, was in a light-hearted mood at the end of the evening. "Say," he told columnist Kiser, "how about sending a couple of wires for me. To Bert James and Alan Leavitt. Just say, 'Having a wonderful time. Wish you were here!'"

An invitational contest at Yonkers Raceway was to be the next meeting of Albatross, Isle Of Wight and friends, but the May 12 event was canceled when the owners, trainers and drivers of the horses involved protested the leanness of the purse—$25,000. Stanley Tananbaum, president of Yonkers at the time, put the blame on Off-Track Betting in New York City. OTB had cut into the track's gate and handle and harmed its purse structure, he said. $25,000 was all the track could offer, and when horsemen complained, he scuttled the race as a sort of dramatic gesture to call attention to the track's plight.

It left Albatross high and dry—without a race for 30 long days. While Super Bird was idle during the period, Dancer was not. He had the balance of his giant stable to campaign, a stable that included the likes of Super Bowl and Silent Majority—leading contenders for three-year-old honors during 1972.

Super Bowl, co-owned by his wife Rachel and by Hilda Silverstein, was his top sophomore trotting threat of the season. After a sputtering start, the Star's Pride son would find himself and go on to win the Triple Crown. Late in the year, Hanover Shoe Farms would pay a flat million dollars for him. Super Bowl would precede Albatross into the Hanover stud barn by about three weeks.

Silent Majority was a different and sadder story. The colt, a Henry T. Adios offspring, was the sport's Two-Year-Old Pacer of the Year in 1971 under the tutelage of handsome, popular Canadian horseman Roger White. Approaching the zenith of his career, White was killed in the crash of a light plane. His widow, who co-owned the colt along with Irving Liverman, had asked Dancer to race him in 1972. Stanley had agreed, not only welcoming Silent Majority into his barn, but turning back half the driving fees he received to Mrs. White.

Albatross, when he returned to action, proved once again that a long layoff had little or no effect upon his performance. He won the $25,000 Adios Butler Pace at Brandywine Raceway with a mile in 1:56.3, scoring by no less than eight and three-quarters lengths over Isle Of Wight and three other free-for-allers. His clocking matched the Brandywine track record set in 1971 by Steady Star.

The victory hiked his career earnings to $851,661 and tuned his mighty motor for the critical $91,000 Realization Pace at Roosevelt

Brandywine Raceway publicist Col. Dave Herman is surrounded by famous racing families during "Dancer-Filion World Championship" event at his track. Dancers, on left, include Stanley, Vernon, Sonny and Ronnie. Filions include Herve, Henri, Renald and Yves. (Brandywine Raceway photo)

Raceway on Saturday night, June 3. Albatross had won Roosevelt's premier stake for two-year-olds (the Futurity) in 1970 and the track's top affair for three-year-olds (the Messenger) in 1971. A victory in the Realization would give him a sweep of the plant's three richest pacing events, and the treasured Roosevelt Founder's Plate to symbolize the feat. Riding along with the Founder's Plate, which honors track founder George Morton Levy, was a $50,000 bonus, with $35,000 of it going to the owners, $10,000 to the driver and $5,000 to the breeders.

The Realization is at a distance of a mile and a sixteenth, although the extra length of the contest did not faze Stanley Dancer. So confident was Mr. Dancer that he also decided to drive Silent Majority in a division of the Battle of Brandywine Pace at Brandywine on the same night. Dancer's task was made easier when Roosevelt racing secretary Larry Mallar scheduled the Realization after the first race. Dancer would drive Albatross, fly to Wilmington, Del-

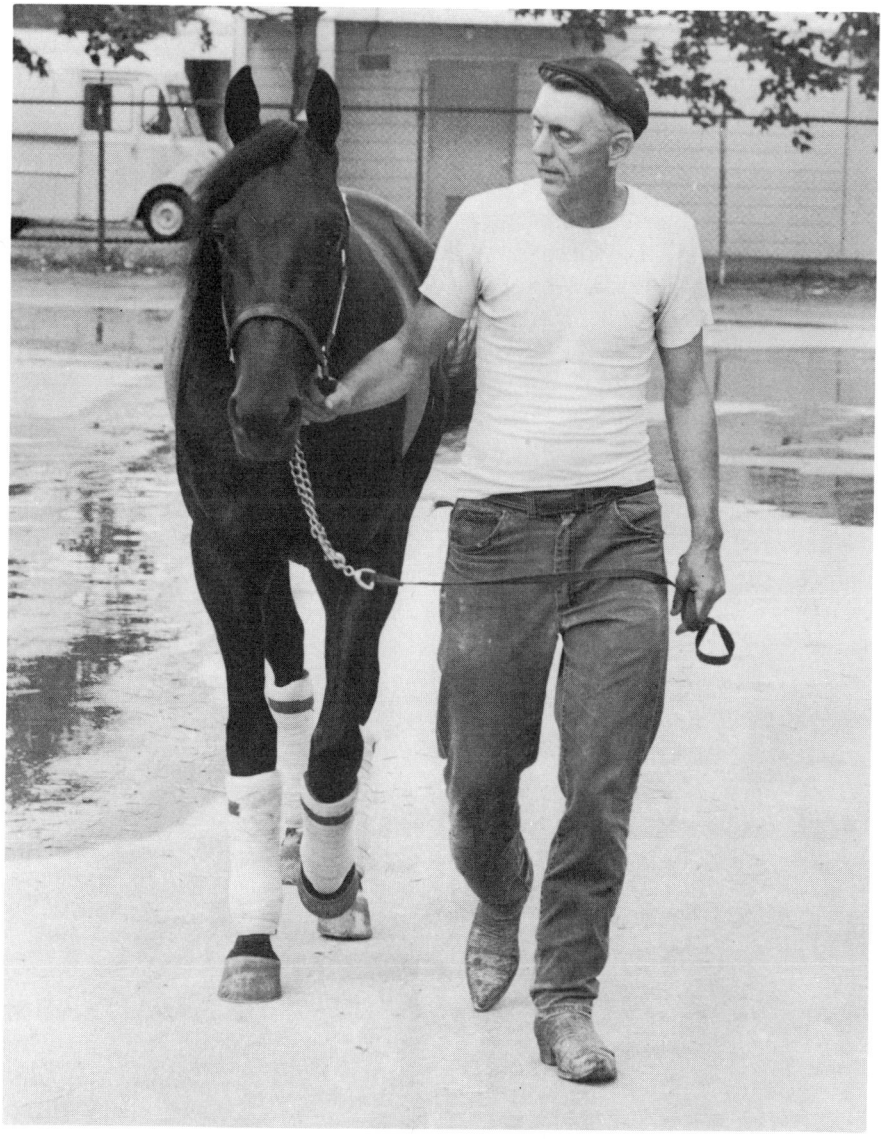

Caretaker Joe Wideman and his favorite pacer enjoy a stroll before the $91,000 Realization Pace. (Roosevelt Raceway photo)

aware, and drive Silent Majority in the eighth race at Brandywine. Shades of Herve Filion.

Only Tarport Skipper (John Chapman), Jake Jackson (Buddy Gilmour), H. T. Luca (Del Insko) and Dexter Hanover (Eddie Wheeler) chose to challenge Super Bird in the Realization, and they were obviously racing for second money. Albatross wrested the lead away at the half and poured it on to win going away in

2:06, earning himself the track, stake and world records for pacers going a mile and a sixteenth over a half-mile oval. Unfortunately, Dancer arrived at Brandywine too late to drive Silent Majority. Brother Vernon did the honors, winning with the fleet colt.

Stanley picked up his $10,000 bonus for winning the Founder's Plate and promptly forwarded $3,333 of it to Harry Harvey, since Harvey had driven Albatross to victory in the 1970 Roosevelt Futurity—the first of the three races making up the Plate trilogy. Ralph Baldwin, contract trainer for Castleton Farm at the time, had done as much for Dancer in 1964. Baldwin was recovering from a heart attack and was unable to drive Dartmouth in the Dexter Cup, final event in the companion Plate series for trotters. Dancer sat in for him, won the race and received a check as his share of the dividend.

Super Bird's decision in the Realization also meant a small bonanza for the five individuals who had bred him. Thousand-dollar checks went to Tic Wilcutts, Elizabeth Peters, Mark Lydon, John Kenney and Charles Kenney. With the bonuses from the Founder's Plate in their pockets, most of the breeders had now cleared $1,072

Meadow Skipper's most famous son wins the mile and a sixteenth Realization Pace in the world record time of 2:06. (Roosevelt Raceway photo)

Albatross and Stan Dancer collect both the race trophy and the Roosevelt Founders Plate after winning the Realization Pace. From left are Liberty Bell Park president Edward J. Dougherty, Amicable Stable representatives John Simpson Sr. and Louis Silverstein, Dancer, and Roosevelt officials S. Harvey Fosner, George Morton Levy and William Hopkins. The prestigious Founders Plate honors Levy. (Roosevelt Raceway photo)

on the sale of Albatross, his dam and his full sister. Wilcutts, the man who had spent considerable time and cash trying to get Albatross's dam to the races, still had a long way to go before he would be even.

The Amicable Stable had enjoyed a big night on the money front. Super Bird's portion of the race purse was $45,500. In addition, the stable had gained the $35,000 owners' premium from the Founder's Plate. There were no plans to share the bounty with James, Leavitt and other unhappy members of the old syndicate. The Amicable group had bought the horse free and clear. And feelings were still running high, very high, against the James gang.

Not that there weren't the faint stirrings of a peace movement from one member of the other side. An olive branch was waving gently at the Lana Lobell Farms in Hanover.

Stanley Dancer, interviewed by Henry Hecht in the *New York Post*, had predictably leveled a broadside at the old owners, training his biggest cannon on Alan Leavitt.

Leavitt, in a personal letter to Dancer on June 29, had turned the other cheek. He told Stanley that he had had numerous opportunities to attack him—Stanley—in public print, but had passed them up. His longstanding friendship with the New Jersey horseman meant more to him than any chance to gain revenge, he said. Leavitt proposed that he and Dancer look each other in the eye, shake hands and forget the feud.

While Leavitt was selling peace, Dancer wasn't buying. He never replied to the youngish master of Lana Lobell.

Thirteen nights after Albatross plundered Roosevelt Raceway in the Realization, he was out in Livonia, Michigan, flashing his fancy form in the $58,295 Matron Stakes for four-year-olds at Wolverine Raceway. Sporting a new five-race win skein, his name was magic again, and 18,273 rabid fans turned out to hand the track an all-time handle record of $1,024,101.

An old foe named Nansemond had slipped out of recent obscurity to renew acquaintances. The Wolverine duel was reminiscent of their monumental war in the 1971 Little Brown Jug, but with a different result. Albatross, awakened by Dancer after a sluggish first half in 1:00.1, had to fly home in 58.1 to stave off a stalking, hard-charging Nansemond and teamster Herve Filion. The 1:58.2 timing was only two ticks off the track record.

A week later, racing in the $25,750 Continental Purse at Windsor Raceway, the Amicable Stable's flashy showboat not only annexed the track mark, but toppled the all-time, all-Canada figure as well. Unpressed, he paced in 1:56.3 to humble Bye Bye Max and Kentucky. Happy Windsor officials Aime DesRosiers, Bill Rowe, Joe DeFrank and Fran Smith were quick to point out that no harness horse had ever traveled so briskly in Canadian racing history. Rubbed from the record book was the 1:57.1 clocking Romulus Hanover had achieved at Blue Bonnets Raceway in 1967.

Anyone taking the trouble to ask Dancer why he had gone such a withering mile when something a little less sensational would have done as well was told the night was fine, the track fast, and Albatross was full of pace. Admittedly, Stanley was also interested in collecting two-minute victories for his horse. Albatross was closing in on Bret Hanover's history-high figure of 31 miracle journeys, and Stanley meant to beat that total before his pacer closed his career.

While Dancer was not advertising it, he was anxious for the Meadow Skipper son to look good at Windsor. The Windsor area was Bert James country, and Stanley could not help but remember that most of his recent problems, the attempted firing and all, had started at Windsor when he was half-crippled and Albatross was not quite Albatross yet.

Big Bird is all alone as he sets Canadian record of 1:56.3 in $25,000 Continental Cup at Windsor Raceway. (Windsor Raceway photo)

Dancer playfully strokes the beak of the Bird during work session at Windsor Raceway. (Windsor Raceway photo)

Sportsman's Park and its five-eighths-mile oval, the scene of Bird's next encounter, brought back pleasanter memories. It was the Chicago area harness plant where the new and infinitely more friendly Albatross ownership team had taken command. It was also the spot where the pacer's current win spurt had been foaled—where happier times had started for Stan Dancer.

Albatross was facing four opponents, Ed Byrd, Nansemond, Song Cycle and Kentucky, in the $25,000 Governor's Cup on Saturday night, July 1. It was likely to be a fast affair—it was a hot, windless night, and Dancer was hoping to give Bird his 28th two-minute win —although no milestone mile was expected.

The truly herculean efforts, the kind that find their way into the history books, traditionally occur over the faster mile tracks like Lexington, Indianapolis and Vernon. And no one in the small field, not even the nifty Nansemond, was liable to push Albatross to *that* kind of journey over a compact five-eighths track. Joe Marsh Jr., the driver of Song Cycle, was stating more fact than fiction when he quipped before the race, "I have a plan to beat Albatross; I'll drive a Honda."

There was a serious question, in looking back on the race, whether the Honda would have done Marsh any good. Albatross and his boss headed straight for the safety of the front end, and lighted there in the middle of the first turn. Dancer looked at his watch at the quarter, read 27.3, and decided to back his horse off some during the next panel. He gave Albatross the breather he deserved, but the clock still read a scorching 57.3 at the half.

At the three quarters, with his horse still fresh and pacing easily, Stanley checked his timepiece for the third time. This time the figures 1:25.4 were there, and Dancer knew Albatross was en route to some headlines. Albatross already owned the world record for four-year-old pacers over a five-eighths track—1:56.2. Still up for grabs, however, was Romeo Hanover's 1:56.1 for pacers of any age, and this was the mark that Dancer felt his pacer would fracture at the end of the mile.

"I figured at the three-quarter pole that we would do maybe 1:55 and a fraction," he told Paul Hofstetter Jr., a sports writer for the *Chicago Tribune*.

More than 18,000 anxious, screaming Chicagoans were on their feet as Albatross slammed down the lane, his legs straining against his hopples, his stride stretched so far it seemed his chest might scrape the ground before he was through. A photo of the finish shows both Dancer and Bruce Nickells, the pilot of Kentucky, the place horse, with their eyes fastened on the electronic timer in the infield. The crowd, too, was waiting for the verdict, and roared its approval when 1:54.3 appeared on the lighted board.

Without really trying, Albatross had succeeded in going the fastest race mile ever recorded by a harness horse of *any age, any gait* and *any sex* over a track of *any size*. He had snipped his own prec-

Super Bird crosses finish to complete world record 1:54.3 mile at Sportsman's Park. (Sportsman's Park photo)

The fastest race mile in the history of harness racing. (Sportsman's Park photo)

Crowd hails the champion and his driver after epic mile. (Sportsman's Park photo)

edent-setting speed badge of 1:54.4, taken at Lexington in 1971.

Not a single soul witnessing his performance, not even Stanley Dancer, had envisioned a clocking like that. Standardbreds simply do not race that fast over the tight confines of a five-eighths track. And Albatross had performed the miracle so easily; never urged, never challenged by another horse. Groom Joe Wideman, collecting his horse after the wild winner's circle ceremonies, was unaware of Albatross's accomplishment until he had led him back to the paddock for saliva tests. "I heard the crowd whooping it up, but then they almost always whooped it up at the end of his races," Joe said. "I couldn't believe the people in the paddock when they told me he'd went in 1:54.3. I thought those kind of miles were only possible in the heat of the afternoon over the big tracks."

The heat of the July night was an important factor in the making of the record. Dancer freely admitted that. So was the track's recent efforts to improve its racing oval. The racing strip had been resurfaced and the turns banked—moves which had paid off handsomely. Sportsman's Park was now the home of the fastest race mile in harness history.

Kentucky, finishing second, was timed in 1:55 flat, winding up

Happiness reigned in winner's circle after record mile. From left are Phil Langley, director of racing, Stanley, Rachel Dancer and Billy Johnston, Chicago Downs and Fox Valley Trotting Club president. (Sportsman's Park photo)

a length and a half in arrears at the wire. Ed Byrd, driven by Harry Burright, finished fifth and last in the race, but managed to set an informal record of his own. No horse in memory had ever traveled a mile in 1:57.3 and lost by 15 lengths!

John Simpson Sr., unable to make the trip to Chicago, received news of Bird's superlative showing by telephone moments after the race. "Paced in *what*?" demanded Simpson, not trusting his ears. The Hanover Shoe Farms' investment was looking stronger, shrewder with every passing race. Albatross was definitely blue-chip stock.

"You're going to hear from a lot of tracks now," Simpson predicted. "They'll all want him for some sort of promotion or the other."

The Hanover president was right. What had been a steady flow of requests for Bird's services now became a flood. Dates had already been arranged with Buffalo Raceway, Saratoga Raceway and Vernon Downs. The new offers, arriving both by mail and phone, were carefully reviewed. Some were accepted, others were gently turned down.

Albatross could only be at one track at a time.

Buffalo Raceway, New York, was next. Only two rivals could be rounded up to face him in the $12,000 Reynolds Memorial, but that did not stop him from putting on a great show for the 12,576 fans. On a cool night, racing in an event that did not go to post until almost midnight, Albatross paced a 1:57.4 mile to chop two full seconds off the 10-year-old record held by Henry T. Adios (who had also been driven by Stanley Dancer).

Gaston Valiquette, Buffalo's general manager and director of racing, presented Dancer with a $2,500 check for setting the new record. Albatross's share of the purse lifted his career earnings to $993,508 and set the stage for him to soar over the million-dollar milestone at his next stop—Saratoga Raceway.

Saratoga President Ernest B. Morris, hoping to give the Meadow Skipper son every possible advantage to break Romulus Hanover's track standard of 1:58.2, carded his race on one of the four matinee programs he had pried out of the New York State Harness Racing Commission. Morris had a warm recollection of what Nevele Pride had done during one of his track's afternoon cards. Pride, with Stanley Dancer at the reins, had trotted the Spa half-mile oval in 1:56.4 to set a world mark that may outlive Saratoga's well-constructed, lovingly cared for grandstand.

Luck had been with Ernie Morris in the Nevele Pride affair. A vicious rainstorm, moving in rapidly, had held off just long enough to get the Pride race in. Rain was pouring down, in fact, when the great trotter was completing his mile.

It looked like Morris had spent his ration of fortune on Nevele Pride however. The best he could arrange for Albatross was a cool afternoon—actually cold for July 8—and some fairly stiff breezes. It was no kind of day for truly fast miles.

Albatross and Dancer gave it their all. They led the field from gate to wire, slashing past the poles in 28.4, 57.2, and 1:26.4. A combination of the ripping pace, dull track and winds got to the Amicable Stable star on the way home, however. He paced the concluding quarter in 30.4.

With conditions a long way from ideal, Albatross had spliced together a mile in 1:57.3—a clocking plenty good enough to cost Romulus Hanover his niche in the Saratoga Raceway archives. And a little more checking by announcer George Miller quickly turned up the fact that Super Bird, as a kind of afterthought, had also snipped a fifth of a second off Bye Bye Byrd's 13-year-old world figure for four-year-old pacers over a twice-around oval.

Miller also offered the assembly a piece of information which elated Stanley Dancer as much as the speed records had. Plucking $8,000 out of the Spa purse, Albatross had now won $1,001,508 during his two and a half-year residency at the races.

The mighty Bird, as a weanling about as good looking as Howard

Cosell, as a yearling practically unsalable, was now the second richest pacing horse of all-time, vaulting ahead of Dancer's game old champion of a few years back, Cardigan Bay ($1,000,837). Only Rum Customer held an edge on him, and it was a slender edge at that—$40. And Albatross was the youngest Standardbred by far to reach the million-dollar plateau.

The speed spree, the long thread of successes, had to end somewhere, sometime. Frank Ervin, the man who had guided Bret Hanover to 35 straight wins before defeat had set in, said it best: "Send a horse to the races enough times and you'll get him beaten eventually. I mean *any* horse."

Albatross's Waterloo went by the name of Brandywine Raceway. It was July 22, and Bird was competing in the $27,750 Adios Harry Invitational, when the string was snapped.

Albatross was in the lead, and the folks who had bet him down to 1 to 20 odds were positive he was headed for his 11th decision in a row. Stanley Dancer wasn't so sure. His horse acted lethargic, laboring to reach the top. Nansemond and Herve Filion made a move at him on the backstretch. Dancer saw them coming and tried to shake up his pacer. To no avail. Super Bird's sting was gone. Nansemond coasted past him and pulled off to an eight and three-quarter-length win. Then Kentucky and Romano Hanover rubbed salt in the wound by slipping past him in the stretch. Albatross was relegated to fourth spot, the first time he had failed to finish in the top three.

It was a question of who was sicker, Stanley Dancer or the thousands of fans who had bet $55,602 on the champion in the three pari-mutuel pools.

As it turned out, it was neither. Albatross was the real ailing party in the affair.

23

Albatross's lackluster performance at Brandywine was in such striking contrast to his recent form that Stan Dancer and John Simpson at first suspected that a bit of skullduggery had transpired. They were afraid some culprit had somehow skirted the 24-hour guard on the horse and tranquilized him.

The "Official" sign was scarcely up on the race when Dancer and Simpson requested saliva, urine and blood tests on their prize pacer. Dancer also put in an urgent call for Dr. Edwin Churchill, the methodical, unflappable veterinarian who had treated Albatross throughout the pacer's long lodging in the Dancer Stable.

It was three days before the results of the tests for drugs came back. They were all negative. In the meantime, Dr. Churchill had rushed to Brandywine and given the champion a complete examination, primarily hunting for signs of a virus—a dripping nose, a high temperature, a cough, throat congestion, loss of appetite, general lethargy. He found none of them.

Churchill ran his own tests on the horse, finding only that Albatross's white blood count was slightly higher than normal. The elevated count signaled a minor infection in the horse somewhere, although Dr. Churchill, one of the nation's premier equine diagnosticians, was at a loss to pinpoint it.

"I can't find anything else wrong with him, so it must be the hidden infection," Churchill told Dancer. "And since I really don't know exactly what I'm treating him for, I'll have to stick to the broad spectrum antibiotics. More than likely a good, long rest will do more for him than any of my drugs."

With Albatross on the shelf at Egyptian Acres, Dancer felt compelled to tell Vernon Downs officials that Super Bird's scheduled bid for a world racing record at the Central New York track on August 11 was in jeopardy. Dancer had planned to send Super Bird after his own 1:54.3 mark in a special $25,000 invitational. The publicity drums were already beating and the field was being assembled when Stanley passed on the gloomy word that his horse might not be fit for the record bid.

Albatross was making progress at the farm—his blood count was gradually returning to normal—but Dancer was wary of trying to yank a 1:53 or 1:54 mile out of him after a three-week layoff. He phoned Vernon general manager Frank O. White and racing secretary Jerry M. Monahan to tell them this.

"I'll be glad to race him on August 11 like we planned," he said, "but I'd rather not publicize it as a shot at the record. He'll be off three weeks by then and I really won't know whether he's fully recovered or not. I'll let you make the decision. We can either race him as scheduled without trying for the record, or postpone it until later and go for the big mile."

"What would you rather do?" Monahan asked him.

"I think I'd rather push it back," Dancer said. "I'd really like to take a crack at the thing, but I'd want everything to be in his favor. I'd want to know the horse is a hundred percent. And I know John Simpson agrees with me."

"Can I get back to you?" the racing secretary asked.

"Sure," said Dancer. "But don't wait too long. I've got to get him back in action, one way or the other. I've got to get him a start somewhere if he's not going to race at your place on the eleventh."

Monahan, White and the rest of the Vernon official family pondered the situation for three days. To postpone the event would disappoint many fans who were looking forward to seeing the champion on August 11. The track already had reservations from people as far away as Canada. By the same token, the same good folks would be frustrated—and very possibly angry—if they came great distances to see Albatross in a listless performance. And, then, Vernon was anxious to bring the world racing record back to its three-quarter-mile track. Adios Harry had taken his 1:55 speed badge there in 1955, and the standard had not been beaten until Albatross shaded it at Lexington in 1971. In the end, the Vernonites decided to postpone the contest. A guaranteed sound Bird in the bush seemed more worthwhile than a questionable Bird in the hand.

Dancer then scouted around for a home for Albatross on Friday night, August 11, and found it at Yonkers Raceway. Racing secretary Ed Parker quickly inherited most of the tentative Vernon Downs field and scheduled the $25,000 Cardigan Bay Pace. Tarport Skipper, Public Affair, El Patron and Bye Bye Max were also in it, but virtually all the interest centered upon the presence of Albatross and Nansemond. Jack Powers, writing in the *Jersey Journal*, termed the affair "the harness race of the year."

The Albatross camp was uniformly confident on the outside, uniformly apprehensive on the inside before the Yonkers race. Dr. Churchill was reasonably certain the Meadow Skipper son had shaken the low-grade infection which had idled him; blood tests showed that. But Stanley Dancer, for one, was not convinced the mysterious infection was the sole cause of his poor showing at Brandywine. He decided to experiment with the horse's equipment, dropping his

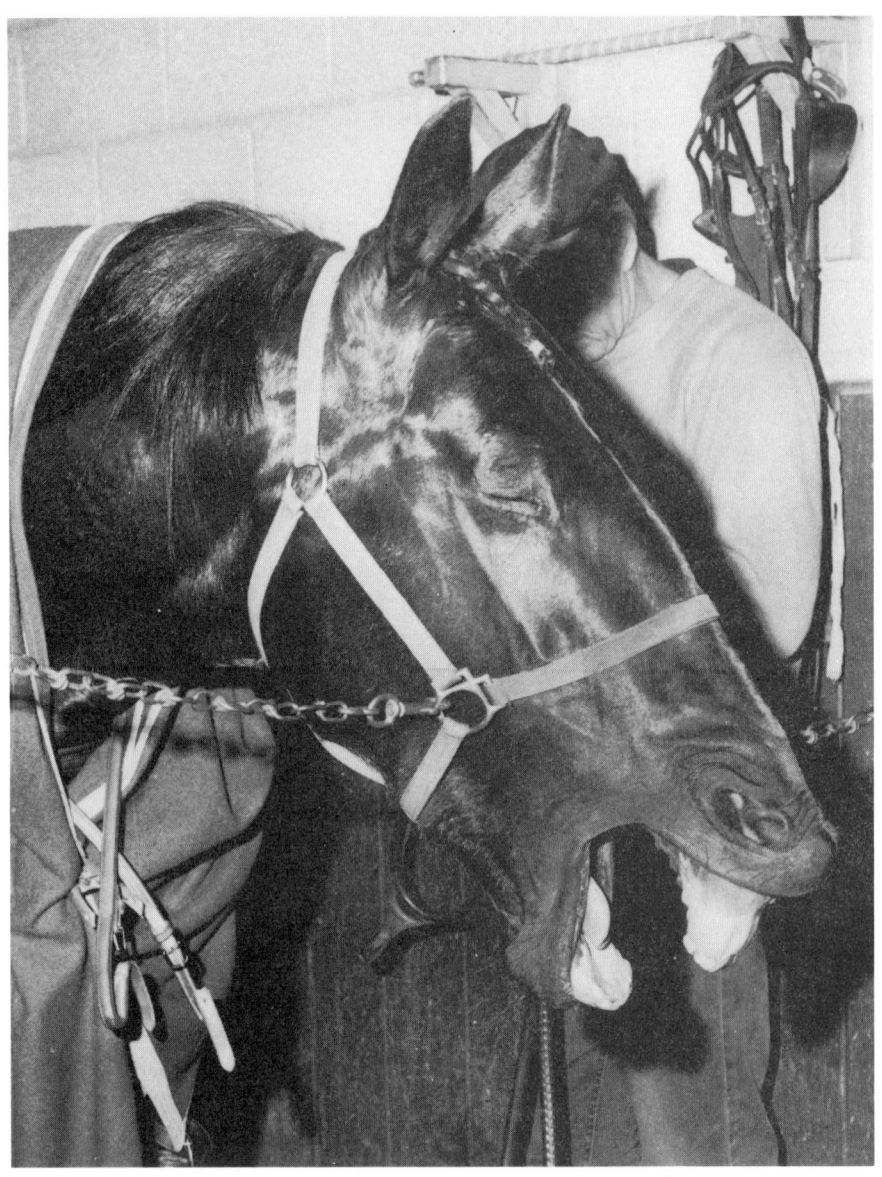

"How come we got to start so early, Joe?" yawns Albatross to caretaker Joe Wideman. (Yonkers Raceway photo)

closed bridle in favor of an open variety, and discarding the headpoles he had worn through the majority of his career.

John Simpson was tied up and could not make the contest. Murray Brown decided to remain in Hanover. Brown, the Shoe Farms' public relations director, had seen all 10 of Albatross's recent wins, but had missed the Brandywine debacle. He opted to sit out the Yonkers test, too—a bad sign.

Albatross, apparently, could not read signs. With great care Dancer kept him near the back of the small pack through the initial four furlongs of the race. Dancer's plan was to keep the wraps on him to the head of the stretch, then test his recuperative powers . . . see if he had his sting back. At the half, however, Bird felt so good, so strong, that Stanley pulled him off the rail and let him go after the pacesetting Nansemond. He sped around his rival with startling ease. Then, pacing up a storm, he flew the last quarter in 28.1 to score by three and a half lengths.

The time for Bird's romp was 1:57.4—the swiftest journey in all of Yonkers's long history. He had also garnered his 31st two-minute victory, matching Bret Hanover's career high for the sport.

Dancer, Simpson, Brown—all the people who knew him best—were astonished. Not one of them had expected such an exalted, swinging performance by a horse who was returning to the racing wars after a 20-day bout with an infection. Squeezing for a win at best, they had drawn a monumental conquest. And Dancer was talking like Albatross could have gone faster. "I don't think he would have had any trouble breaking the world record (Bret's 1:57 over a half-mile track) if we were going for it," Stanley announced joyfully.

Up in Vernon, New York, track officials heard the results of the race and groaned. Vernon had enjoyed a hot, muggy night, an evening seemingly tailor-made for record attempts. If things had gone right, Albatross would have been ripping up the world record book at Vernon instead of flirting with it at Yonkers.

There was no doubt in Dancer's mind that his horse was at full strength again, and an unfortunate defeat at Hawthorne Race Course, Illinois, seven nights later did nothing to alter his conviction. Nansemond and Herve Filion were the villains again.

Filion immediately sent his pacer to the front in the $44,450 Suburban Downs Pacing Derby. Albatross, still dressed in an open bridle and racing without headpoles, was back in fifth. Dancer's horse was trailing an outclassed entry named Miles Dares and fell far off the pace when the longshot could not keep up with the leaders. When Stanley sent his charge to the outside for his run at the pacesetter, it was too late. Nansemond hustled the last half in 57.1 and was uncatchable. Albatross had to settle for second as his rival chewed up the Hawthorne track standard with his 1:57.1 tour.

Dancer couldn't decide whether he was more peeved at Miles Dares or himself. He vowed that he would not permit his champion to get caught in a bind like that again.

Racing him in the $59,400 Canadian Pacing Derby at Greenwood Raceway on August 26, he bullied his way into the lead early in the affair and turned back Nansemond in 1:58.2. From Hawthorne on, Dancer would take his chances at the head of the field, avoiding the risk of being trapped in traffic.

It was a time of celebration for the Albatross hierarchy. The

Big Bird had not only gobbled up the Greenwood speed banner for four-year-olds, but harvested his 32nd victory in two minutes or less as well. He was history's leader now, replacing the mighty Bret Hanover. Stanley Dancer had planted the seed for that milestone moment months before, carefully nurturing it to its fruition.

The Amicable Stable star, bouncing back from illness, sets a new Yonkers Raceway mark of 1:57.4 to capture the Cardigan Bay Pace. (Yonkers Raceway photo)

Albatross breezes to 1:57.4 victory at Brandywine Raceway to gain revenge over arch-rival Nansemond (3). (Brandywine Raceway photo)

And if Stan Dancer were the drinking sort, he would have also popped the cork on a magnum of bubbly four days later. On August 30, on a parched afternoon at DuQuoin, Illinois, he won the 1972 Hambletonian Stake with Super Bowl, collecting five world records in the process. It was Mr. Dancer's second Hambletonian win in five years.

Back in the sulky behind Albatross, he scored airily over Nansemond in 1:57.4 at Brandywine, then sent his pacer on to Vernon Downs. Vernon, straining at the leash to display the red-hot pacing king before its patrons, had fashioned a $20,000 special invitational around him. An extra $5,000 bonus was earmarked for any driver who set a world record in the event—mainly Stanley Dancer. Four rivals, all nice pacers but hardly in his league, were corralled to face the champion. The idea was for at least one of the outgunned quartet to volunteer a blistering pace for as far as he could go, with Albatross to pick up the baton at that point. At the end of the mile, it was hoped, Albatross and Vernon Downs would own the fastest race mile in harness racing annals. Dancer would own the $5,000 bonus.

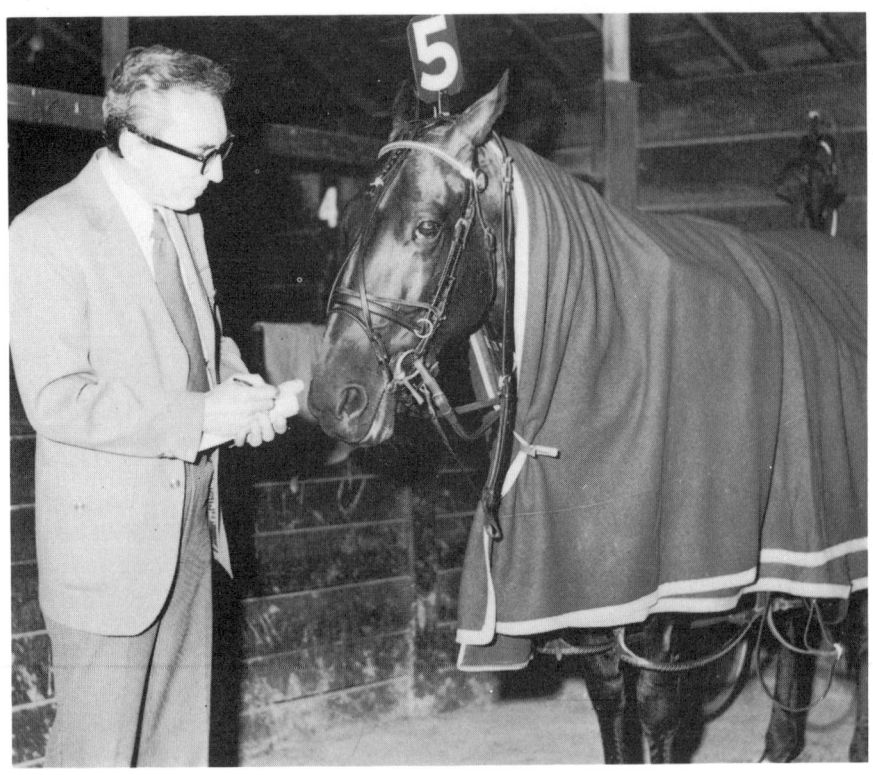

Author Donald Evans interviews Albatross before Vernon Downs record bid. Big Bird wasn't talking. (Auburn Citizen photo)

Leaving as little as possible to chance—giving Super Bird every conceivable advantage—the track scheduled the September 9 record bid for 8 p.m., before the regular Saturday night racing card was slated to get under way. The earlier the race, the faster the track, went the thinking.

It was a thoughtful, heady plan that promptly fell apart in the face of unfavorable weather. It poured on Friday night. Then it turned cold on Saturday, preventing the track from drying out. Charles (Deac) Thurston, the track superintendent, scraped the big three-quarter-mile oval, but the surface remained a little damp, chilled and dull—perhaps a pair of seconds off its peak. When the sun finally broke through late in the afternoon, it was too late to heal the damage.

Dancer, surveying the racing strip from the paddock, was game but doubtful. "We'll have a go at it," he said. "I don't know, maybe if the pace is quick enough . . ."

Sureshot Hanover, handled by George (Buddy) Regan for the Hickory Way Stables and co-owner Leo Glickberg, was the entry who

The sun finally broke through to dry Vernon Downs track, but it was too little and too late for Bird's try at world mark. (Auburn Citizen photo)

was expected to provide the early foot in the race. Sureshot was to be the "rabbit." He had the credentials for the role. A week before he had won at Vernon in 1:57.4, pacing to the first two poles in 26.3 and 56.2. The same sort of trip, complete with the blistering early fractions, was exactly what Dancer needed to turn a slim chance into success.

The tall, raw-boned Sureshot was a bitter disappointment, however. He had apparently left his big mile on the track in his last race. Driver Regan had trouble getting him away from the gate, had trouble getting him over to the rail, and had trouble getting him to pace at all. He was never a factor in the contest, other than the fact that he got in Albatross's way. Dancer had to discard his strategy and go it on his own. By the time he was able to steer Albatross into the lead, the half-pole was upon him. The timer read 58.4 and track announcer Jim Moran had trouble keeping the disappointment out of his voice. Moran, Dancer and a good share of the Vernon fans realized that Bird's slender hopes for the record had gone by the boards. Albatross sped home in 57.3 to complete his mile in 1:56.2. It was Vernon's nattiest clocking of the year, but it wasn't nearly enough. History's swiftest race mile still belonged to Sportsman's Park.

"It seems it wasn't meant to be," Dancer told the dejected Vernon management family.

Bird flies home at Vernon Downs, but weather and a slow early pace costs him world record. (Bill Taylor photo)

The track managers felt no worse than Stanley Dancer. Dancer was longing to add the pacing race record over a three-quarter-mile track to his burgeoning collection. Few people were aware of it, but Stanley Dancer-driven trotters (Noble Victory, Nevele Pride and Super Bowl) had gone the fastest race miles ever over half-mile, five-eighths-mile, three-quarter-mile and mile tracks. On the pacing side, Albatross had given him records over mile and five-eighths-mile tracks. He needed only the pacing marks over three-quarter-mile and half-mile ovals to complete his one-man sweep. Failure in the Vernon effort would be the only hole in his grand design, since the half-mile standard would fall to him and Albatross 10 days later.

It was fitting and proper that Albatross's last and possibly greatest world record should come over the track where he had suffered his most bitter defeat—the Delaware, Ohio, Fairground. It was there that Nansemond and Filion had outgunned him in the Little Brown Jug, spoiling his bid for the Triple Crown of Pacing.

Reparation was one of the motives prompting Dancer to accept an offer to race his super sidewheeler at Delaware on September 19.

Dancer collects jewel box trophy from Vernon Downs president Sen. George R. Fearon despite the fact that weather and a slow pace halted Bird's chances for a world record. (Bill Taylor photo)

That and the chance to pick up another major mark for his horse and himself.

It certainly wasn't the money luring him out there. The good folks at Delaware could muster only $2,000 for the invitational starring Albatross. It was the smallest pot Super Bird had scrapped over since June 17, 1970, when he was a two-year-old competing in an overnight contest at Northfield Park, Ohio.

There were no Nansemonds, Isle Of Wights, Kentuckys, Bye Bye

Maxes or Winning Worthys within sight. The field, instead, consisted of three journeymen crowd-pleasers called Cissy T. Adios, Steady April and Bloom. All three were mares, but the Women's Liberation Movement would claim no victories that afternoon. Even the most zealous of Women's Libbers had to admit that the Ms. Cissy, Ms. Steady and Ms. Bloom were hardly the equal of Albatross.

Competition was not the point. The object of the affair was a mile faster than Bret Hanover's 1965 record of 1:57 over the same Delaware half-miler, and Dancer was working toward that end from the opening bell. Albatross was down to the quarter in 28.3, over to the half in 58, and around to the three quarters in 1:26.4. The three mares had practically vanished as Bird turned for home, the Fairground throng rising *en masse* to help root him to the wire. With the crowd screaming and Dancer working on him with both hands, the king of speed paced the rest of the way in 28.4 to halt the clock in 1:55.3. He had not only beaten Bret's figure, but obliterated it.

"It was a truly great performance, for he had no company at the end, no prompters to spur him on, only his own speed and heart," Elizabeth Rorty wrote, singing his praises in *Horseman & Fair World* magazine. "As he hit the wire in 1:55.3, 30 or more lengths on top, he had not only established a world race mark for half-mile tracks, but . . . given Delaware a new track mark for coming generations to shoot at."

John Simpson, glancing back at the race months later, was of the opinion that the Amicable Stable star would have turned in an even greater mile had the event been held a day later. "The weather was quite a bit better the next day, and I sincerely believe he'd have beaten 1:55 had his race been contested then."

Stan Dancer agreed with the Hanover president. A breeze estimated at 15 miles an hour had probably cost Albatross the better part of a second, he said, whereas the following day had turned out to be as perfect as a horseman bent upon making racing history could order. No less than 13 changes were made in the record book at Delaware on Wednesday.

Not that Dancer wasn't content with his horse's 1:55.3 timing. He was. Content and proud. "When we got to the three quarters in 1:26.4, I knew a 30-second last quarter would break Bret's world record. He got home more than I thought he would," he reported. "You know," he added wistfully, "Albatross really didn't deserve to lose the Brown Jug last year. I think this kind of makes up for that loss."

It was the last time Dancer and Simpson would send the powerful pacing machine after a world record despite a strong appeal from the potent racing people who operate the Lexington Red Mile.

"They weren't offering enough money—a thousand dollars, as I recall—and Albatross already owned the 1:54.3 mark they wanted him to shoot at. We'd have looked like donkeys had something happened and he got hurt chasing his own record," Simpson explained.

"And besides, it was getting pretty late in the game."

It was, indeed, getting late in the game. The signs of autumn were everywhere as caretaker Joe Wideman packed Albatross's gear for his next journey. The clock was running down on the super pacer's tumultuous racing career. The Hanover Shoe Farms' stallion barn was beckoning.

Leaving the tiny Ohio fairground, Albatross and Dancer traveled to Batavia Downs in Upstate New York, where they whipped Nansemond and Filion in 2:00.3 over a damp and thoroughly chilled track. Then they went on to Liberty Bell and lost a tight 2:00.2 decision to the same combination. Nansemond and Filion got a big jump on them and couldn't be overhauled in the driving finish.

Revenge came two weeks later on October 21 when Albatross, sharp from a brief rest, ignored raw weather and a dull track to demolish the Freehold, New Jersey, record with a 1:57.3 victory. Nansemond and the rest of his rivals were 17 or more lengths back as he sliced through the electronic beam.

Murray Brown hailed it as his greatest performance as a four-year-old. "Several horsemen commented that the Freehold track, which isn't very fast in the first place, was at least two full seconds off that day," Brown recalled. "And Stanley never touched him as he pulled away from the field."

At Roosevelt Raceway a week later, Albatross proved once again that he was a champion for all tracks and all distances. He drew the number one post in the mile and a quarter National Pacing Derby and led all the way, was never really threatened, as he coasted to a three-length triumph over Nansemond and Banner Ranger. The time for the extra distance event was 2:33.3.

And then the racing opportunities grew sparse, the pickings slim. It was late October and many of the nation's harness tracks had closed up shop for the year. Those that were running—in the East, at least—were playing to smaller and smaller houses, tightening their belts and catering to the hardy hard-core fans who would turn out to watch racing goats if the mutuel windows were open to them. The fair-weather fan, the fellow who appreciated the spectacle of racing, the gentleman who made it worthwhile for a track to offer an Albatross, had packed it in for the season. He was watching "Monday Night Football," refinishing furniture in his basement, or attending PTA meetings.

There was nothing left for Albatross but a pair of races out in California. Dancer sent him back to his New Egypt farm to await his trip to the West Coast. The end of his racing career was in sight.

24

In a way, it was the best part of the year for Stanley Dancer. Much of the pressure was off. Most of his better horses, the Grand Circuit colts and fillies, had called it a season, were lounging about Egyptian Acres, waiting to be shipped to Pompano Park. Dancer still had a couple of horses to race—Albatross and Super Bowl—but in the main, he, too, was through for the season.

Stanley and most of his lieutenants, son Ronnie, Bill Bain, Jim Harrison, Jean-Guy Lemarre, Jack Smith and Walter (Pee Wee) Welch, were assembled at the farm, line-breaking and training the yearlings the stable had plucked out of the fall sales.

The rest of the Dancer clan was there as well—Vernon, Harold Sr., Harold Jr. and James—either training horses over Stanley's inestimable farm track or showing up to swap racing tales and to pat, probe and ogle the new crop of yearlings. Sort of like kicking the tires on each other's new cars.

Albatross, of course, was jogged daily and worked periodically. And while the champion was on the track, being put through his training paces to keep him tight for his California starts, Stanley would occasionally hand the reins to one of his kin—son Ronnie or brothers Vernon and Harold Sr.

For Ronnie Dancer, young, articulate, eager to learn, in love with Standardbred horses and Standardbred racing, it was the sublime treat. "It was the first and only time I'd held pacing perfection in my hands," he reported enthusiastically. "His gait was so smooth I could imagine a glass of water sitting on his hopple spreader and not spilling. I had a sort of sad feeling that I'd never have the opportunity to sit behind his equal because there'd never be another like him."

Vernon Dancer was an old hand at riding behind Albatross. He had trained him several times and warmed him up on a number of occasions when Stanley was struggling with his back and neck injuries. Yet Vernon never missed a chance to climb into the jog cart when his brother offered. "My God what a horse," Vernon said. "He just seemed to glide over the ground. When you spoke to him to go faster, he didn't seem to change his gait, he simply stretched his

A well-bundled Stanley Dancer works out colt at his New Egypt, New Jersey, headquarters. (Bill Taylor photo)

stride. I've never had a horse in my stable over the years that had that kind of feeling."

Harold Dancer Sr. is a trotting man who barely acknowledges the existence of the pacing gait. But he had his eyes opened—and opened wide—when he was called on to handle Albatross. "I'd never driven or never seen a pacer like him before," the eldest of the Dancers confessed. "He was simply smoother, more powerful than anything I'd ever sat behind. A real machine, with every foot landing where it was supposed to. I thoroughly enjoyed working him, and that's something, coming from a man who isn't too fond of pacers."

Stanley Dancer, leaning on the track fence, squinting into the autumn sun, watching his son or one of his brothers cruising past with Albatross, couldn't help but reflect on his turbulent yet infinitely satisfying months as trainer-driver of the world champion.

He remembered Alan Leavitt's phone call to Pompano Park, the catalytic call which had set the whole chain of events into motion.

He remembered the early victories—the Romeo Hanover Pace at Rockingham, the Messenger at Roosevelt, the Prix D'Été at Blue Bonnets, the Cane at Yonkers and the Adios at The Meadows.

And he remembered the shock, the ache of the smarting loss at Delaware, when his horse's bid for the Triple Crown had gone up in a puff of dust raised by the flying hoofs of Nansemond.

He recalled his injuries late in 1971 and again in early 1972, when he had tried to ignore his throbbing neck and back, his useless right hand, to take his great pacer to post in rich and crucial contests on both coasts.

He recalled the treatment he had received from Bert James, Alan Leavitt and Glen Brown, the nightmare session in the hospital, the surly telegram which had arrived to inform him that he was fired as the horse's handler.

And he was not likely to forget the awesome faith Louis Silverstein had demonstrated in him by purchasing Albatross without the faintest idea of who might join him in the expensive venture. Nor would he forget the support he had received from Hilda Silverstein, Hazel Shriner and John Rollins.

John Simpson and the Hanover Shoe Farms? He would be forever in their debt for the way they had plunged into the syndication on his word alone that Albatross was perfectly sound and ready to resume his domination over all the pacing horses in the land.

Sure as hell, there'd been some rocky moments during the 19 months he'd had Albatross, Dancer mused, but the horse had made every blessed one of them worthwhile. What an incredible, incomparable, wondrous, spectacular, superior, rare animal he was! If he managed to win his last two matches in California—the $50,000 Western Pace and the $100,000 American Pacing Classic—Albatross would retire with a lifetime record of 71 starts, 59 wins, eight seconds, three thirds and a fourth. His career earnings would stand at $1,201,470, the most ever for a pacing horse. He would retire with 11 major world records and more track and stakes standards than any horse of any breed in history. His two-minute victories would total 37, an even half-dozen more than any Standardbred who had come before him. And, unless all the eligible voters had spent the year in the heart of African bush country, he would most assuredly repeat as Harness Horse of the Year.

Campaigning him all those months had been a real physical and mental grind, Dancer had to admit. He was relieved, truly and genuinely relieved, that it was almost over, that he would no longer be wearing an Albatross around his neck. Yet Dancer knew in his heart that if some owner came walking down the road, tugging another like him by a lead shank, looking for a trainer, that he would be the first one to get his hand in the air. That's the way it is with Stanley Dancer.

When Albatross went to post in the Western Pace at Hollywood Park on November 24, he was coming off a 27-day vacation. Most harness horses, despite the jogging and work miles they would receive in the interim, would be rusty, flat, in need of a start or two to put the deep breath back in their lungs, the tone back in their muscles. Not Albatross. A layoff only made him tougher. Lining up for the Western, he was fit and fresh, full of zip and fight, and there wasn't a horse in the field who could come close to him—not Kentucky, not El Patron, not Silent Majority (now handled by Billy Haughton), not Bye Bye Max, not Banner Ranger, not Horton Hanover, not Isle Of Wight and not Nansemond.

Albatross, at the peak of his powers, paced as he pleased, ripping

Hollywood Park publicity montage featured Big Bird after 1:56 victory late in pacer's final season. (Hollywood Park photo)

up the first quarter in 27.2, coasting the next four furlongs to arrive at the three quarters in 1:28.2, then hustling home in 27.3 to finish in 1:56 flat with nearly five lengths over the old familiar duo of Nansemond and Filion. Otto Sunder's Bye Bye Max, with jaunty Jack Bailey in the bike, was another length back in third.

It was the second fastest mile in 26 years of harness racing competition at Hollywood Park, and a new stakes record by a full second. Dancer was convinced the Bird could have eclipsed Adios Butler's 1960 track mark of 1:55.3 had he—Dancer—been so inclined.

And then there was but one start left in Albatross's racing career.

Stanley jetted back to New Egypt, leaving Albatross at the Inglewood harness headquarters to train a little and loaf a lot in the warm California sunshine. Faithful Joe Wideman was with him, although West Coast horseman Eddie Wheeler was asked to work the pacer in his one strenuous session between races. The perennially boyish-looking Wheeler was joining a select club. Outside of the Dancer clan, only John Simpson Jr. had worked the champion since his departure from the Harry Harvey Stable.

Dancer returned to Los Angeles a week later. Hollywood publicists Bob Wellman and Warren Eves had done such an excellent job of pushing Albatross and the American Classic that Dancer was a celebrity aboard the jumbo 747 carrying him and Rachel back to the West Coast. Stanley ended up inviting the aircraft's entire crew to the race, arranging free passes for anyone wanting them. There were many takers.

Nostalgia was in the air as Albatross prepared for the final competitive event of his three-season campaign over North America's race tracks. The drivers of the great horses who had faced him over the years were lavish in their praise as they reminisced.

Bruce Nickells, the driver of Kentucky, recalled that his horse had come close to beating Super Bird at Hollywood Park in 1971. "But the more I race against him, the more I know I can't beat him," Nickells said frankly. "Some people call him 'freak' and other names, but I think they're wrong. He's simply a great, great horse . . . a horse that people will always remember."

Jack Bailey, whose Bye Bye Max had chased Bird for two full seasons, termed the Dancer pacer "a super horse. It's funny," Bailey added, "you finish up close to him and you figure, 'Maybe the next time I can beat him.' But, when the next time comes, he just runs off and hides on you."

And Herve Filion, the man who had defeated Albatross more than any other? "I beat him occasionally, but I really don't think he was 100 percent those times," Filion reported. "As far as I'm concerned, Albatross is the super horse of harness racing. A horse is not a machine, I realize, but Albatross was the next thing to one."

The most flattering tribute of all was contained in the U.S. Trotting Association's weekly newsletter, *In Harness*. "A mark of a great

Bruce Nickells, trainer-driver of Albatross rival Kentucky. (USTA photo)

athlete, and Albatross qualifies as an equine athlete of Olympic stature, can be measured in many ways," the USTA said. "Fans remember mighty achievements like Babe Ruth's 60 home runs, but few can recall the name of the man (Roger Maris) who hit 61 in a single season.

"The same is true of great horses. Albatross, who has rewritten the U.S. Trotting Association record book in three seasons, has the same charisma as Babe Ruth. Fans know Albatross, and in his three

Jack Bailey, the driver of Albatross rival Bye Bye Max, has a bit of fun with the Vernon Downs photographer. (Mike Taylor photo)

years of campaigning, more people have seen the Big Bird in actual competition than any Standardbred in history . . ."

A more unusual token of honor came the great pacer's way when the City of Industry, a community about 30 miles outside of Los Angeles, obliged the Hollywood Park management and named a main artery in a new shopping center "Albatross Street."

Nearly 20,000 racing devotees, many from hundreds or even thousands of miles away, flocked to the huge and handsome harness racing palace on Friday night, December 1, 1972, to offer a sentimental adieu to Albatross. It was a crisp, cool night for Southern California, and you could see the steam shooting out the nostrils of the eight entries in the American Pacing Classic as they went their warm-up miles.

Stanley Dancer, killing time in the driver's lounge, seemed calm and relaxed as he watched television, chatted with writers and drivers, and accepted the offers of good fortune from well-wishers. Beneath the veneer, however, he was tense and tight, anxious for the

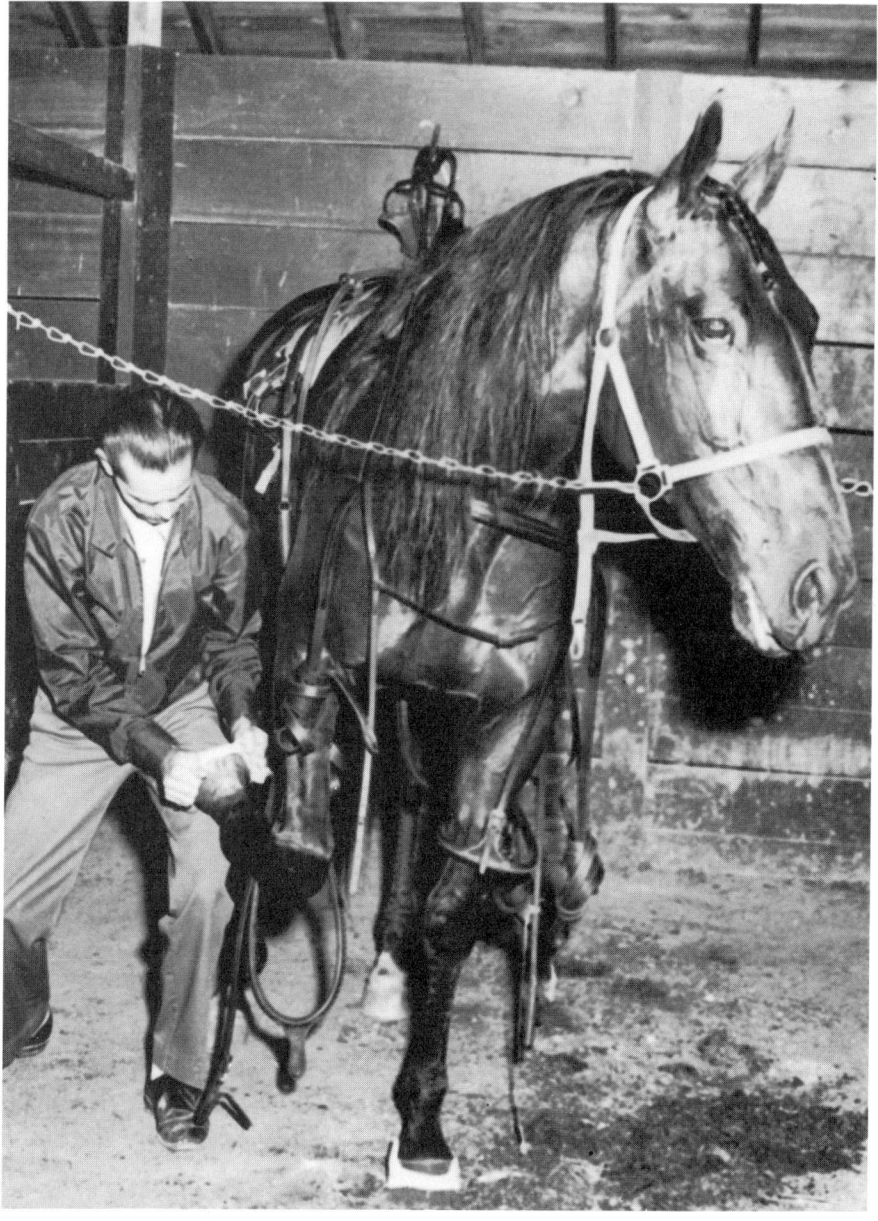

Night watchman Roger Pritchard puts scalpers on the world champion for the last time prior to the pacer's final race at Hollywood Park. (Bill Taylor photo)

race to go to post, anxious for it to be over. Only three weeks earlier he had faced a similar situation with Triple Crown trotting champion Super Bowl. Super Bowl, sporting a win skein of 12 straight seemed like a cinch to close his career with a win in the $100,000

Dancer, Wideman and Pritchard put the final touches to Bird's rigging before his career-ending start in the American Pacing Classic. (Bill Taylor photo)

American Trotting Classic over the same oval. Yet the great Star's Pride son had drawn a wet, sticky track, not to his liking at all, and had gone down to defeat.

And Dancer had Bret Hanover in mind as he awaited the start of the mile and an eighth American Pacing Classic. Bret, closing out his racing career in the 1966 edition of the same race, had lost his poise and bowed unceremoniously. Frank Ervin, in misery from an abscessed jaw, had been too weak to control and rate his beloved Big Bum. Bret had set his own frantic pace and tired in the final eighth. Two horses roared past him. Instead of winding up his three-year campaign in a blaze of deserved glory, Bret had finished third. It was the only time in 68 races that he had ended up worse than second.

Stanley Dancer was only too happy to abandon the blaring TV set when the paddock judge summoned the Classic field.

Minutes later, the eight contestants were on the track—Albatross with Dancer, Nansemond with Filion, Kentucky with Nickells, Bye Bye Max with Bailey, Isle Of Wight with Tom Wilburn, Horton Hanover with Stan Bayless, Banner Ranger with Lucien Fontaine and El Patron with Eddie Wheeler.

Stanley climbs into sulky to take Albatross to post in the last race of his career. (Bill Taylor photo)

Announcer Roy Shudt was offering a litany of Albatross's accomplishments. It took a while. Finally, with the crowd pressing closer to the apron fence, the race was under way.

Dancer was being conservative. He tucked Albatross in fourth

Albatross steams across the finish wire for the last time in winning the 1972 American Pacing Classic. (Hollywood Park photo)

It's time to say farewell after Albatross closes his career with a victory in the $100,000 American Pacing Classic in California. (Hollywood Park photo)

while Kentucky and Nansemond battled furiously for the lead. Kentucky won it and led the eight down to the quarter in 27.4. Then Nansemond swept around him to steal it away. Filion wanted his horse on the front end. It would cost Albatross something to get around him.

The big, rolling thunder of the crowd's roar began when Dancer pulled his horse off the fence. It grew louder as Albatross made his charge. If Filion had hoped to park him out, he was whistling in the dark. Within seconds Albatross was on top, slicing through the cool night air, ruling the roost, leading his subjects, winning the Pacing Classic. By five lengths.

The half was in 59 seconds. The three quarters in 1:29.2. The mile in 1:56.3. The mile and an eighth in 2:11.3.

The timing was well off the 2:09.1 world mark set by True Duane in the 1966 Classic. Stanley Dancer couldn't have cared less. Neither could the 20,000 screaming harness buffs. The throng had seen a super horse in a great performance. That was enough to earn him a booming, standing ovation. A vociferous vote of appreciation.

The winner's circle was jammed. Rachel Dancer was there. The Hanover crew—John Simpson Sr., Hal Jones, Murray Brown and others—was there. Track chieftains Marvin Shapiro, David Butler and Pres Jenuine were there. Various and sundry county and state officials were also there, squeezing into the fringes of the gathering, hoping to be included in the pictures.

In the heart of the mass, in the eye of the storm, stood Stanley Dancer, a giant blanket of flowers draped around his neck, cascading down the front of him to his knees so that it looked as if he were wearing a bulky floral overcoat. A broad slash of a grin was painted across his face. It signified happiness, certainly, but it also advertised relief.

It was over.

Almost.

Col. Dave Herman, public relations director of Brandywine Raceway, and John W. Rollins, one of the faithful band who had stood firmly beside Stanley Dancer through his bitter struggle with the Bert James forces that spring, had asked him to ship Albatross back to Dover Downs for a farewell ceremony on Sunday. Dancer was happy to accommodate them.

Albatross was flown back East on Saturday. The next afternoon a record 5,024 fans jammed the small Delaware track to bid their own farewell to history's most successful pacing horse. Most had never seen Albatross in competition, but they were aware of his massive reputation, cherished his greatness and wanted to be a part of his official retirement rites.

All the men and women who had come to Dancer's rescue in the spring were present—Rollins, Louis Silverstein, Hilda Silverstein, Hazel Shriner and John Simpson. Stanley, choosing simple yet power-

Royal treatment for the champion at Dover Downs. (Dover Downs photo)

ful words, struggling to control his emotions, thanked them publicly for their faith and loyalty.

He jogged Albatross once around the track before turning the reins over to Simpson, the man who guides the fortunes of the Hanover Shoe Farms. Then Simpson, in a gesture overflowing with symbolism, drove the great pacer slowly up the track.

Dancer's work was done. Hanover's was only beginning.

Stanley presents Albatross whip to David Buckson, president of Dover Downs. The whip had hardly been used. (Dover Downs photo)

Albatross, with sulky and all his tack headed for the Hall of Fame of the Trotter, is paraded for the last time at Dover Downs. (Dover Downs photo)

With "Auld Lang Syne" being played in the background, Albatross heads for the van that carried him to Hanover Shoe Farms and the start of his new career. (Dover Downs photo)

APPENDIX

ALBATROSS'S LIFETIME RECORD

LIFETIME EARNINGS—$1,201,470 71 Starts 59 Wins 8 Seconds 3 Thirds

ALBATROSS b h, 4, by Meadow Skipper, Voodoo Hanover by Dancer Hanover
Amicable Stable, Hanover, Pa.   (Tr. S. Dancer)

FOUR-YEAR-OLD RACING RECORD

SPK 5/8 1972 1:54 3/5 26-20-4-1 \$459,921

Dec1-72 Hol 1 1/8 :27 4/5 :59 1:29 2/5 1:56 3/5 2:11 3/5 ft 1-10 1 4-1½ 4-1½ 1-½ 1-4 1-5 DancerS FFA 2:11 3/5 Albatross Nansemond Horton Hanover

Nov 24-72^{6}Hol	1	:27^{2}	:59	1:28^{2}	1:56	ft 1-5	▲	1	1	$1^{1\frac{1}{2}}$	1^{4}	$1^{4\frac{3}{4}}$			DancerS^{8}	FFA 1:56	Albatross Nansem'd ByeByeMax
Oct 28-72 RR	1¼	:29^{2}	1:02	1:33^{4}	2:33^{3}	ft NB		1	1	1	$1^{2\frac{1}{2}}$	$1^{2\frac{3}{4}}$			DancerS^{6}	Dby 2:33^{3}	Albatross Nansem'd Ban'rR'nger
Oct 21-72 Fhld	1	:28	:57	1:26^{4}	1:57^{3}	ft 1-3	▲	1	1	1	1^{11}	1^{17}			DancerS^{4}	FFA 1:57^{3}	Albatross Nansem'd SundanceD.
Oct 7-72 LB	1	:29^{3}	1:00^{4}	1:30^{4}	2:00	gd 1-5	▲	2	2	2	$2^{\frac{3}{4}}$	$2^{1\frac{3}{4}}$			DancerS^{1}	Inv 2:00^{1}	Nansemond Albatr's Fr'd'mNow
9-30 Btva	20000 gd Inv mi	28^{4}	1:01	1:32^{1}	2:00^{3}		5	1	1	1	1^{2}	$1^{1\frac{1}{4}}$	2:00^{3}	*.20	(S.Dancer)		Albatross, Nansemond, GeneBloss
9-19 Dela	2000 ft FA mi	28^{3}	:58	1:26^{4}	1:55^{3}		1	1	1	1	1^{40}	1^{33}	1:55^{3}	N.B.	(S.Dancer)		Albatross, CissyT.Adios, Stdy.April
9- 9 VD¾	20000 gd Opn mi	27^{4}	:58^{4}	1:27^{3}	1:56^{2}		5	2	2	1	1^{8}	1^{9}	1:56^{2}	N.B.	(S.Dancer)		Albatross, SteadyBrave, Dean Butler
9- 2 Brd⅝	25000 ft FA Inv mi	27	:59^{3}	1:29^{3}	1:57^{4}		2	1^{0}	1	1	1^{3}	$1^{1\frac{1}{2}}$	1:57^{4}	*.40	(S.Dancer)		Albatross, Nansemond, Kentucky
8-26 GrR⅝	59400 ft Stk mi	29^{1}	1:00^{2}	1:30^{3}	1:58^{2}		5	1	1	1	1^{1}	1hd	1:58^{2}	*.65	(S.Dancer)		Albatross, Nansemond, Kentucky
8-18 Haw^{1}	44450 ft Stk mi	29^{2}	1:00	1:30	1:57^{1}		5	6	6	4	$4^{3\frac{1}{2}}$	2^{3}	1:57^{4}	*.30	(S.Dancer)		Nansemond, Albatross, Kentucky
8-11 YR	25000 ft FA mi	29^{2}	:59^{3}	1:29^{3}	1:57^{4}		4	5	4^{0}	1^{0}	$1^{2\frac{1}{2}}$	$1^{2\frac{1}{2}}$	1:57^{4}	*.50	(S.Dancer)		Albatross, Nansemond, Tar.Skipper
7-22 Brd⅝	27750 ft FA mi	28	:58^{4}	1:27^{3}	1:56^{1}		2	1^{0}	1	2	2^{6}	$4^{8\frac{3}{4}}$	1:58	*.05	(S.Dancer)		Nansemond, Kentucky, RomanoHan.
15Jly 72 Stga ft	16000 Inv m	:28^{4}	:57^{2}	1:26^{4}	1:57^{3}		7	1^{0}	1	1	1	1^{14}	1:57^{3}	N.B.	(DancerS)		Albatross, Jonathan Han, Nifty Nelse
8Jly 72 BR ft	12000 4yr Stk m	:29^{1}	:59^{1}	1:29^{2}	1:57^{4}		3	1^{0}	1	1	1^{5}	1^{15}	1:57^{4}	N.B.	(DancerS)		Albatross, Airy Way, Anchor Boy
1Jly 72 Spk(⅝) ft	25000 FFA m	:27^{3}	:57^{3}	1:25^{4}	1:54^{3}		3	1	1	1	$1^{2\frac{1}{2}}$	$1^{1\frac{1}{2}}$	1:54^{3}	*.20	(DancerS)		Albatross, Kentucky, Nansemond
23Jun 72 WR(⅝) ft	25750 FFA Inv m	:28^{1}	:58^{3}	1:28^{2}	1:56^{3}		3	1^{0}	1	1	1^{1}	1^{3}	1:56^{3}	*.35	(DancerS)		Albatross, Bye Bye Max, Kentucky
16Jun 72 Det(1) ft	58295 4yr Stk m	:29^{3}	1:00^{1}	1:30	1:58^{2}		1	1	2	1	1^{1}	$1^{\frac{1}{2}}$	1:58^{2}	*.30	(DancerS)		Albatross, Nansemond, Trpt Skppr
3Jun 72 RR ft	91000 4yr Stk 1$\frac{1}{16}$	:29^{1}	1:29^{4}	1:58^{2}	2:06		1	4	1	1	1^{1}	$1^{1\frac{1}{4}}$	2:06	N.B.	(DancerS)		Albatross, H.T.Luca, Dexter Hanvr
28May72 Brd(⅝) A ft	25000 FFA m	:28^{4}	:58^{1}	1:28^{2}	1:56^{3}		5	5	3	$^{0}1\frac{1}{2}$	1^{3}	$1^{7\frac{1}{2}}$	1:56^{3}	*.20	(DancerS)		Albatross, IsleOfWight, FrdmNow
29Apr 72 LB(⅝) ft	40000 FFA m	:28^{3}	:58^{2}	1:27^{4}	1:56^{2}		5	1^{0}	1	1	1^{1}	$1^{\frac{3}{4}}$	1:56^{2}	*.90	(DancerS)		Albatross, ByeByeMax, Kentucky
4-20 May	25000 sy Inv mi	31^{2}	1:05	1:36^{4}	2:07^{4}		2	1	1	1	$1^{1\frac{1}{2}}$	1^{nk}	2:07^{4}	*.30	(S.Dancer)		Albatross, HailToAll, CafineKid
4-10 Spk⅝	80425 ft 4yr Stk mi	29^{2}	1:01^{3}	1:30^{1}	2:00		2	2	1	1	$1^{3\frac{1}{2}}$	1^{3}	2:00	*.20	(S.Dancer)		Albatross, ProperTime, ElPatron
3-25 LB⅝	40000 ft FA mi	29^{1}	:59^{3}	1:29^{1}	1:59		5	7	7	6^{0}	$6^{2\frac{1}{2}}$	$2^{1\frac{1}{2}}$	1:59^{2}	*.50	(S.Dancer)		IsleOfWight, Albatross, ByeByeMax
3-19 WR⅝	50000 ft FA mi	28^{1}	:59^{1}	1:28^{4}	1:59^{4}		6	1^{0}	1	1	1^{2}	2^{1}	2:00	*.40	(S.Dancer)		Is.OfWight, Albatross, RoyCountN
3-11 LB⅝ ft inv	m	:30^{3}	1:02^{4}	1:31^{2}	2:00^{2}		5	5	3	2^{0}	$2^{\frac{1}{4}}$	3^{ns}	2:00^{2}	*.10	(S.Dancer)		IsleOfWight, MissConnaAdios, Albat's

THREE-YEAR-OLD RACING RECORD

Lex (1) 1971 1:54 4/5 28-25-2-1 $558,009

11-12 Hol^1 ft FA		1⅛	:28^3	1:01^1	1:32^2	2:13^4	1	3	1	1	1^2	1 1¾	2:13^4	*.20	S Dan	Albatross Kentucky RumCustomer
11- 5 Hol^1 ft cd		m	:27^3	:57	1:29^1	1:57^4	12	4^0	5^0	3	1^6	1 3½	1:57^4	*.70	S Dan	Albatross HortonHanover RumCustomer
10-29 Hol^1 ft 3yr		m	:28^2	:58^4	1:30^1	1:58^2	8	7^0	1	1	1^2	1¾	1:58^2	*.30	S Dan	Albatross WinningWorthy Nansemond
10-23 Hol^1 ft inv		m	:28^4	:58^1	1:27^2	1:57	2	1^0	2	2	2nd	1 ns	1:57	*.20	S Dan	Albatross Kentucky BuckeyeBill
10- 9 LB⅝ ft 3yr-inv		m	:29	:59^2	1:30^1	1:58^3	4	4	4	4^0	3^1	1 1¾	1:58^3	*.40	S Dan	Albatross Nansemond Scrooge
10- 2 Lex^1	23789 ft Stk	mi	30	:58^4	1:26^2	1:54^4	1	8	3^0	1	1^3	1^3	1:54^4	BAR	(S.Dancer)	Albtrss.(bar), Win.Wrty., Sprngfld.
10- 2 Lex^1	23789 ft Stk	mi	27^2	:57^2	1:26^4	1:54^4	9	10	7^0	6^0	2^2	1^4	1:54^4	BAR	(S.Dancer)	Albtrss.(bar), Win.Wty., DexterHn.
9-23 Dela	10296 ft 3yr Stk	mi	31^2	1:03^1	1:36^2	2:04^2	2	2	2	2	2½	2¾	2:04^3	N.B.	(S.Dancer)	Nansemond, Albatross, H.T.Luca
9-23 Dela	30889 ft 3yr Stk	mi	29	:59^1	1:29	1:57^2	1	2	1	1	1½	2^1	1:57^3	BAR	(S.Dancer)	Nansmnd., Albtrss.(bar), ElPatron
9-23 Dela	30889 ft 3yr Stk	mi	29^1	:59^3	1:29^4	1:58^1	7	4	4	1^0	1 nk	1 ns	1:58^1	BAR	(S.Dancer)	Albtrss.(bar), Nansmnd., Sprngfld.
9-17 Det^1	25000 ft 3yr Stk	mi	28^4	:57^4	1:28	1:58^2	3	3^0	3^0	1	1^1	1^3	1:58^2	*.20	(S.Dancer)	Albatross, Win.Worthy, Springfield
9-13 ScD⅝	23000 gd 3yr Stk	mi	29^4	1:01^2	1:33^4	2:03^3	7	4^0	1	1	1^1	1 1¾	2:03^3	*.10	(S.Dancer)	Albatross, HighIdeal, VeriSpecial
8-14 Mea⅝ ft Adios Stk		1	29.3	:59.1	1:29.3	1:59.3	1	2	1	1	1 2½	1^3	1:59.3	*.20	(S.Dancer)	Albatross, H.T.Luca, PaulasHanover
8-14 Mea⅝ ft Adios Stk		1	29	:58.2	1:28.2	1:58.3	10	9	6^0	2^0	2 1½	1 1½	1:58.3	*.20	(S.Dancer)	Albatross, H.T.Luca, DexterHanover
8-6 RR ft Stk		1	29.1	:59.4	1:30	1:59.4	6	5	4^0	4^0	3^1	1 2½	1:59.4	*.10	(S.Dancer)	Albatross, DexterHanover, H.T.Luca
7-31 VD¾ gd 3 yr ec		1	29.3	1:02.2	1:31.4	2:00.3	1	1	1	1	1 1½	1 3½	2:00.3	barred	(S.Dancer)	Albatross, PaulosHanover, PatTaylor
7-24† GrR⅝ ft Stk	24800	m	29.2	1:01.2	1:32.4	2:00.4	5	1^0	1	1	1/1½	1/1¾	2:00.4	*.05	(S.Dancer)	Albatross, HighIdeal, Springfield
7-16† YR ft Fut	106795	m	29.3	1:01.3	1:31.3	2:00	7	1	1	1	1/1	1/1½	2:00	*.10	(S.Dancer)	Albatross, H.T.Luca, HighIdeal
7-10† Rich ft Stk	34400	m	30	1:01.1	1:30.4	1:58.3	3	1^0	1	1	1/2	1/1¼	1:58.3	*.05	(S.Dancer)	Albtrss, HighIdeal, RobRonTarios
6-27† BB⅝ ft open	36050	m	29.2	58.3	1:28	1:57.2	1	2	1	1	1/2½	1/3¾	1:57.2	*.05	(S.Dancer)	Albtrss, RobRonTarios, Nansemd.
6-20^1 BB⅝-8a	ft 3yr Inv.	m	.28^3	.59^4	1.29	1.57^2	3	2	1	1	1^6	1 4½	1.57^2	0.10†	(DancerS)	Albtrss, DexterHanover, SetonHanover
6-10^1 H.P.(⅝)	ft 3yr Stk	m	.29^2	1.00^1	1.30	1.59^3	7	5	2^0	1	1 1½	1 2½	1.59^3	0.10†	(DancerS)	Albatross, DebAdios, SlyHeel
6- 5^1 Brd(⅝)	ft 3yr Stk	m	.28^4	.58^4	1.28^1	1.57^1	11	6	2^0	2^0	1^1	1 2½	1.57^1	0.40†	(DancerS)	Albatross, Nansemond, DexterHanover
5-28^1 Y.R.	ft 3yr Stk	m	.29	1.00^2	1.30^4	1.59^3	6	1^0	1	1	1 2½	1 3½	1.59^3	0.20†	(DancerS)	Albatross, Springfield, H.T.Luca
5-22^1 R.R.	ft 3yr Stk	m	.29^1	1.01	1.31^3	2.00^2	5	1^0	1	1	1 2½	1 3½	2.00^2	e0.20†	(DancerS)	Albatross, Nansemond, TarportSkippe
5-18^1 R.R.	ft 3yr Stk	m	.29^3	.59^4	1.31^2	2.01^2	7	2^0	1	1	1 1½	1 1½	2.01^2	0.30†	(DancerS)	Albatross, Nansemond, Springfield
5- 8^1 R.R.	gd JFA AA	m	.30^1	1.01	1.30^4	2.01	6	6	4^0	4^0	3 2½	3½	2.01^1	0.20†	(DancerS)	Colonial, CarbineHanover, Albatross
5- 1^1 Rock	ft 3yr Inv.	m	.29^3	1.00^3	1.31^3	2.01^3	5	6	4^0	1^0	1^6	1 10¾	2.01^3	0.30†	(DancerS)	Albatross, TarportSkpr., MountainSkpr.

VD (3/4) 1970 1:57 4/5 17-14-2-1 $183,540

10-31^{0} R.R. ft 2yr Stk m .29^{3} 1.00 1.31^{1} 2.00^{4} 5 3^{0} 1 1 1^{2½} 1^{4} 2.00^{4} 0.20†(HarveyH) Albatross, SetonHanover, Nansemond

10-24 R.R. ft A-1 10000 m 30 1:00:3 1:30:4 2:01:1 5 3 2 2^{0} 1/^{nk} 1/^{nk} 2:01:1 *.30 (Hrvy) Albatross, NardinsLuck, ShreWill

10- 3 Y.R. sy 2yr Stk 53495 m 30:3 1:01:1 1:31:3 2:02 8 5 1 1 1/2 1/2½ 2:02 *.30 (Hrvy) Albatross, Nansemond, Springfield

9-28Y.R. ft 2yr Stk 27747 m 29:4 59:4 1:30:3 2:00:1 9 5 6^{0} 1^{0} 1/5 1/8 2:00:1 *.70 (Hrvy) Albatross, HighIdeal, Nansemond

9-15 Det(1) sy 2yr Stk 12500 m 30:2 1:01:4 1:32:1 2:02:3 5 2^{0} 1 2 2/1 1/3 2:02:3 *.60 (HHrvy) Albatross, SlyHeel, SprngsPride

9- 6 Ind(1) gd 2yr Stk 31378 m 28:2 58:2 1:28:3 1:58:3 1 5 3^{0} 1 1/1¼ 1/1 1:58:3 N.B. (HHrvy) Albatross, RaceByrd, CountBret

9- 6 Ind(1) gd 2yr Stk 31378 m 28:3 58:2 1:28:3 1:59 8 3^{0} 1 1 1/½ 1/4½ 1:59 N.B. (HHrvy) Albatross, LoclTime, Trprt Skppr

8-14 Mdws(⅝) ft 2yr Stk 17370 m 29 1:00:3 1:30:3 2:00:2 8 1 1 1 1/2 2/^{ns} 2:00:2 *.70 (HHrvy) SetonHn, Albatross, TrprtSkppr

8- 8 PcD(⅝) ft 2yr Stk 11445 m 28:4 59:2 1:29:4 1:59:1 1 1 1 1 1/1½ 1/3½ 1:59:1 *.60 (HHrvy) Albatross, DexrHn, Springfield

7-27 VD¾ 9400 ft 2yr Ec mi 27 :57^{3} 1:27^{4} 1:57^{4} 4 1 1 1 1^{1½} 1^{1} 1:57^{4} *1.90 (H.Harvey) Albatross, PaulosHan., RaceByrd

7-10 Rich 16610 ft 2yr Stk mi 32 1:04^{2} 1:35^{2} 2:03^{3} 2 2 2 2 2¼ 2^{nk} 2:03^{3} 1.05 (H.Harvey) HighIdeal, Albatross, TimelockLob.

7- 4 GdnC⅝ ft Stk mi 30 1:04^{2} 1:33^{2} 2:03^{3} 4 1 1 1 1 1^{1¾} 2:03^{3} e1.65 (H.Harvey) Albatross, HighIdeal, Gr'tDreamer

6-25 Lau⅝ 8133 ft 2yr Stk mi 30^{2} 1:02^{1} 1:32 2:02^{3} 3x 8x 6 5 5^{7¾} 3^{5¼} 2:03^{3} *1.00 (H.Harvey) JollyRoger, RaceByrd, Albatross

6-17 Nfld 1000 sy 2yr mi 30^{2} 1:05^{1} 1:37^{2} 2:06^{4} 1 1 1 1 1^{4} 1^{10} 2:06^{4} *.20 (H.Harvey) Albatross, OpenUp, EverytimeAnn

6- 4 Spk⅝ 9500 ft 2yr Stk mi 32^{2} 1:04^{2} 1:34^{4} 2:04^{3} 6 1 3 1 1^{3} 1^{3½} 2:04^{3} *2.00 (H.Harvey) Albatross, Bret'sBrat, GoldTrick

May 28-70 H.P⅝ 1:31^{4} 1:03^{3} 1:35 2:06^{3} ft 4½ 6^{0} 4^{0} 4 1½ 1^{nk} HarveyH^{7} st 13550 2:06$^{3/5}$ Albatross, Jolly Roger, Tar Adios

May 20-70 Mea⅝ 1:33^{1} 1:06^{1} 1:36^{1} 2:07^{2} ft N.B. 7 2^{0} 1 1^{2} 1^{3½} HarveyH^{7} 2y300 2:07$^{2/5}$ Albatross, Game Cash, Justarrived

INDEX

Adapter, 88
Adios, 32, 34, 63
Adios Butler, 224
Adios Butler Pace, 195
Adios Harry, 56, 135, 138, 209
Adios Harry Invitational, 207
Adios Scarlet, 160
Adios Stake, 116–17, 124, 221
Adora's Dream, 100
Airliner, 124, 126
Airy Way, 124
Albatross Stable, 13, 77, 90, 149, 153, 173, 177
Albatross Street, 226
Albatross Syndicate, 102, 154–55
Alcindor, Lew, 83
Almahurst Farm, 30
Almahurst Stake, 136
Alnoff and Gargreve Stables, 124
American-National, 51, 153, 167, 169, 173, 176–77, 188, 191
American Pacing Classic, 149–51, 222, 224, 226, 228, 230–31
American Trotting Classic, 228
Amicable Stable, 175, 188, 199–200, 212, 218
Amtrak, 173
Andy Kerr Memorial Pace, 57–59, 68
Apache Stable, 124
Arden Downs, 63
Arden Downs Stake, 60
Arden Fairground, 41, 43, 66, 68, 73, 79, 85, 87
Arden Hills Farm, 32
Armbro Flight, 30
Armbro Laddie, 48
Armstrong Brothers, 30, 77, 91–93, 167–68, 179
Armstrong, C. Edwin, 77
Armstrong, H. Charles, 77
Armstrong, J. Elgin, 37, 77, 149
Arthur, James, 32, 84
Atlantic City Raceway, 48, 50
Ault, Mr. and Mrs. Chester V., 133
Aurora, Ohio, 140

Avella, Pennsylvania, 27, 30, 40
Avery, Earle, 20
Ayres, 181

Babb, Ben, 160
Bailey, Jack, 9, 193, 224, 226
Bain, Bill, 220
Baldwin, Ralph, 56, 63, 198
Baltimore Raceway, 18
Bancroft, 30
Banner Ranger, 219, 223, 228
Batavia Downs, 117, 219
Batavia, New York, 117
Batman (horse), 149
Batman (television character), 149
Battle of Brandywine Pace, 104, 196
Bayless, Stan, 228
Beaulieau, Roland, 74, 136
Beaver Stakes, 107–8
Bergstein, Stan, 9, 188–89
Berry, Thomas S., 32, 34, 44, 63
Beslove, Bob, 9
Best Of All, 63, 181
Betty Hanover, 84
Big Bum: The Story of Bret Hanover, 8
Blackhurst, Randy, 66, 79, 94
Bloom, 218
Bloomfield Hills, Michigan, 124
Blue Bonnets Raceway, 106–8, 200, 221
Blue Chip Farms, 83
Bob Hanover, 37
Boehm, Edward Marshall, 116
Bonafice, Walter, 57–58
Bonjour Hanover, 83, 187
Boring, Chris, 119
Brampton, Ontario, Canada, 30, 77
Brandywine Raceway, 18, 27, 64, 93, 104–6, 195–98, 207–9, 213, 231
Brenna Hanover, 187
Bret Hanover, 7, 36, 50–52, 55–57, 63, 74, 86, 95, 98, 102–3, 111, 122, 129, 133, 135–38, 143, 148, 152, 169, 187, 200, 207, 211–12, 218, 228
Breton Hanover, 37
Bret's Brat, 51

Broglio, Eligiol (Lee), 174–78
Brown, Dave L. Estate, 133
Brown, Dr. J. Glen, 7–8, 14, 91–92, 153–54, 165, 167–70, 172, 179, 186–87, 222
Brown, Murray, 8, 139, 187–88, 210–11, 219, 231
Buckley, Dr. E. R., 46
Buck, Leonard, 37
Buckson, David, 233
Buffalo Raceway, 205–6
Bullet Hanover, 58, 63, 65, 122, 181
Burright, Harry, 205
Burton Livestock Exchange, 56
Butler, David, 231
Buxton, Dick, 155
Bye Bye Byrd, 206
Bye Bye Max, 171, 193, 200, 209, 217, 223–24, 226
Bye Bye Sam, 100
Byram, Connecticut, 74

Cafine Kid, 191
Camden Fibre Co., 166
Camden Trust Co., 166
Cameron, Del, 37, 88
Camper, Bob, 124
Camp, William M., Jr., 125, 160
Canadian Juvenile Stakes, 54
Canadian Pacing Derby, 211
Cane Futurity, 100, 108–11, 125, 221
Cantor, Allan, 172
Capital Hill Farm, 69, 125
Carbine Hanover, 96
Cardigan Bay, 83, 85, 88, 109, 149, 161, 169, 207
Cardigan Bay Pace, 209, 212
Carney, Les, 56
Castleton Farms, 18, 30, 124, 134, 198
Celanese Corp., 166
Chamberlain, Wilt, 18
Chamber of Commerce, Broward County, 81
Chapman, John, 102, 197
Charlebois Brothers, 56
Chicago Downs, 205
Chicago Tribune, 9, 202
Childs, Joe, 133
Churchill, Dr. Edwin, 9, 78–79, 82, 85, 87, 115, 156, 208–9
Cissy T. Adios, 218
City of Industry, 226
Claridge, 171
Clark, Charlie, 50, 58, 62, 98
Clearview Stables, 20
Clemson College, 182

Cobb, Eddie, 70
Cohen, Leonard, 113
Coldstream Stud Thoroughbred Farm, 24
Coleridge, Samuel Taylor, 24–25
Colgate University, 57
Colonial, 96
Columbia George, 74, 138, 152, 181
Commodore Pace, 113–14
Common Pleas Court, Philadelphia, 177, 179
Connelly Container, Corp., 166
Connors, William C., 50
Continental Purse, 200–201
Cooke, S. Jay, 13–16, 167, 173–75, 177, 179
Cool It, 48
Copeland, Leroy, 94
Cosell, Howard, 206
Count Bret, 65
Countess Adios, 30
Countess Vivian, 20, 34
Country Don, 20
Cox, Bob, 119
Crank, Vernon, 171
Crilley, Paul, 20
Crown Cork and Seal, 166

Dahle, Dudley C., 37
Daily News, New York, 100, 114
Daily Sentinel, Rome, New York, 9
Dale Frost, 20, 34, 43
Dam, Jim, 56
Dancer Hanover, 18, 84, 108, 181
Dancer, Harold (Sonny), Jr., 66–67, 196, 220
Dancer, Harold, Sr., 9, 49, 220–21
Dancer, James, 220
Dancer, Rachel, 83, 100, 136, 140–41, 144–47, 150, 155, 157, 161, 177, 195, 205, 231
Dancer, Ronnie, 9, 94, 142, 144, 196, 220
Dancer, Vernon, 9, 143, 161–62 171, 178, 196, 198, 220
Daniel C. Parish Memorial, 191–92
Dan Patch, 191
Dartmouth, 198
Dayton *Daily News*, 123
Decker, Richard, 108
Decorum, 83, 112, 136, 138, 174
Dee, Bobbie, 111
Deer Park, N.Y., 148
DeFrank, Joe, 200
Delaware County Fairground, 85, 117, 216–18
Delaware, Ohio, 100, 117, 121, 222

DesRosiers, Aime, 200
Dexter, Arthur W., Jr., 124
Dexter Cup, 113, 198
Dexter Hanover, 37, 65, 84, 95, 106, 108, 117, 124, 127–28, 132, 134, 197
Dexter, Mildred, 124
Dexter, Thomas A., 37, 124
D. Judge, 132
Doc's Fritzi, 26, 74
Dottie's Pick, 30
Dougherty, Edward J., 199
Downing, Richard, 122
Dover Downs, 231–34
Dufty, Dale, 119
Dunnigan, Eddie, 61–62
Du Quoin Fairground, 117
Du Quoin, Illinois, 117, 122, 213

Eaton, Tom, 137
Ed Byrd, 202, 205
Effrat, Louis, 68, 96
Egan, Fred, 182–83
Egan Hanover, 183
Egyptian Acres Farm, 94, 113, 152, 159, 208, 220
Egyptian Candor, 83
Egyptian Jody, 102
El Patron, 124, 126–28, 132, 209, 223, 228
Empire Standardbred Sales, 73
Ervin, Frank, 37, 56, 63, 74, 86, 102, 155, 207
Evans, Donald P., 214
Evans, Jane, 9
Evans, Larry, 9, 65, 120, 138
Evans, Marta, 9
Eves, Warren, 9, 224
Experimental Championship Ratings, 94
Express Rodney, 32

Farmington, Connecticut, 37
Farmstead Acres, 57
Fearon, Sen. George R., 217
Filion, Henri, 196
Filion, Herve, 9, 37, 70, 100, 124–31, 142, 162, 171, 174, 177, 191–92, 196–97, 200, 207, 211, 216, 219, 224, 228, 231
Filion, Renald, 196
Filion, Yves, 196
First Lee, 88
Flag Time, 36–37, 40–41, 43, 54
Fleming, Vic, 63
Flora, Earl, 9
Flying Bret, 49–51, 58, 62, 98–99

Foley, Red, 114
Folger, Henry, 53
Fontaine, Lucien, 228
Foodland Store, Vernon, N.Y., 56
Forsyth, Earl, 124
Fortune Hanover, 48
Fosner, S. Harvey, 114, 199
Founder's Plate, 27, 70, 196, 198–99
Fox Stake, 63–65, 102, 182
Fox Valley Trotting Club, 205
Franklin, Virginia, 125
Fraser, Terry, 75
Freehold Raceway, 191–92, 219
Fresh Yankee, 153
Froelich Hanover, 37

Galt, Dr. Raymond M., 158–59
Galt, Jane Falley, 100
Galvin, Bill, 9
Game Cash, 48–49
Gamecock, 48, 181
Gamely, 124–28, 132, 134
Garden City Raceway, 54
Garnsey, Glen, 18, 119, 125, 134–35, 148
Garrett, Joe, 44
Geers Stake, 49–50, 117
Gerber, Gordon W., 177, 179
Gilmour, William (Bud), 70, 96, 127, 197
Glen Head, New York, 57
Glickberg, Leo, 214
Gochneaur, Vernon, 140
Goldberg, Rube, 142
Goldstein, Joseph, 78
Good Humor Man, 140
Goshen, New York, 63, 88, 124
Governor Armbro, 30
Governor's Cup, 202
Grand Central Station, 117
Grand Circuit, 32, 48–51, 56–58, 68, 88–89, 112–13, 117, 120, 131, 155
Grant, Hugh, 20, 30
Great Neck, New York, 77
Greenwood Raceway, 112, 191–92, 211–12
Greenwood Stake, 112
Gunner, 153

Hail To All, 191
Hall of Fame of the Trotter, 63, 90, 234
Hal Oaks, 141
Hambletonian Society, 117
Hambletonian Stake, 21, 32, 88, 117, 122, 181–82, 186, 213
Hammett, Philip, 179
Hampshire House, 13–14, 173
Hanover-Hempt Stake, 60, 124

Hanover, Pennsylvania, 49, 181
Hanover Shoe Farms, 14, 30, 49, 59, 75, 84, 181–90, 195, 205, 210, 218–19, 222, 232, 234
Harness Horse, 9, 30, 49, 68
Harness Tracks of America, 188
Harrisburg, Pennsylvania, 18, 36
Harrisburg Standardbred Auction, 37, 43–44, 70, 115
Harrison, Jim, 220
Hart, Margaret, 9
Harvey, Harry, 8, 31–38, 40–44, 46–55, 57–70, 72–75, 77–79, 85, 87–88, 91, 94–95, 98, 102–03, 112, 133, 178, 198, 224
Haughton, Bill, 37–39, 56–57, 62–63, 88, 99, 125, 148, 155, 158, 223
Hawthorne Race Course, 211
Hayes, Bill, 117
Hayes, Christy S., 20
Hazel Park, 50, 105–6
Hecht, Henry, 200
Helicopter, 32, 88
Helman, Ira, 14, 77, 165, 167, 170, 179
Hembach, Jean, 68
Hempt, Max C., 38
Henry T. Adios, 83, 85, 125, 195, 206
Herman, Col. Dave, 9, 196, 231
Hewlett, New York, 124
Hialeah Park, 24
Hickory Smoke, 181
Hickory Way Stables, 214
High Ideal, 51, 54–55, 95, 108, 112
Hill, Charley, 117
Hirsh, Judge Ned L., 177, 179
Hodgins, Clint, 56
Hoffstetter, Paul, Jr., 9, 202
Holiday Park Apartments, 21
Hollins, Virginia, 183
Hollywood Park, 89, 97, 144–48, 222–31
Hoof Beats, 9, 32, 75
Hope Time, 29
Hopkins, William, 199
Horseman & Fair World, 9, 49, 122, 137, 218
Horseman Futurity (Indianapolis), 122, 124
Horse of the Year, 174
Horton Hanover, 149, 223, 228
Howlett Harbor, New York, 50
H. T Luca, 57, 102, 108, 116–17, 124, 126–29, 132, 188, 197
Hudson Stake, 102
Hult, Arthur, 136
Hutt, George, 174

Hutt, Van, 79, 90, 120

Imperial Hanover, 182–83
Imported Messenger, 36
Indianapolis Fairground, 63, 102, 135, 142, 202
Indiana State Fair, 63
Insko, Del, 124, 127, 197
Isle Of Wight, 14, 149, 153, 160, 162, 164, 170–72, 191–93, 195, 217, 223, 228

Jake Jackson, 99–100, 102, 197
Jambo Adam, 30
Jambo Adonis, 30
Jambo Allan, 30
Jambo Andrea, 74
Jambo Bell, 30, 178
Jambo Byrd, 30
James, Albert, 30
James, Bert, Jr., 30
James Bert V., 7–8, 14, 28–32, 34, 36–38, 41, 43–45, 49–51, 54, 59–61, 64–66, 68–70, 73–79, 82, 88, 91, 93, 98, 110, 112, 114, 116, 119–20, 127, 130, 136, 149, 153–55, 162–63, 165–69, 170, 172, 174–75, 177–79, 181, 186–87, 195, 199–200, 222
James Boys Farm, 30, 33, 36–37, 40–41, 73
James Clark Memorial, 171
James, David, 30, 37, 43
James, Donna, 30
James, Jeffrey, 30
James, Judy, 30
James, Mary, 30
James, Peter, 30
Jenuine, Pres, 145, 150, 231
Jersey Journal, 209
Joe Neville Memorial Stake, 105
Joeys Byrd, 43
Johnston, Billy, 205
Johnston, David R., 20
Jolly Roger, 49–51, 53–54, 57, 83, 95, 98–100, 102
Jones, Hal S., 187, 231
Justarrived, 48–49

Karl, Adolph, 114
Kennedy, Dr. Robert L., 66
Kenney, Charles, 8, 21–28, 30–31, 34–35, 38, 136, 198
Kenney, Dr. John S., 22–23, 26, 198
Kennilworth Farms, 148
Kentucky (horse), 145, 148–50, 193, 200,

202, 204, 207, 217, 223–25, 231
Kentucky Derby, 122
Kentucky Futurity, 182
Keys, Ed, 9
Keystone Andy, 149, 171
Keystone Journal, 124, 127–28, 132, 134
Keystone Memento, 83, 95
Keystone Pat, 171
Kimbred Farms, 136
Kingspoint, New York, 148
Kiser, Jack, 192, 195
Knight Dream, 63, 181
Kopas, Jack, 127
Koufax, Sandy, 146
Kristel, Alan, 50
Kristel, Ira, 50

Lafayette, 63
Lagoy, Lee, 56
Lamarre, Jean-Guy, 144, 220
Lana Lobell Farms, 14, 75, 77, 82, 92, 136, 139, 184, 199–200
Langley, Phil, 205
Laughing Girl, 50
Laurel Raceway, 18, 53–54
Laverne Hanover, 63, 72, 187
Lavish Hanover, 187
Lawrence B. Sheppard Pace, 67–68
Law, Willie, 56
L-Bar Farms Corporation, 124
Leavitt, Alan J., 7–8, 14, 73, 75–77, 81–83, 85, 91–92, 110, 135, 139, 153–54, 162, 165, 167, 170, 172, 177, 179, 181, 185–87, 195, 199–200, 221–22
Lehigh Hanover, 48, 83, 85, 122, 125, 181
Lemay, Raymond, 107
Levy, George Morton, 70, 196, 199
Lexington, Kentucky, 24–25, 36, 74
Lexington Red Mile, 20, 25, 48, 50, 56, 68, 131–38, 202, 204, 218
Liberty Bell Park, 18, 20–22, 27, 34, 88–90, 125, 142–43, 160, 162–63, 165, 167–68, 170–71, 174, 176–77, 185, 191, 193, 199, 219
Lieberman, Hilda, 166
Lindsay, Mayor, 114
Little Brown Jug, 100, 117, 122–32, 142, 160, 168, 182, 187, 200, 216, 218
Little Brown Jug Trial, 117–19, 129
Liverman, Irving, 195
Living Hall of Fame, 165, 182
Livonia, Michigan, 200
L.K. Shapiro Stakes, 148
Local Time, 65, 99, 102, 124
Long Island Press, 100

Lowry, Biff, 9
Lubitsh & Bungarz, 115, 143
Lucky Creed, 88
Lull, 24
Luster, Joe, 42
Lydon, Mark, 8, 21–24, 26–27, 34, 38, 49, 198

MacCormac, Michael, 107
MacDonald, Morris, 100
Machiz, Leon, 14, 77, 153, 165, 167, 170, 179
McGlyn, Denis, 9
McIntyre, J. J., 182–83
Madison Square Garden, 73
Majestic Hanover, 32
Mallar, Larry, 69, 96, 196
Mancuso, Louis and Connie, 148
Man O' War, 17
Maris, Roger, 225
Marsh, Joe Jr., 202
Mate, 24
Matron Stake, 65, 118–20, 129, 200
Maywood Park, 191, 194
Meadow Lands Farm, 32
Meadows Lands, Pennsylvania, 32
Meadow Skipper, 20–26, 28, 34–35, 39, 42, 50, 53, 59–60, 84–85, 121, 135–37, 140, 161, 188, 200, 206
Meadows, The, 45–48, 53, 60, 78, 116, 221
Messenger Stake, 70, 95–96, 98–102, 119, 122, 182, 196, 221
Messenger Trial, 99, 119
Miles Dares, 211
Milestone Pace, 160
Miller, Delvin, 20, 30, 32–34, 37, 43, 63, 68, 84–85, 88, 95, 112, 117, 171, 179
Miller, Dr. Bert, 9
Miller, George, 206
Mirror, New York, 100
Miss Conna Adios, 160, 171
Mitzi Stable, 136
Monahan, Jerry, 57, 59, 209
Moran, Jim, 214
Morgantown, West Virginia, 116
Morris, Ernest B., 206
Morrow, Ralph, 123
Morton, Paul F. II, 140–41, 161–62
Most Happy Fella, 50, 83, 86, 100, 102–3, 108, 116, 125, 140, 174
Mountain Skipper, 95
My Birthday, 182

Namath, Joe, 83

Nansemond, 54, 69, 71, 98–100, 106, 108, 124–25, 127–32, 142, 148–49, 152, 160, 200–202, 207, 209, 211, 213, 216–17, 219, 222–24, 228, 231
Nanuet, New York, 124
Nason, Art, 95
National Bank of Vernon, 56
National Pacing Derby, 219
Nevele Pride, 7, 52, 83, 88, 91, 97, 109, 111, 142–43, 148, 152–53, 174, 206, 215
Nevele Pride: Speed 'N' Spirit, 8
Newark Star-Ledger, 100
New Egypt, New Jersey, 14, 49, 78, 95, 108–9, 116–17, 144, 151, 219, 221, 224
New England Pacing Derby, 182
New Hope, Pennsylvania, 77
Newport Champ, 88
Newsday, 70, 100
New York Post, 100, 114, 200
New York State Harness Racing Commission, 206
New York Times, 68, 96, 100, 122
Nickells, Bruce, 9, 145, 148, 202, 224–25
Noble Gesture, 95
Noble Victory, 82–83, 87, 91, 97, 216
Northfield Park, 51, 217
Nutshell Inn, 56

Oaklands Yank, 44
Obenchain, Dick, 37
O'Brien, Joe, 37, 63, 93, 124, 128, 133, 136, 155, 168–69
O'Brien Paddock, 42
Old Orchard, Maine, 182
Orlando, Florida, 124
Overcall, 114
Overtrick, 20, 48
Owen, K. D., 37
Ozzie Hanover, 149

Painesville, Ohio, 46
Palin, Sep, 63, 182–83
Palms, California, 150
Paramount Studios, 191
Paris, Kentucky, 20–21, 136
Parker, Ed, 209
Pat Taylor, 113
Paulos Hanover, 57–58, 65, 108, 113, 117, 124, 132, 148
Pearl River, New York, 124
Peg's Lady, 21
Pennsylvania Station, 14, 174
Perry, Fermer, 125, 160
Peters, Dr. John, 21–23, 25–27

Peters, Elizabeth, 21, 23, 198
Phelps, Gene, 159
Philadelphia Daily News, 192
Pinehurst, North Carolina, 18, 20
Pittsburgh Steelers, 34
Pocono Downs, 60, 124
Pompano Park, 13, 50, 56, 81, 83, 90, 157–58, 220–21
Ponter, James, 33, 39, 61, 79
Popfinger, Bill, 96
Powers, Jack, 209
Powers, Pete, 116
Pretty Boy, 36–37, 70
Pritchard, Roger, 9, 97–98, 130, 148, 154, 176, 192, 227–28
Prix D'Été, 106–7, 221
Provincial Cup, 161, 163–64
Public Affair, 209

Quaker City Stable, 148
Queen Air, 83, 140, 161
Queen City Stake, 112
Queen's Blue Chip, 83, 136
Quick Pride, 83, 95, 112–13, 142, 158–59

Race Byrd, 53, 57–58, 65
Ravdin, Dr. I. S., 166
Reading Futurity, 53–54
Realization Pace, 70, 195–200
Red Pluto, 63
Reed, William F., 78
Regan, George (Buddy), 214–15
Reigel, Gene, 119, 155
Resnick, Louis, 37, 91
Resnick, Mrs. Jackie, 150
Review Futurity (Springfield), 117, 124
Rexall Drug Store, Vernon, 56
Reynolds Memorial, 206
Richelieu Raceway, 54, 58, 64, 106–7
Right Time, 36
Rime of the Ancient Mariner, 24
Ring Leader, 124
Rivaltime, 71
Robbinsville Airport, 140
Rob Ron Tarios, 106
Rockingham Park, 18, 78, 94, 96, 98, 221
Rodney, 183
Rollins, John W., 14, 77, 85, 127, 165, 168, 173–74, 179, 187, 222, 231
Rollins, Mrs. John W., 127
Romalie Hanover, 84, 136, 138, 187
Romano Hanover, 207
Romeo Hanover, 63, 84
Romeo Hanover Pace, 94, 96, 187, 202, 221

Romola Hanover, 187
Romulus Hanover, 84, 106, 187, 200, 206
Rooney, John, 34
Rooney, Timothy J., 34, 38, 40
Roosevelt Futurity, 68–71, 73, 196–98
Roosevelt Raceway, 27, 68–70, 72–73, 96, 98, 100–102, 113, 115, 130, 195–96, 200, 219, 221
Rorty, Elizabeth, 137, 218
Ross, Frank, 86–87
Rowe, Bill, 200
Royal Count N, 171–72
Ruby's Sterling Farm, 116
Rum Customer, 138, 148–50, 153, 207
Ruth, Babe, 225

Saint Clair Bill, 36–37
Saint Clair Bit, 36–37
Salem, New Hampshire, 94
Saratoga Raceway, 205–6
Saucy Wave, 57, 74, 77–78, 88, 112, 178
Schenkel, Chris, 176
Schmidt, Alice, 124
Schmidt, Dr. Erwin R., 141–43, 159–61
Scioto Downs, 18, 56, 117, 119, 129
Scot Time, 60
Scottish Bret, 124, 132, 137
Senator Eric, 29
Seton Hanover, 39, 57, 59–60, 62, 65, 70, 95, 99, 102, 106, 108, 114, 116
Shadow Wave, 74
Shapiro, Marvin, 231
Sheena Hanover, 74
Sheppard, Charlotte, 184
Sheppard, Lawrence B., 182–85
Shoemaker, Bill, 146
Sholty, George, 37, 57, 148, 158
Shriner, Hazel D., 14, 77, 85, 153, 165, 168, 173, 177, 179, 187, 222, 231
Shriner, Marlin L., 84
Shudt, Roy, 229
Silent Majority, 195–98, 223
Silverstein, Hilda, 8, 14, 16, 77, 82, 85, 87, 153, 155, 165, 168, 173, 175, 177, 179, 181, 187, 195, 222, 231
Silverstein, Louis, 8, 13–16, 82, 85–86, 165–70, 173–74, 176, 178–80, 184, 188, 199, 222, 231
Silverstein Pavilion, 166
Simpson, John F., Jr., 32, 56, 124, 127, 129, 183, 186, 224
Simpson, John F., Sr., 8, 49, 58–59, 63, 100, 139, 182–90, 199, 205, 208, 210–11, 218, 222, 231–32
Sisti, Tony, 70

Slutsky, Ben J., 91
Slutsky, Julius, 91
Sly Heel, 119
Sly Yankee, 88
Smallsreed, George, 9
Smart, Curly, 63, 128
Smith, Dr. George A., Jr., 74
Smith, Fran, 9, 162, 200
Smith, Horace E., 184
Smith, Jack, 144, 158, 220
Songcan, 155
Song Cycle, 202
Spears, Paul E., 184
Speedy Count, 181
Speedy Crown, 117, 153
Sports Illustrated, 78, 171, 178
Sportsman's Park, 51, 169, 176, 188, 191, 202–4
Springfield (horse), 95, 98, 102, 112, 119, 124, 127–28, 132, 134
Springfield, Illinois, 117
Spring's Pride, 132
Stafford Family, Cherry Hill, N. J., 40
Standardbred Sales Company, 18, 36
Star Beacon, Ashtabula, Ohio, 123
Star Pointer Pace, 65, 67
Star's Chip, 83
Star's Pride, 181, 195, 228
Steady April, 218
Steady Beau, 71, 133
Steady Glow, 132, 137
Steady Star, 133, 153, 181, 195
Stearns, Bruce, 9
Steele, Dr. John, 9, 108, 114
Stehmann, Kurt, 9
Stokes, Charles, 9, 117
Stoner Creek Stud, Inc., 20–21, 23–25, 34–35, 91
Suburban Downs Pacing Derby, 211
Suffolk, Virginia, 125
Su Mac Lad, 83, 97, 109, 153
Sunder, Otto, 224
Super Bowl (football), 82
Super Bowl (horse), 83, 88, 112, 143, 153–55, 157, 195, 213, 216, 220, 227
Sureshot Hanover, 214–15
Swinebroad, George, 18
Syracuse Fairground, 142

Tananbaum, Stanley, 195
Taneytown, Maryland, 14, 77
Tar Heel, 125, 127–28, 160, 181
Tarport Skipper, 57, 65, 95, 99, 102, 197, 209
Tattersalls Pace, 131–33, 137

Tattersalls Standardbred Auction, 24, 74, 140
Taylor, Bill, 9, 228–29
Taylor, Mike, 226
Taylor, Ted, 99, 124
The Old Maid, 84
The Widower, 63
Thomas, Henry, 63
Thomas P. Gaines Memorial Pace, 113
Thomson, Hank, 128
Thor Hanover, 100
Thorpe Hanover, 36, 48, 84
Thurston, Charles (Deac), 214
Timely Beauty, 136
Timothy T., 32
Titus Hanover, 84
Toledo Hanover, 18
Torpedo Hanover, 84
Torpid, 63
Trans-Canada Pace, 106, 108
Triple Crown (pacing), 50, 83, 100, 102, 108, 125, 129, 140, 216, 222
Triple Crown (trotting), 195, 227
Trottier, Albert, 9
Trotting and Pacing Guide, USTA's, 138
Trotwood Willie, 48
True Duane, 231
Truthful Waverly, 95

United Press International, 123
United States Harness Writers Association, 152, 185
United States Trotting Association, 9, 19, 25, 45, 52, 56, 71, 76, 83, 92, 94–95, 112, 122, 138, 152, 155, 189, 224–25
Universal Driver Rating System, 46, 155
University of Pennsylvania Hospital, 15, 141, 143, 145, 148, 151, 159, 162, 166, 173

Valiquette, Gaston, 206
Van Lennep, Fred L., 37, 119
Van Ridell Stake, 112
Veri Special, 70, 95, 119, 124, 132
Verna Rainbow, 83
Vernon Downs, 9, 48, 56–60, 84, 105, 108, 113, 124, 135, 202, 205, 208–9, 211, 213–17, 226
Vernon, New York, 56
Vicar Hanover, 32

Village Inn, Vernon, 56
Voodoo Hanover, 18, 20–21, 23–28, 31, 33, 35, 39, 74–75, 84

Wallkill, New York, 83, 136
Walnut Hall, 30
Walsh, Ed, 9
Waples, Keith, 54–55
Wasserman, Dave, 9
Watson, Earl, 59–60
Welch, Walter, 143, 158, 220
Wellman, Bob, 9, 148, 224
Werner, Sacher, 102
West, Adam, 149
Westchester Pace, 102–3, 108
Western Pace, 148–49, 222–23
Wheeler, Eddie, 197, 224, 228
Whitcomb, Gov. Edgar D., 65
White, Ben, 182–83
White, Frank O., 209
White, Mrs. Roger, 195
White, Roger, 195
White, Tom, 9, 32
Wideman, Joe, 9, 79, 88–90, 94–95, 97–98, 120, 127–30, 133–34, 137–39, 145, 154, 175–77, 192, 197, 204, 210, 219, 224, 228
Wilburn, Tom, 228
Wilcutts, John (Tic), 8, 17–23, 25–28, 38, 49, 74, 198–99
Wilkes Barre, Pennsylvania, 88
William Penn Racing Association, 24, 34
Williams, Dick, 61
Wilmington, Delaware, 14, 77, 104
Wilson, Dick, 117
Windsor, Ontario, 29–30, 40, 68
Windsor Raceway, 29, 161–65, 169, 171, 200–201
Winning Worthy, 57, 108, 119, 124, 132, 134–37, 148, 218
Winthrop, Maine, 20
Wolverine Raceway, 65, 118–21, 129, 200
Woolworth, Norman S., 20, 37
World Driving Championship, 191
Worth Seein, 83

Yonkers Raceway, 34, 65–68, 100–103, 108, 110–11, 124, 140, 158–61, 195, 209–12, 221